Police Powers and Citizens' Rights

Police detention is the place where suspects are taken whilst their case is investigated and a case disposal decision is reached. It is also a largely hidden, but vital, part of police work and an under-explored aspect of police studies. This book provides a much-needed comparative perspective on police detention. It examines variations in the relationship between police powers and citizens' rights inside police detention in cities in four jurisdictions (in Australia, England, Ireland and the US), exploring in particular the relative influence of discretion, the law and other rule structures on police practices, as well as seeking to explain why these variations arise and what they reveal about state-citizen relations in neoliberal democracies.

This book draws on data collected in a multi-method study in five cities in Australia, England, Ireland and the US. This entailed 480 hours of observation, as well as 71 semi-structured interviews with police officers and detainees. Aside from filling in the gaps in the existing research, this book makes a significant contribution to debates about the links between police practices and neoliberalism. In particular, it examines the police, not just the prison, as a site of neoliberal governance.

By combining the empirical with the theoretical, the main themes of the book are likely to be of utmost importance to contemporary discussions about police work in increasingly unequal societies. As a result, it will also have a wide appeal to scholars and students, particularly in criminology and criminal justice.

Layla Skinns is a reader in criminology in the Centre for Criminological Research, University of Sheffield, having formerly worked and studied at the Institute of Criminology, University of Cambridge and the Institute for Criminal Policy Research, King's College London. She has a long-standing interest in police and policing, in particular in how policing agents use their authority. A key focus of her research has been on police detention in England and Wales, but also in other parts of the anglophone world. In this setting, she is interested in police powers and their relationship with the law, police cultures and police discretion, and furthermore, how they impact on equality and state-citizen relations. She is also interested in how the public – particularly detainees – perceive the police, which links her research to discussions about police legitimacy and 'good' policing.

Routledge Frontiers of Criminal Justice

Critical Perspectives on Coercive Interventions
Law, Medicine and Society
Edited by Claire Spivakovsky, Kate Seear and Adrian Carter

The Anthropology of Police
Edited by Kevin G. Karpiak and William Garriott

Criminal Justice and Regulation Revisited
Essays in Honour of Peter Grabosky
Edited by Lennon Y.C. Chang and Russell Brewer

The Pixelated Prisoner
Prison Video Links, Court 'Appearance' and the Justice Matrix
Carolyn McKay

Prisoner Resettlement in Europe
Edited by Frieder Dünkel, Ineke Pruin, Anette Storgaard and Jonas Weber

Restoring Harm
A Psycho-Social Approach to Victims and Restorative Justice
Daniela Bolívar

Police Powers and Citizens' Rights
Discretionary Decision-Making in Police Detention
Layla Skinns

For more information about this series, please visit: https://www.routledge.com/Routledge-Frontiers-of-Criminal-Justice/book-series/RFCJ

Police Powers and Citizens' Rights

Discretionary Decision-Making in Police Detention

Layla Skinns

Routledge
Taylor & Francis Group

LONDON AND NEW YORK

First published 2019
by Routledge
2 Park Square, Milton Park, Abingdon, Oxon OX14 4RN

and by Routledge
52 Vanderbilt Avenue, New York, NY 10017

Routledge is an imprint of the Taylor & Francis Group, an informa business

British Library Cataloguing-in-Publication Data
A catalogue record for this book is available from the British Library

Library of Congress Cataloging-in-Publication Data
Names: Skinns, Layla, author.
Title: Police powers and citizens' rights: discretionary decision making in police detention / Layla Skinns.
Description: Abingdon, Oxon; New York, NY: Routledge, 2019.
Identifiers: LCCN 2018049160| ISBN 9780415642309 (hardback) | ISBN 9780203080979 (ebook)
Subjects: LCSH: Criminal justice, Administration of. | Detention of persons. | Police. | Civil rights.
Classification: LCC HV7419 .S585 2019 | DDC 363.2/3—dc23
LC record available at https://lccn.loc.gov/2018049160

ISBN: 978-0-415-64230-9 (hbk)
ISBN: 978-0-203-08097-9 (ebk)

Typeset in Bembo
by codeMantra

For my parents, Laura and David Skinns, an important constant in my life.

Contents

List of tables

Preface

The legal powers of the police are arguably their defining feature. The most influential and persuasive approach to defining the police was formulated nearly 50 years ago by Egon Bittner. Police are "equipped, entitled and required to deal with every exigency in which force may have to be used" (Bittner 1974: 35). They are the specialist repositories of that monopolisation of legitimate force in a territory which Max Weber analysed as the essence of a state.

In a recent sympathetic critique of this "police-use-of-force" paradigm, Jean-Paul Brodeur developed the concept in a variety of ways (Brodeur 2010: Chapter 4). Crucially, he built upon a common observation about, and indeed a tenet of, effective policing. The use of force must be minimised to be legitimate, deployed only when absolutely necessary, and calibrated proportionately to the threat that justifies it. Identifying the police primarily through the use of legitimate force is misleading in that it postulates as their essence a capacity that is seldom actually resorted to. What marks the police out on a more regular basis is their endowment with a battery of special legal powers beyond those of the ordinary citizen, intended to enable them to maintain order and enforce substantive criminal law. These powers are of course all underpinned by the potential use of legitimate force, but this is relatively infrequently necessary.

The strongest of these legal powers is the ability to deprive people of their liberty, by arrest and its regular corollary, detention in the police station. In what purport to be democratic societies, the use of these powers is subject to some sort of legal constraints to safeguard citizens from unwarranted or unfair intrusions on their liberty. Thus, the topic of this remarkable book goes to the very heart of key issues concerning human rights, effective and fair government and social justice.

Dr Layla Skinns has become the leading authority on police custody in Britain since the publication in 2011 of her monograph *Police custody: governance, legitimacy and reform in the criminal justice process*. In the last few years, she has researched and written prolifically on police custody, as well as police powers and policing policy, and reform more generally. Her large body of important research and publications makes her one of the outstanding police scholars of her generation, a position that will be consolidated by this fine book.

Police powers and citizens' rights: discretionary decision-making in police detention is a major achievement in a number of ways. At an empirical level, it presents data from pioneering comparative research on police custody in England, the US, Ireland and Australia. The fieldwork combined observation with qualitative interviews and offers rich insights into the variations in, as well as similarities between, these different jurisdictions. These findings are embedded in sophisticated theoretical chapters seeking to understand the differences by a combination of historical, cultural and sociolegal perspectives with a fundamental grounding in political economy, in particular stressing the consequences of the hegemony of neoliberalism since the 1970s.

As Skinns describes it: "The book began with a 'research puzzle.' Whilst collecting data in police detention in an American city in 2009, I was fascinated by why it was that police officers provided varying responses to the question of how long they were entitled to detain someone without charge. This was particularly so given that the same question in the other cities in the research in Australia, England and Ireland elicited a straightforward answer and possibly also a reference to the relevant piece of legislation."

This puzzle led to the extensive fieldwork in the four jurisdictions. It examines the extent to which citizens held as suspects by the police were accorded their rights and entitlements. Both the legal rights themselves, and the extent to which they were respected in practice, varied across the four countries. So too did the manner in which suspect citizens were treated. In all sites, the police handled suspects with a mixture of coercive authority wielding sanctions, and procedural justice based on transparency and fairness. They deployed, in addition, a tacit background resource of respect for police authority, which varied between jurisdictions and citizens. There were systematic differences between the jurisdictions, but also in the degree of discretion exercised by officers, leading to variations in practice within them.

The police in all four jurisdictions have somewhat similar historical origins, as all were at one time colonies of England, and their forces' development reflects this in varying ways. Nonetheless, their legal systems and modes of police organisation have developed in different directions, and this is reflected in their treatment of suspect citizens in police custody. What emerges as a key finding is the outlier status of the US. The legal protection afforded to suspects in the US is far weaker, both by the law in the books and the law in action as practised by the police.

The overarching explanation of this, argues Dr Skinns, is the much tighter grip of neoliberalism in the USA, historically, and accentuated after the worldwide spread of neoliberalism since the 1970s. At certain points in the 19th and early 20th centuries, there were nascent socialist and radical movements in the US, and, from Franklin Roosevelt's 'New Deal' in the 1930s until Lyndon Johnson's 'Great Society,' some social democratic policies without the label. Nonetheless, Sombart's question a century ago, "why is there no socialism in the United States?" remains pertinent.

Neoliberalism, the exaltation of free-market economics and curbing of the scope of the state in all but its coercive aspects, is relevant to policing and citizens' rights in a number of ways. Above all, it widens economic and social inequality and exclusion. The deep racial divisions and oppression throughout US history make this more visible and more bitter. Culturally, neoliberalism also promotes greater egoistic individualism and undermines any sense of the general public good.

As the data in this book show, the result is less restraint of police coercive tactics by law protecting citizen rights. This is especially the case for those who are tacitly excluded from full citizenship as analysed by T.H. Marshall, i.e. enjoying civil, political and socio-economic rights on a par with dominant elites. In the US, the laws regulating police powers are not defined by statute in most areas, with the only national input being the jurisprudence of the Supreme Court, which has allowed even more discretion to the police since the liberal heyday of the 1960s Warren Court.

The English police seemed the most bound by law, following the codification embodied in the Police and Criminal Evidence Act 1984 (PACE) (although this still left scope for much apparent deviation from the full spirit of legality). The Irish and Australian cases were in between the US and UK. In all places, there had been some deterioration in the position of suspect citizens, since neoliberalism became more hegemonic, and in particular as a result of the austerity policies practised since the 2008 economic crash. For example, the average time spent in custody increased, whilst access to legal advice and representation fell in the 21st century.

Dr Skinns' book is a major contribution to understanding policing today. It provides us with pioneering comparative empirical evidence, rigorously gathered and analysed. Its account of the policing practices observed is formulated through a sophisticated theoretical framework. This moves between the levels of micro interaction and choice, the meso influences of law, physical and social organisation of stations, and varying force policies, to the underlying macro political economy and cultures of different states. All this is accomplished with exceptional clarity and coherence. This book will consolidate Dr Skinns' reputation internationally as one of the leading contemporary authorities on police powers and policing generally.

Robert Reiner, Emeritus Professor of Criminology, Department of Law, LSE, 4 September 2018

Acknowledgements

This book was written over a more protracted period than originally envisioned, in part, because the writing of it was happily interrupted by two-year-long periods of maternity leave, as well as by the demands of being the principal investigator on a large Economic and Social Research Council-funded study of police custody in England and Wales. As a result, there are a large number of people who have variously supported and encouraged me over the years, to whom I wish to offer a few words of thanks.

First of all, thanks must go to all those who participated in the research across five cities and four jurisdictions, including both staff and those detained in police custody. Moreover, I must also acknowledge the Economic and Social Research Council (RES-000–22–1719) and the British Academy (RG54278) for generously funding the research studies on which the book is based. A number of colleagues also read and commented on the book, or parts of it, at various stages of its development, and I am exceedingly grateful to them for their wise words. This includes Vicky Conway, David Dixon, Bethan Loftus, Peter Manning, Alpa Parmar and Charles Weisselberg.

In the early stages of this project, both when writing grant applications and whilst preparing for and then collecting the data, I must also thank former colleagues from the Institute of Criminology, University of Cambridge, in particular, Katrin Muller-Johnson and Lawrence Sherman, as well as from the Institute for Criminal Policy Research, in particular, Mike Hough and Tiggey May. I was also fortunate to hold visiting positions at a number of institutions whilst collecting the data, on which this book is based, and I must, therefore, thank David Dixon, Leanne Weber, Chris Cunneen, Jill Hunter, Ian O'Donnell, Deirdre Healy, John Jackson and Aogan Mulcahy.

I must also extend my gratitude to all of my current and some former colleagues at the University of Sheffield who have supported me in various ways throughout the writing of this book, including during the study leave, research buyouts and periods of maternity leave, where they were left covering for my absences. I must thank in particular Matthew Bacon, Cormac Behan, Stephen Farrall, Sara Grace, Tara Lai Quinlan, Lindsey Rice, Gwen Robinson, Joanna Shapland, Gilly Sharpe, David Thompson and Andrew Wooff.

Two other people who deserve a special thanks are Alpa Parmar and Bethan Loftus, who have been a continual source of support and encouragement.

It was also at the University of Sheffield that, following the retirement of Simon Holdaway, I was given carte blanche from 2010 to develop a series of undergraduate and postgraduate policing modules, one of which was particularly instrumental in developing my ideas for this book. Therefore, I must thank all of my wonderful students over the years, but particularly those on Police and Policing in a Global Context (LAW3021) in 2011, 2012, 2014, 2017 and 2018. I only hope they learned as much from taking this module as I did from teaching them.

Thanks must also go to Routledge for bearing with me, particularly Tom Sutton, Jake Rainbow, Hannah Catterall and Heidi Lee. I hope the wait has been worth it!

Finally, last but not least, I am grateful for the patience and forbearance of my family, including my children, Emile and Selda, who are still too little to appreciate the sense of grounding that they provide. Making a flying saucer birthday cake in the midst of writing the conclusion to this book helped no end to keep my feet firmly on the ground! I must also thank my sisters, Marsha and Jessica, and my mother, Laura. My father, David Skinns, was, as ever, a tremendous sounding board for ideas and willingly read various drafts of the book throughout. For this, I am exceedingly grateful. However, the biggest thank you of all is owed to my partner, Matthew Stancombe, whose gentle and unwavering support helped see me through.

Introduction

On my first day of observation in a police detention facility in the American city that was one part of the comparative research on which this book is based, I asked what I thought would be a straightforward question, based on my experiences of collecting data in other countries.[1] I asked first a sergeant and then a corporal who I encountered there, "What is the maximum permitted length of detention without charge for those detained by the police?" The sergeant told me that the maximum length of detention was 12 hours, which contrasted with what the corporal told me later, which was that the maximum length of detention was 72 hours. This was puzzling to me. How was it that staff could give such contrasting answers to a question which would have elicited a fairly standard response about legally permitted upper time limits in the other cities in the research? Perhaps one of these two initial research participants was mistaken. And thus, I posed the same question time and again during my participant observation and interviews with staff across all seven of the police detention facilities that I visited and spent time observing in this American city. As discussed in more detail in Chapter 6, responses to this question continued to vary wildly.

This seemingly minor matter about what police officers understood to be the length of detention and how they applied it in practice in this American city, compared to the other cities in the research, was the starting point for the present book. At the forefront of my mind was the question of *why* these differences arose and what the implications were for police-citizen relationships, particularly in jurisdictions with differing social, political and economic conditions. My initial hypothesis was that for police officers, in this American city, there was a lack of familiarity with legal rules and that this might be suggestive of a larger gulf between the law in the books and the law in practice in this American city, compared to the other cities in the research. Perhaps these ambiguities in what police officers understood about the length of detention were also rooted in greater discretionary decision-making for police officers, connected to the historical, social and political conditions in which discretion had developed in the US. In relation to the length of detention, this high degree of discretion was unlikely to be in the interests of detainees, many of whom would have no doubt been craving certainty about when they would be released.[2] This prompted a further hypothesis, this time about the nature of the relationship between police powers and citizens' rights. In the American city, which formed a part of the research, perhaps the police wielded a significantly higher degree of power than those they detained.[3] Together, these are some of the issues animating the present book.

The police have a broad range of powers at their disposal including those used to stop, search, arrest, detain and interrogate citizens. These powers can therefore transform an innocent party into a suspect, then a defendant, and, if convicted of a criminal offence, an offender (McConville et al., 1991: 16–22), and then possibly even a prisoner or probationer and so on, with many of these labels outlasting the period in which they are ascribed. The powers that the police have at their disposal are also a part of the broader process of governance, in which the police are central players in the processes of crime control and social order maintenance. As the gateway to the criminal justice process, the police help to construct who is or is not criminal, as well as shaping who may or may not make claims to citizenship and to a valued place in society (Loader, 2016; Lerman and Weaver, 2014: 12–13; Waddington, 1999b: 30). Through their concept of "custodial citizenship,"[4] for example, Lerman and Weaver (2014: 28) argue that police-citizen interactions result not just in exclusion from certain rights and benefits, but also the active construction of a different kind of citizenship, given that, for many people, interactions with the police are their only tangible experience of the state. Those in Lerman and Weaver's study were entitled to register to vote and were formally equal before the law.

> However, because of their race, their income, and the characteristics of the neighborhoods in which they live, these individuals are systematically more likely to be exposed to public institutions that deny them voice, treat them as a suspect, do not respond to their needs, and are unaccountable to their complaints. We join others who suggest that criminal justice delimits citizenship, its meaning and practice.
>
> (2014: 28)

These roles of the police in shaping social order and conceptions of citizenship are especially potent, in part, because of the widespread existence of discretionary decision-making. It exists both, vertically, from the top to the bottom of the police organisation, and horizontally, across all areas of policing including with regard to the use of police powers (Bronitt and Stenning, 2011; Lipsky, 2010: 16, 18–23; Finnane, 1990: 218; Goldstein, 1960). Police discretion – which is described in more detail in Chapter 2 – refers to police officer perceptions of the quantity and nature of their authorised capacity to make choices about different courses of action or inaction, which are structured by and structuring of the legal and administrative rules, as well as by the wider social structures that surround their work. Police discretion enables the police to choose who enters the criminal justice process, as well as how, when, where, with whom, etc., albeit these decisions are hemmed in by legal, administrative and informal working rules associated with police cultures. Hence, it has long been noted that discretion enables but also undermines fairness and the equitable distribution of policing. It has been implicated, for example, in the over-policing of minority communities, both in the past and present and across different countries, including those in the present research, with catastrophic consequences for police–citizen relations and also for the over-representation of non-white citizens in the criminal justice process.[5]

As the foregoing discussion reveals, police work is intimately connected to social, political and economic conditions, which can further constrain police decision-making and behaviour. Of particular interest to this book is neo-liberalism. This concept is defined as a series of interlinked ideas, including free-market fundamentalism and the idea that the state should play a more limited role in the lives of citizens, for example, through the rolling back of the welfare state, the deregulation of markets (e.g. for banks or stock markets) or through outsourcing (e.g. of police duties). In addition, and of particular importance to police discretion, is the growing emphasis placed on individ-ualism and the personal responsibility of free-willed 'rational' social actors, who can be held responsible for perceived failings, including personal dif-ficulties or allegations of lawbreaking. Moreover, neoliberalism can also be understood as involving an intensifying gaze and growing grip on certain cit-izens by the state, in particular, those engaged in the criminal justice process, namely, young minority ethnic men from deprived neighbourhoods (Lerman and Weaver, 2014: 181; O'Neill and Loftus, 2013).

The purpose of this book is to explore, in a comparative perspective, the relative influence of discretion, the law and other rule structures on police practices in police detention and, furthermore, to highlight what it reveals about the state's relationships with its citizens in neoliberal democracies. It will also tentatively theorise why these variations arise, pointing to the political economy of these jurisdictions, in particular, the varying way that neoliberalism has manifested itself in police detention practices, as well as to the role of the law in regulating police practices and the history of the police institution. In so doing, the book makes an original contribution to the field of criminology and criminal justice, as accounts connecting neoliberalism to criminal justice practices have tended to focus on the prison – not the police – as the primary coercive agency (Reiner, 2017; Squires and Lea, 2013; Wacquant, 2009b: xix).

The empirical chapters of this book are informed by data collected in five cities in four jurisdictions in 2007–2009 in Australia, England, Ireland and the United States of America. Henceforth, the latter is referred to as the US. For reasons of confidentiality, these cities will not be explicitly named in the book. The research as a whole entailed 480 hours of observing and talking informally to staff and a selection of detainees across 18 detention facilities and 59 shifts. These observational data were supplemented by 71 semi-structured interviews with police officers, as well as other criminal justice practitioners and detainees in England. Further detail about the data collection and analysis, as well as its challenges, is set out in Appendix 1 (see also Skinns, forthcoming). However, it is important to note here that due to the small scale and to some extent exploratory nature of the data collection, these data cannot be seen as generalisable much beyond the cities in which they were collected. They nonetheless provide a valuable contribution to debates about police powers and citizens' rights in a comparative context.

Why citizens' rights?

Before summarising each of the chapters of the book, I wish to briefly reflect on why the book is about police powers and citizens' rights, rather than police powers and suspects' rights. The "standard narrative" on modern forms of citizenship is associated with T.H. Marshall's classic essay first published in 1950 (Bellamy, 2008: 45). He conceptualised citizenship as including: civil rights, such as freedom of speech and the right to work and to justice;[6] political rights, such as equal access to vote or to stand to be elected; and social rights, such as access to social security by the unemployed or ill and, more generally, the right to "live the life of a civilised being, according to the standards prevailing in society" (Marshall and Bottomore, 1992: 8). Marshall regarded these rights as once intertwined, for example, in feudal and medieval periods, but subsequently separated and thus able to develop at a different pace, with civil, political and social rights approximately emerging in the 18th, 19th and 20th centuries, respectively. For Marshall, by bestowing citizenship rights on all, citizenship was synonymous with the pursuit of equality, which he saw as having been eroded by the capitalist class system from the latter part of the 17th century (Marshall and Bottomore, 1992: 18).

Marshall's conceptual framework was not just an intellectual exercise; aspects of it became institutionalised. In Britain, for example, the institutionalisation of social citizenship was partially evident in the use of Keynesian macroeconomic policies to stimulate the economy in times of recession and in the 1942 Beveridge Report, which proposed a new system of social rights to unemployment, disability, retirement income and healthcare services (Humpage, 2015: 21). The introduction of legal aid in England and Wales can also be seen as evidence of the institutionalisation of Marshallian civil rights. Sommerlad remarks, for example, that

> legal aid represented the beginning of a new stage in the relationship between law and society and was thus fundamental to the development of an inclusionary form of citizenship ... As such it provided a significant basis for social democracy....
>
> (2004: 348)

However, under conditions of neoliberalism from the 1980s onwards, the inclusive and egalitarian form of citizenship that Marshall conceptualised and, indeed, advocated has become increasingly far removed from the lived realities of many citizens in Western democracies,[7] such as the US, England, Ireland and to a lesser extent, Australia (see Chapter 3). Whole communities and families can find themselves socially excluded and part of an underclass living in ghettos of acute deprivation (Cavadino and Dignan, 2006a; Young, 1999: 19), with "policing by consent being most difficult to establish and sustain" in these kinds of communities (Loader and Mulcahy, 2006: 12). Though they do not mention it, these changing social, political and economic conditions are, in part, causative of the growing number of "custodial citizens" that Lerman and Weaver (2014: 55–56) note. These shifting conditions have also had a marked effect on the importance attached to active, not passive, social citizenship. Marshall recognised that citizenship entailed a set of duties – most notably to pay taxes and insurance contributions, as well as to work hard – not just a set of rights (Marshall and Bottomore, 1992: 45–46). Neoliberalism has placed growing expectations on citizens to actively, rationally and responsibly perform these duties, with access to social citizenship rights becoming increasingly seen as conditional on this (Humpage, 2015; Evers and Guillemard, 2012; Lister, 2012; Standford, 2012).[8] This has had a polarising effect, further contributing to notions of deserving and undeserving citizens. This deserving/undeserving distinction is no longer based only on whether someone is welfare-dependent or has had contact with the criminal justice system or not, but also on whether or not they actively perform their duties as a citizen, such as by looking for work whilst they receive unemployment benefits (Humpage, 2015: 234–5).

For the purposes of the present book, it is important to recognise suspects *as* citizens. This is for two main reasons, which reflect the contradiction between the normative and empirical realities of citizenship in neoliberal democracies. Firstly, in principle, those detained by the police should continue to have the full range of civil rights, as well as access to a full range of political and social rights. This understanding of suspects as citizens humanises them and encourages them to be seen as a full and valued part of society irrespective of the allegations of lawbreaking. That is, it encourages us to look beyond reified binary categories of criminal / innocent party or good guy / bad guy. Secondly, the emphasis in the book on suspects as citizens helps to locate police custody within the political economy. As noted above, citizenship was originally conceived as synonymous with equality, albeit these intentions have been eroded, in part, by growing neoliberalism. These conditions make it more likely that police practices add to existing social inequalities and increase the grip of the state over criminal justice populations. To put it another way, recognising suspects as citizens enables an understanding of how "*restrained* the application of police authority is to those who enjoy [full] citizenship" (Waddington, 1999b: 30). Ultimately, my focus on citizens', not suspects', rights is about recognising the political nature of police work in unequal societies in which the ideals of citizenship are undermined by the realities of citizen contact with the police (Lerman and Weaver, 2014: 28).

The remainder of the book

Chapter 2 – Theorising police powers and citizens' rights

In Chapter 2, I examine the power of the police, police discretion and accountability. Its main purpose is to examine the theorisation of police powers and citizens' rights, thereby providing a conceptual framework for the chapters which follow. In terms of the power of the police, I differentiate legality and *whether* police officers abide by legal rules from styles of authority, that is, *how* the police employ their authority. I then set out the origins, influences on and arguments for the necessity of discretion in police work whilst also recognising discretion as a form of human agency. Finally, I examine the evidence for Ericson's (2007) conceptual framework of the role played by the law and other rule structures in discretionary decision-making.

Chapter 3 – The police in context: neoliberalism in the selected countries

This chapter builds on the conceptual framework developed in Chapter 2 whilst also marking the first of three chapters that place the police in the cities/jurisdictions of interest in context, the aim being to go from the macro- to the micro-level over the course of Chapters 3, 4 and 5. In Chapter 3, I explore neoliberalism in the selected countries, examining how the cities/jurisdictions of interest have been classified in terms of their neoliberal tendencies, as well as looking at data and evidence to examine the extent to which such classifications apply. The cities/jurisdictions of interest are compared in terms of their social demographic patterns, economic and social policies, income differentials, the status of egalitarian values and citizen–state relations. This is in order to build a picture of the political economy in which the police exist and thus to also develop an idea of how this might affect discretionary police practices in police detention.

Chapter 4 – The police in context: patterns of police work

This chapter provides a narrower contextual frame of reference than Chapter 3. It explores the way that police work is organised and delivered in each of the cities/jurisdictions of interest. It examines the localised nature of police work and its historical origins, as well as examining data on police–citizen relations and how the police are held to account, legally speaking, particularly when it comes to the treatment of detainees in police custody. Chapters 3 and 4 are deliberately descriptive, as their overarching aim is to provide a platform for understanding how police powers and citizens' rights, explored in the rest of the book, are put into practice in the cities in the research. Such a descriptive account is also necessary given that the comparative study of police work is an underdeveloped area of research (de Maillard and Roché, 2016; Body-Gendrot and de-Wenden, 2014: 2, 9–10; Mawby, 1990: 4–5).[9] As a result, there are no other systematic comparative examinations of the organisation and context of police work encompassing *all* of the four selected countries within one publication.

Chapter 5 – Inside police detention: conditions, routines, rituals and rules

Drawing on the empirical material, this chapter provides an even narrower contextual frame of reference than Chapters 3 and 4. Here the focus is on the microcosm of police detention facilities in the cities in the research, examining the terminology used, the physical conditions, routines and rituals in police custody, and staff perceptions of the formal and less formal rules surrounding their discretionary decision-making. It is argued that, to an extent, all the detention facilities in the research involved the exercise of coercive control over detainees as a result of the conditions, routines, rituals and rules. Along with the styles of authority that the police exhibited, as discussed in Chapter 7, these have a bearing on detainees' capacity to exercise their rights.

Chapter 6 – Abiding by the rules? Legality in police detention

The purpose of this chapter is to examine the extent to which the police abided by legal rules, police policies and procedures with regard to detainees' rights in police detention and, furthermore, to examine the role that discretion played in any departures from the rules. This chapter focuses on three key rights, which were of importance across all the cities in the research: (i) the right to silence, (ii) the right to custodial legal advice and (iii) the right to not be detained indefinitely by the police. A further purpose of this chapter is to examine the extent to which the coercive custody environment, outlined in Chapter 5, was moderated by the bestowing of rights and entitlements on detainees. To do this, this chapter draws on the data collected in the present research as well as relevant existing research. In essence, it examines the legality of police custody in the cities in the research.

Chapter 7 – Styles of authority

The focus of this chapter is on how staff understood and used their authority in police detention. Drawing on the empirical material and the conceptual framework set out in Chapter 2, I reflect on the extent to which police authority and detainee compliance with it, were rooted in coerced, legitimate and symbolic forms of authority and/or inducement by staff. It is argued that staff across the cities in the research exhibited all of these styles of authority but to varying degrees. For instance, the authority of staff in the American city seemed to rest, to a greater extent, on the symbolic authority of the police.

Chapter 8 – Meeting individual needs? Vulnerability and police custody

Chapter 8 is the final empirical chapter, which also draws on sociolegal notions of vulnerability. Its purpose is to examine the ways in which police custody was adjusted for detainees deemed to be vulnerable. I explore how vulnerability was defined, identified and responded to in police custody in the cities in the research, as well as examining the implications of this. Here the focus is on children, detainees who had medical conditions, mental health conditions or learning disabilities, as well as women and the culturally and linguistically diverse (e.g. those from non-English-speaking backgrounds). My argument is that the effects of the coercive custody environment and coercive styles of authority were only partially mitigated for vulnerable detainees: adaptations of police custody tended only to occur when detainees visibly demonstrated their vulnerability.

Chapter 9 – Conclusion

The aim of this chapter is to provide a complete account of the material contained in the book. I start by summarising each of the chapters, along with my overarching thesis. In the remainder of the conclusion, I further elaborate upon and unpack this thesis. I also examine the implications of the book for how the relationship between neoliberalism and police authority might be conceptualised in future research, as well as for state-citizen relations in neoliberal countries. Finally, I end by offering some suggestions about what might be done about the entrenchment of inequalities, as a result of individualised and neoliberal-influenced forms of discretionary decision-making in police detention.

Notes

1 By this point I had already collected data in two cities in England (in 2006–2007), one Australian city (in August 2009) and in a city in Ireland (in September 2009).
2 As previous research has shown, one of the more difficult aspects of police custody for detainees is the deprivation of certainty; a key thing that detainees want

to know is what is going to happen to them and when (Wooff and Skinns, 2017). Yet, this information is not always forthcoming and this is especially likely if there are no established rules about the maximum permitted period of detention.

3 Another way of thinking about this is as an imbalance between police powers and citizens' rights. However, this can be misleading (Ashworth and Redmayne, 2014: 41–45; Dixon, 1997: 47). For instance, the length of time someone is detained in police custody is not simply a product of police practices but also detainee choices (e.g. to request legal advice) and the speed at which other criminal justice practitioners (e.g. legal advisers) respond to the choices that detainees make (Skinns, 2010). See also Chapters 3 and 7 for further discussion of this.

4 In essence, custodial citizens are those brought into contact with the criminal justice system, often by dint of their socio-economic circumstances and where they live, but who are neither charged nor convicted and who subsequently develop a warped view of the nature of state authority. By contrast, criminal citizens are those convicted of crime. Lerman and Weaver (2014: 56) note that they do not intend to reify these two categories, but there is a sense in their book that criminal citizens are somehow less deserving than custodial citizens.

5 In the US, for example, in the prohibition era, African Americans were seen as an easy target for discretionary police practices due to their lack of political influence (Muhammad, 2010: 215). In the 21st century, African Americans similarly feel that they have a "target on their back" (Lerman and Weaver, 2014: 181). This is due to discretionary police practices, such as stop-and-frisk, because of their skin colour, their socio-economic status, where they live, and due to any prior contact with criminal justice institutions (Eterno and Barrow, 2018; Engel and Cohen, 2014; Brunson and Miller, 2006; Bass, 2001). See also Bowling and Weber (2011) for a review of the international evidence included in their special issue on stop-and-search in a global context.

6 With regard to the right to justice, Marshall and Bottomore (1992: 8) say it is "of a different order from the others, because it is the right to defend and assert all one's rights on terms of equality with others and by due process of law." For the purpose of this book, Marshallian notions of civil rights, in particular the right to justice founded on due process and equality before the law, are the most relevant.

7 This incongruence between Marshall's conceptual framework and the empirical reality of citizenship in the 21st century may partly be because this framework set out ideal-types. However, it may also be because his account is outdated. For example, the Marshallian notion of citizenship, linked as it was to national identity, as well as to the relatively consensual and socially homogenous context of the 1950s and 1960s, has become outmoded. This is in light of growing diversity and processes of globalisation, which have transformed us into global citizens (Evers and Guillemard, 2012; Turner, 1990), albeit such global citizenship is largely only available to those in Western democracies (Aas, 2013: 13). Gender and the more limited access that women have to citizenship were also largely absent from discussions about citizenship in the period in which Marshall was writing (Evers and Guillemard, 2012; Walby, 1994).

8 This was seen, for example, in the UK under New Labour, where receiving Job Seekers Allowance (which had been introduced by the previous Conservative government) became conditional on certain kinds of behaviour, such as actively looking for work and acquiring the skills needed to work, with sanctions if people did not (Lister, 2012).

9 There are exceptions to this observation about limited comparative research on the police. See for example de Maillard et al. (2016), Body-Gendrot and de Wenden (2014), Manning (2011), Ross (2007) and Bayley (1996).

Theorising police powers and citizens' rights

This chapter sets out the conceptual framework of the book, examining the way police powers and citizens' rights can be theorised. It starts by setting out the meaning of the power of the police, distinguishing legality, that is, *whether* legal rules are abided by, an approach which is typically associated with sociolegal scholars, from *how* the police use their authority, an approach which is associated more with sociologists and criminologists. This is an original way of conceptualising police powers as, in the past, theorists have tended to think of the powers of the police mostly in terms of one or the other. Second, it examines the discretionary nature of the power of the police, as well as conceptualising how such power is held in check. This chapter also sets out the main thesis contained in the book and its contribution to comparative police studies.

The power of the police

Legality

The legality of police behaviour is judged in terms of whether it conforms to established rules in particular societies (Tankebe et al., 2016; Bottoms and Tankebe, 2012) and, thus, whether detainees access the rights that are available to them as a result of these legal rules. The powers the police have include the right to search citizens and their property, seize goods, arrest and detain and use force, all of which are implicated in order maintenance and in the pursuit of security and are what separate the police from ordinary citizens (Brodeur, 2010: 133). As discussed in Chapter 4, in the common-law countries that are of interest to the present book, these legal rules are primarily set down in statutes and their associated codes of practice – such as the Police and Criminal Evidence Act 1984 (PACE) and its Codes of Practice in England – and/or in case law.[1] This results in the possibility that evidence may be excluded from court if police officers are found to breach the legal rules. This is one way of ensuring that the police comply with the demands of legality (Bittner, 1970: 35). As will be made clear in Chapter 6, inevitably, given the socially situated nature of the law and police institutions, these legal rules vary from place to place. They vary in terms of the extent and nature of these provisions, as well as how they are put into practice and the extent to which they accord with shared societal beliefs and values (Bottoms and Tankebe, 2012; Dixon, 1997: 274).

One of the most important sociolegal accounts used to understand legality in the criminal process is provided by Packer (1968) in his influential crime control and due process model. This is an abstract model which specifies two ideal-types,[2] as a way of examining the key elements of the criminal process. It does not therefore necessarily describe how crime control and due process values do or should operate in practice. Crime control values refer to "the system's capacity to apprehend, try, convict, and dispose of a high proportion of criminal offenders whose offences become known" (Packer, 1968: 158). Packer goes on to say that this presupposes "an administrative, almost managerial model" akin to a conveyor belt or an assembly line, involving a series of routinised operations and hurdles, with success being gauged by whether the case reaches the end of the line (1968: 159–60). By contrast, due process refers to the idea that there should be a set of rules, often written in law, which are publicly known and embody values – such as the presumption of innocence and equal access to defence counsel – that emphasise fairness (Packer, 1968: 165–6). In the crime control / due process model, the idea is that due process acts as a break on the crime control "conveyor belt." In police custody, due process and crime control can respectively be compared with suspects' rights and police powers. Suspects' rights, in theory, act as a break on the way the police use their powers in relation to those detained in police custody.

Though highly regarded, influential and often used by sociolegal scholars to conceptualise the criminal process, Packer's crime control and due process model has also been widely criticised (Ashworth and Redmayne, 2014: 40–41; Macdonald, 2008; Dixon, 1997: 45–57). One of the most important criticisms of it, for the purposes of this book,[3] is the lack of explanation Packer provides about the nature of the relationship between crime control and due process. For example, though implicit in his account, he does not say whether crime control should be seen as the main purpose of the criminal process, and due process as secondary to this, acting to set limits on the way crime control is achieved. This lack of explanation of the nature of the relationship between crime control and due process encourages an unhelpful tendency to essentialise these different dimensions of his model and to treat them as straightforwardly dichotomous. In fact, they are deeply intertwined, with due process *limiting* crime control,[4] as well as sometimes being *for* crime control. For example, with regard to the latter point, McBarnet argues that though it may seem as if the police are to blame for subverting the law,[5] in fact, it is the law itself that is to blame, as "deviation from the rhetoric of legality and justice is institutionalised in the law itself" (1981: 155–6).[6] Hence, she argues that "due process exists *for* crime control" (McBarnet, 1981: 156). Taking all of this together, this suggests that there is a "constant and inevitable tension between due process and crime control which cannot be reduced to the simplistic accounts of conflict or searches for 'balance'" (Dixon, 1997: 47).

More recently, debates have shifted beyond the crime control / due process dichotomy, as evident in Sanders et al.'s (2010: 47–56) freedom model and in Ashworth and Redmayne's (2014: 48–51) human rights model.[7] This shift is also evident in the growth of the legitimacy paradigm in police studies, which I shall touch on briefly here, and then in the next section of this chapter. As a result of this recent paradigm shift in police studies, the legality of police actions has come to be seen as an important, albeit non-constitutive, component of police legitimacy (Tankebe et al., 2016; Jackson et al., 2013: Chapter 11; Bottoms and Tankebe, 2012; Reiner, 2010: Chapter 3).[8] Beetham asserts that "power can be said to be legitimate, in the first instance, if it is acquired and exercised in accordance with established rules" (1991: 16). Moreover, the subordination of the police to the rule of law is regarded as an important feature of policing in democratic societies (Dixon, 1997: 289).

However, aside from the impossibility of enforcing all laws all of the time (Dixon, 1997: 3), such full enforcement of the law is not always a legitimate course of action for the police. To the contrary, it can lead to a sense of injustice and unfairness, as illustrated by the full enforcement of stop-and-search laws during the unfortunately-named Operation Swamp in 1981. This police operation resulted in high levels of stops in the black community in Brixton in London, one of which directly contributed to the Brixton Riots, in the context of already simmering tensions between the police and the community (Scarman, 1981: 37). This is where conceptions of legality link to notions of discretion: discretion is one of the means through which the police can balance the enforcement of the law and the maintenance of public order. As Lord Scarman, the senior judge responsible for the report on the Brixton Riots, shrewdly noted, this balance can be achieved through:

> The constant and common-sense exercise of police discretion. Indeed the exercise of discretion lies at the heart of the policing function. It is undeniable that there is only one law for all: and it is right that this should be so. But it is equally well-recognised that successful policing depends on the exercise of discretion in how law is enforced. The good reputation of the police as a force depends on the skill and judgement which policemen [sic] display in the particular circumstances of the cases and incidents which they are required to handle. Discretion is the art of suiting action to particular circumstances. It is the policeman's daily task.
>
> (1981: 63).

That said, such discretionary decisions need to be taken in ways that secure the approval of the communities in which they operate (see section 'Discretion: its origins, meaning and importance' for a fuller discussion).

Whilst legality is increasingly thought to be one component of police legitimacy, what is less clear is the relative importance that citizens and the police attach to legality. Bottoms and Tankebe (2012) argue that for citizens, perceptions of illegality – not legality – are key, with citizens becoming resentful if those in positions of authority do not adhere to the law. In addition, they also argue that for power-holders such as the police, perceptions of their own legality are only a desirable rather than an essential component of whether they regard themselves as legitimate. However, this position is not borne out by recent empirical research. Meares et al. (2016) argue that there is a disconnect between how the police and citizens evaluate police authority. Police officers largely evaluate their legitimacy through the prism of lawfulness, and they are socialised into this way of thinking both in training (Meares and Neyroud, 2015: 10–11), as well as on the job (for example, where unlawful, not procedurally unfair, conduct is punished). Lawfulness is thus seen by the police as conferring protection, though Meares et al. (2016) do not provide any empirical data to support this point. By contrast, the public focus on the procedural fairness of an encounter, rather than its lawfulness, by which they mean the non-legal normative standards that exist, such being spoken to politely and treated with dignity and respect (see also section 'How the police use their authority in police custody' for a more detailed definition). In particular, based on a national (non-representative) survey of Americans, Meares et al. (2016) found that for respondents to their survey, perceptions of lawfulness were based largely on whether they perceived an encounter to be procedurally fair rather than on its actual lawfulness. Thus, they go on to say that "there is a fundamental disconnect between the lawfulness frame that characterises police-thinking about the propriety of their conduct and the procedural fairness frame through which the public evaluates police and their actions" (Meares et al. 2016: 301). Skinns and Sorsby (2017) also found a similar disconnect between police and suspect understandings of police authority in police detention in England and Wales. For staff, acting according to legal rules was paramount, whilst for detainees, the quality of interpersonal treatment was key, in particular being treated with kindness, which was strongly correlated with detainees' overall sense of satisfaction with their detention.

How the police use their authority in police custody: coerced, normative, symbolic ('taken-for-granted') and manipulated/induced

The recent paradigm shift in police studies, marked by the growth of interest in police legitimacy, points to a need to look at not just *whether* the police uphold the law and citizens' access their legal rights, but also *how* they uphold it and in particular whether the police act in procedurally just ways. This involves the interlinked concepts of the quality of treatment and the quality of decision-making (Donner et al., 2015; Tyler et al., 2015; Jackson et al.,

2013: 10). For example, if citizens are treated by the police with dignity and respect, this is likely to enhance police legitimacy and citizen cooperation. Next, I examine theories about *how* the police use their authority, arguing that legitimate forms of citizen compliance with the police are only one part of the picture, coexisting alongside coerced, symbolic and induced forms of compliance.

Drawing on existing research, police authority and citizen compliance are conceptualised in the present book as multipronged,[9] entailing four main components: coercive compliance; normative compliance (police legitimacy); a kind of taken-for-granted compliance based on the cultural and symbolic significance of the police; and compliance based on manipulation and inducement. Moreover, in the context of police custody, there is evidence to suggest that these forms of authority / citizen compliance coexist. For example, though police officers in police detention may begin by using softer, more legitimate forms of authority, if detainees do not comply with them, they then switch to firmer forms of authority involving coercion (Skinns, 2011a: 196–9). This interweaving of forms of authority and compliance has also been found in prisons. For instance, Crewe (2009: 85–86) notes that threats and veiled suggestions by prison officers constitute a form of "psychic violence" that is suggestive of both coercive and symbolic forms of power.

First, with regard to coercive forms of police authority, police powers, including the power to use force, mean that if detainees do not wish to do something that is asked of them, then they may be compelled to do so. However, what is also important is not just that coercive powers exist, but rather that there is a constant and pervasive sense of the *possibility* that they may be used, therefore underscoring all interactions between citizens and the police (Bittner, 1970: 26). This possibility is of paramount importance when it comes to what some regard as the police power that defines their role in society, that is, their monopoly over the use of legitimate force. According to Bittner, for example, the role of the police in society is "as a mechanism for the distribution of non-negotiably coercive force employed in accordance with the dictates of an intuitive grasp of situational exigencies" (1970: 46). It is their unique capacity to use force in a largely unrestricted range of circumstances that defines their role. This capacity to use force also distinguishes them from other agencies, such as the military, who also have an authorised capacity to use force. The implication of Bittner's thesis is that the possibility of using force – whether to effect an arrest or a strip search – underscores all police powers and inculcates in the population an obligation to obey the police. That is to say, it has a deterrent effect on citizens who weigh up the consequences of obeying police orders, and this compels most of them to accede to the demands of the police. This also has the effect of turning the police into an agency of last resort, who are called on to deal with situations involving "something-that-ought-not-to-be-happening-and-about-which-someone-had-better-do-something-now" (Bittner, 1990: 249).

At the same time, this utilitarian understanding of police powers – where the recipients of them rationally weigh up the costs and benefits – does not capture the diverse circumstances in which the police are called on to act and in which coercive powers are not used at all. Research over the last 50 years has exposed the mythological status of the police solely as crime-fighters (and by implication as law enforcers). It has also pointed to their importance as, amongst other things, social workers, negotiators and mediators, and in safe-guarding not just social order, but the well-being of individual citizens and wider society (Millie, 2013; Brodeur, 2010: 155; Reiner, 2010: 244; Bayley, 1996; Bittner, 1990: 237; Punch, 1979). However, this research has failed to dislodge this mythological status. Politicians and the police have continued to cling on to this belief. This is partly a consequence of the law-and-order po-litical climate from the late 1970s onwards, as well as due to the more recent decline in crime, which has enabled the police to claim they are effective as crime-fighters, even though this does not always marry up with the realities of the job.

Nor does this utilitarian understanding of police power capture the im-portance of police-citizen interactions as "teachable moments" in which pro-cedurally just interactions – founded on the respectful, polite and dignified treatment of citizens by the police – are key (Tyler et al., 2014: 4). This points to the second way in which the police and their associated powers can be con-ceptualised, namely, as a legitimate authority. Police legitimacy is generally thought to mean the sense of obligation that citizens feel to obey the police. However, drawing on Beetham (1991: 15–16), scholars have extended this understanding of police legitimacy to include more than simply an expressed consent to being policed by citizens. They point as well to the importance of the normative justifiability of power, that is, whether the rules policing agents employ are premised on shared beliefs between them and policed pop-ulations, such as about what constitutes an appropriate social order (Jackson et al., 2013: 13–14; Tyler, 2011; Tyler, 2004; Sunshine and Tyler, 2003). Fur-thermore, they point to the legality of police actions, that is, whether their behaviour conforms to established rules (Bottoms and Tankebe, 2012).[10] An extensive array of recent research has pointed to the overriding importance of procedural justice – notably the fair and respectful decision-making and treatment – to citizen conceptions of police legitimacy and their cooperation with the police and compliance with the law (Donner et al., 2015; Tyler et al., 2015; Mazerolle et al., 2013). However, the fact that legitimate forms of authority can coexist, in reality, alongside coercive forms of authority under-scores an unresolved tension in theories about police powers (which stretches back to the work of Weber), about the relative balance of coercive and legit-imate forms of power, that is, between the "iron fist and the velvet glove" (Skinns, 2012).

The relative balance between coercive and legitimate police power is not the end of the story either. As Loader and Mulcahy (2006: 39–40) note, too often in literature on the sociology of the police, the police have been reduced to their coercive powers, with less recognition being given to the cultural resonance of the police institution and its symbolic power, which is the third way in which police power can be understood. In terms of the culture of English policing, this refers to "the institutions, practices and policies, myths, memories, meanings and values that, at any given time, constitute the idea of policing within English society" (Loader and Mulcahy, 2006: 55).[11] This leads to a taken-for-granted sense of the police role in society and a kind of 'dull compulsion', in relation to police power. This is manifest, so Loader and Mulcahy (2006: 55) argue, in a set of durable, entrenched and preconscious ways of seeing and feeling about the police. This dull compulsion is also manifest in the perceived legitimacy of the police to diagnose, classify and make pronouncements, not only about social disorder and criminality, but also about power, morality, social norms and personhood, all of which are taken for granted (Loader and Mulcahy, 2006: 55). In light of the history of the police institution in Australia, Ireland and the US, in which, at least for some, the police became seen as saving fledgling postcolonial societies from descending into disorder (see Chapter 4 for further details), there is reason to think that the police will have a similarly important cultural significance.

This taken-for-granted aspect of power has also been documented in work on the sociology of prisons. Crewe (2009: 80–86), for example, notes the habitual, ritual and fatalistic resignation that some prisoners express, which he argues comes from a sense that there are no alternatives and that one's subordination is inevitable and unalterable. He goes on to argue that it is a mode of power that is taken for granted within the prison context, as part of prisoners' routines and habits; for example, it comes from prisoners' observance of prison rules, which act as symbolic reminders of institutional domination.

The prison studies literature, which is of particular relevance to the analysis of the use of police power in the quasi-prison-like environment of police custody (Skinns, 2011a: 200–2), also points to a fourth dimension of compliance, namely, manipulation or inducement (Crewe, 2009: 80–86). This form of compliance emerges through the use of official and unofficial rewards and sanctions; for example, seemingly trivial rewards can acquire an elevated status given the sparseness of the prison environment. Such seemingly trivial rewards have been shown to exist in the similarly sparse police custody environment. For example, hot drinks and cigarettes have been found to be used by the police as bargaining tools to persuade detainees to do things that they may not wish to do, whether that is to go to their cell or speak to the police (Skinns, 2011a: 98–99). Such inducement means that detainees/prisoners actively seek them out, even if this means acting in disingenuous ways, so as to secure them. That is, they may ostensibly 'toe the line' but not because of a commitment to shared moral values, as might be expected with legitimate forms of compliance, rather because it is a way of accessing extra privileges. Equally, staff may manipulate detainees, making them do as they wish because, if they do, detainees will be given an extra hot drink, for example. To some extent, this use of power can be seen as a form of coercion, albeit the sanctions and rewards employed are less obviously coercive than the use of force described above.

Discretion: its origins, meaning and importance

Regardless of whether the police are abiding by legal rules or not, or whether they are employing different styles of authority whilst they do this, their actions in police detention or in other policing contexts are, in part, influenced by discretion.

The origins of discretion

Discretion permeates all aspects of the police institution, meaning that it is a central topic in the field of police studies and, as will be argued, to the examination of police powers and citizens' rights. Yet, it was only relatively recently 'discovered' by American scholars; as described later in this chapter, Goldstein (1960) 'discovered' discretion, with Davis (1975, 1969) then setting the terms of the debate about how it should be controlled (Dixon, 1997: 300).[12] During the ascendancy of the police in England, for example, ideologies about the full enforcement of the law (as discussed in the section above on legality), helped establish police legitimacy. They were used to overcome any scepticism about the impartiality of the police, as it could be assumed that the police were a neutral social institution which was there to protect the rights of all citizens equally (Reiner, 2010: 243).[13] This understanding of the police institution ruled out the possibility that discretion occurred. It was presumed that the police simply followed the rules and that to understand the police one only had to look at the laws and administrative rules that regulated them (Ericson, 2007; Dixon, 1997: 1–9).

However, it was with the emergence of police studies, in the 1950s and the 1960s, that scholars began to note the highly discretionary nature of police decision-making. In fact, Dixon (1997: 3) argues that modern academic work on the police only began with the 'discovery' that police work is highly discretionary and that mostly it does not revolve around law enforcement. This acknowledgement of police discretion was logically accompanied by growing scepticism about police adherence to legal and administrative rules, which was shortly followed by an acknowledgement of the role played by informal rules, values and norms that comprise police cultures. It was also no coincidence that this questioning attitude towards the police arose in the 1960s, at a time when deferential attitudes towards those in authority were beginning to wane (Loader and Mulcahy, 2006: 18; Reiner, 1995, 1992). However, the development of more social science-oriented conceptions of discretion were somewhat stymied by the legal origins of the concept. Discretion was a concept which initially received a great deal of attention by legal scholars (e.g. Hart, 1994: 124–36; Dworkin, 1977: 31) who aimed to develop prescriptive theories. This made the development of descriptive theories and the empirical investigation of discretion difficult (Nickels, 2007).[14] Yet, as Nickels (2007) also notes, such empirical examination of discretion is essential for the development of social science understandings of the police institution, including in the present book.

Defining discretion

> Sometimes when I know a guy is 10–30 [wanted], I like to say, 'Pick a number between one and ten'. He'll say, 'Six!' And I'll say, 'put your hand behind your back'. 'That ain't fair man!'. But you gotta have fun.
>
> (Moskos, 2008: 115).

This description by a police officer of how he sometimes decided whether to make low-level non-drug-related arrests in areas known for high levels of drug dealing in Baltimore offers an insight into the way in which police discretion operates, in practice, and the sometimes farcical but also cruel way in which arrest decisions are made. This process is unlikely to be "fun" for the arrestee, whilst probably also serving as a crude way for this officer to establish some degree of personal power in front of the arrestee, colleagues and bystanders.

From an academic perspective, in a pioneering and influential study of discretion by Davis (1969),[15] discretion was defined as when the effective legal limits on a public officer "leave him [or her] free to make a choice among possible courses of action or inaction" (p. 4). In his 1975 study of discretion in the Chicago Police Department, he similarly defined police discretion as being about variations in the extent to which the police enforced the law, noting that "some law is always or almost always enforced, some is never or almost never enforced, and some is sometimes enforced and sometimes not" (Davis, 1975: 1).[16] Lustgarten (1986), also a legal scholar interested in public law and criminal justice, defined discretion in the same way as Davis (1969), adding that the "room for decisional manoeuvre" is a matter of degree, which varies "with the precision of the standards governing an official's discretion" (Lustgarten, 1986: 10). Furthermore, he added that though they may not break criminal or civil laws (e.g. by accepting a bribe or assaulting someone), police officers act with an almost infinite range of lawful possibilities. For example, if they are called to break up a fight between two parties, in which one may be guilty of common assault, they can choose to break it up and give an informal warning. Alternatively, they might break it up, enquire about the cause and attempt to reconcile them. Or they could inquire into the cause and arrest the party they believe to be guilty. A further option is that they arrest both parties on other charges and investigate further. Therefore, he dealt with a key criticism of Davis' definition of discretion, namely, that he failed to distinguish authorised from illicit forms of decision-making. The point is that the police have the *"authority* to make a choice" (Nickels, 2007: 573), suggesting that "discretion is not simply a capacity to make choice … but a permission, privilege or prerogative" (Kleinig, 1999: 6), which is embedded in the legal and administrative rules constraining their work.

Though legal scholars may dispute this on the basis that discretion is primarily about legal responsibility, not human action, more generally (Nickels, 2007), discretion can also be defined in sociological terms, as a form of human agency. As with other forms of human agency, police discretion cannot be seen as entirely separate from the cultural and social structures that continually shape, influence and guide social action. Police officers like all other social actors have a 'choice'. That is, the decisions that police officers make – such as about how they use their authority – are affected by the immediate context (including legal rules and policies), but also structural circumstances in which those decisions are taken. For example, drawing on Giddens' structuration theory, Campbell (1999) argues that, from a social scientific standpoint, police discretion, like any form of human agency, is rarely free from constraint. Rather, behaviour is structured and structuring, with the law being only one of a number of limitations imposed on it. This means that once these cultures, including police cultures, and social structures are taken into account, discretion is never as unfettered as it appears (Campbell, 1999).[17]

Discretionary decision-making arises at all levels of the police organisation, albeit the discretionary decisions taken by officers on the street are regarded as the most significant by some, in part, because of their frequency, but also because of their low visibility, often taking place in circumstances away from the gaze of superior officers (Lipsky, 2010: 16, 18–23; Goldstein, 1960). However, the gulf between operational and managerial discretionary decision-making may not be as great as Goldstein (1960) suggests. Lustgarten (1986), for example, notes that policy decisions taken by managers can turn out to be operational ones; for instance, stop-and-search policies eventually become manifest in everyday contact with the public. Indeed, for Lustgarten (1986: 20), such policy decisions may be *more* significant than those taken at the operational level. This is because managerial discretionary decisions affect matters that are fundamental to the police institution, like the definition of the crime problem, the style of policing (hard vs. soft), the deployment of staff (number and where deployed) and the use of certain technologies. Unlike the decisions taken by officers on the street, these managerial decisions are inherently political, entailing judgements about moral values, favouring certain interests over others and weighing up competing claims for scarce resources. Though these policy decisions may not be as evidently politicised as those on the street, as Lustgarten (1986: 20) suggests, it is helpful to recognise the continuum of discretionary decision-making that exists from officers out on the street to those at the apex of the organisation.

The necessity of discretion

Though undoubtedly problematic, police discretion is also regarded as a necessary part of the police role. Davis, for example, saw it as

> absolutely essential. It cannot be eliminated. Any effort to eliminate it would be ridiculous. Discretion is the essence of police work, both in law enforcement and service activities. Police work without discretion would be something like a human torso without legs, arms, or head... But that proposition is entirely consistent with two other essential propositions – that excessive or unnecessary discretion can and should be eliminated, and that necessary discretion should be properly controlled.
>
> (1975: 140–1)

The necessity of discretion can be seen as partly rooted in the vagaries and misunderstandings of the police role in society (Millie, 2013; Brodeur, 2010: 155; Reiner, 2010: 244; Bayley, 1996; Bittner, 1990: 237), meaning that discretion is required to pursue these different mandates, enabling them to at times prioritise other matters over strict enforcement of the law. Though the police are thought of by the public, politicians and often by the police themselves as 'crime-fighters', this belies the complexity and wide-ranging nature of the role, including peacekeeping, social order maintenance, acting as a social service and an agency of last resort, as well as enforcing the criminal law. Indeed, these purposes may be sometimes competing and, therefore, at odds with each other, thereby requiring discretion to disentangle this complexity and enable the police to act. For example, as noted above, Scarman (1981: 63) regarded discretion as a key way of resolving the conflict between the need for public tranquillity and the excessive enforcement of the law, as happened prior to the Brixton Riots in London in 1981. This makes discretion a necessary part of the role of the police in society. The varied role of the police furthermore means that the situations they encounter are idiosyncratic, making it hard to draw up any preordained rules for them to apply (Bittner, 1974: 18, cited in Lustgarten, 1986). Moreover, when in these situations, police officers also have to make decisions at speed, which also does not lend itself to the application of rules. What is more, particularly in the current climate of economic austerity, limited police resources provide a further reason why under-enforcement of the law through the use of discretion is a necessity in some circumstances. For example, Moskos (2008: 112–3) attributes the necessity of decision-making to the lack of supervisors immediately at hand when officers are out on the streets, such that "the idea that officers should be allowed to make their own decisions is never in question." In a nutshell, the complex role of the police in society and the complex situations they encounter, combined with limited resources, means that it is impossible to enforce all laws against all offenders all of the time, and that discretion is essential.

The necessity of discretion is also connected to the complexity but also to the vagaries of the law itself. Discretion is required to overcome such complexity and uncertainty. In terms of its complexity, no legislature has succeeded in formulating laws that encompass all conduct which could be construed as criminal, or in excluding all other conduct that is not. In most countries, there is a tendency for obsolete and poorly drafted legislation to continue to exist on the books, even if it is not used much, thereby also necessitating discretion. What is more, the law is vague itself. Contrary to the certainty suggested by the notion of the "rule of law," the "law in modern society ... is as elusive and as adaptable as a chameleon" (McBarnet, 1981: 165). These complexities and vagaries of the law mean that there cannot be a straightforward way for police officers on the street to interpret the law and put it into practice. Public order offences, such as offensive language and behaviour in parts of Australia, for example, are so broad that virtually any behaviour could be included in this offence, and so the police are in a position to either under-enforce or over-enforce these laws. This raises the possibility of selective enforcement against some social groups more than others and therefore unfairness and injustice (Lustgarten, 1986: 16).

This points to a third and final reason why discretion is a necessity, which is connected to the consequences of the law. Whilst discretionary practices may lead to unfairness and injustice depending on which laws are under-enforced and against whom, equally, overly zealous and strict enforcement of the law could have a similar consequence, resulting in harsh and intolerable results, with differential consequences for some social groups (Bronitt and Stenning, 2011: 323). As such, discretion becomes a necessity in order to avoid such harsh consequences and to try to ensure that (socially) just outcomes can prevail.

The definition and importance of discretion in this book

As the foregoing discussion suggests, police discretion is a potent part of police work affecting action as well as inaction, yet it is also an ambiguous concept. It potentially includes a range of dimensions such as

> The capacity to make a work-related decision; the authority to make a legal decision; the use of judgement or interpretation in legal decisions; the relative indeterminacy of the law in legal outcomes; the relative salience of extralegal factors; the sheer variability of outcomes across similarly situated legal contexts; the individual agency presumed to drive that variation; the decision making process, per se; and more.
>
> (Nickels, 2007: 570)

For the purposes of this book, discretion is defined as police officers' perceptions of the quantity and nature of their *authorised* capacity to make choices about different courses of action or inaction, which are structured by and structuring of the legal and administrative rules, as well as the wider cultural and social structures that surround their work. This definition draws on the individualised perception-driven forms of police discretion found in Davis' (1969, 1975) work, as well as the importance placed on the relationship that police discretion has with the law and thus the distinction between authorised and illicit forms of discretionary decision-making (Kleinig, 1996). At the same time, this definition also adds a more social science-oriented understanding of police discretion found in the work of Campbell (1999), acknowledging that discretion is more than a mere legal responsibility; it can also be seen as a form of human action embedded within cultural and structural contexts. Drawing on Nickels (2007), this definition also emphasises that discretion might vary in its quantity, but also in its quality and the form that it takes, in any given policing situation.

In terms of the importance of discretion in the present book, as argued above, discretionary decision-making exists throughout police organisations and, moreover, it is a necessity, for example, in order for the police to be able to put the law into practice. It is therefore central to the way that the power of the police operates, as described earlier in this chapter. It likely influences the style of authority the police employ, including coercive authority. Indeed, this was something that Bittner was aware of, saying "our expectation that police men will use force, coupled by our refusal to state clearly what we mean by it (aside from sanctimonious homilies) smacks of more than a bit of perversity" (Bittner, 1990: 122). It also implicated when the police induce citizen compliance, for example, using cigarettes and hot drinks as bargaining tools (Skinns, 2011a: 98–99). In this context, discretion becomes a kind of 'soft power', in which seemingly mundane material goods of any kind potentially become instruments of control, which contribute to the dispersal of power throughout custodial settings (Crewe, 2009: 104–9).

Sociological understandings of police discretion/agency are also important to this book because of their implications for state-citizen relations in neoliberal societies. The agentic potential of the police through their discretionary powers means that they become a mechanism through which neoliberal discourses, values and expectations – such as about the importance of active, responsibilised citizens – may impact on how police use their authority with those who are alleged to have broken the law. Police agency/discretion is potentially part of the process by which the police become a site of neoliberal governance, in which they both embody and reproduce the values of neoliberalism. To an extent, this is examined by Kaplan-Lyman (2012), who notes that the valorisation of individual responsibility means that the neoliberal state does not solve the problems it creates.[18] Instead, lawbreakers are blamed, individually, for the 'poor' choices they have made and find themselves on the receiving end of punitive policing practices, such as order-maintenance policing, which "functions structurally as one of the neoliberal state's primary technologies to deal with the effects of poverty through the individuation of crime" (2012: 209–10). The present book adds further empirical evidence to this. It is argued that discretionary decision-making in police detention seemed to be greater in the American city in the research, which was partially a consequence of a climate in which neoliberal values were more commonplace.

Ultimately, discretion is an important concept in the present book, as discretionary decision-making affects the equitable distribution of the benefits and impositions of policing. It also impacts on patterns of social ordering, in which citizens become cognisant of their sense of citizenship and their place in society relative to others (Lerman and Weaver, 2014: 2; Herbert, 2006a: 7, 2006b). The many discretionary decisions that the police make on a regular basis about who to stop, search and arrest influence the flow of different social groups into the criminal justice system, based on their ethnicity, social class, age, gender, etc. In turn, this influences who comes to be regarded as 'criminal', perhaps reinforcing (or not) stereotypes about typical and atypical offenders and expectations about the orderliness of their behaviour (e.g. Hall et al., 1978: 389–97). That is, discretionary police decisions – such as about policing tactics and how and where they are deployed – can shape and even construct the crime problem, as well as limiting access to but also reconstructing the meaning of citizenship for those in contact with criminal justice institutions (Lerman and Weaver, 2014: 28). Rather than the benefits and impositions of policing being equitably distributed across society, therefore, they become concentrated amongst particular social groups and in particular geographical areas.

Accountability: playing it "by the book"?

Thus far it has been argued that the police have a wide array of powers at their disposal to stop, search, arrest, detain, investigate and surveil. If ordinary citizens were to do some of the things that the police do, then they would be regarded as illegal. The police have specific legal exemptions from certain prohibitions, providing them with powers to do certain things (in the interests of wider society's safety and security), and this is what separates them from the rest of society. *Whether* the police abide by the rules relating to these powers amounts to legality. That the police have authority is a given, but *how* they use this authority is less clear-cut. Sometimes they use their authority in a coercive manner, compelling citizens, such as through the use of force (coerced authority). However, by and large, they rely on citizens complying with them either because citizens feel they have no choice, given the cultural and symbolic authority of the police (symbolic compliance) or because they feel that they have been treated fairly and trust the motives of the police (legitimate compliance). *Whether* and *how* the police use their powers is a discretionary matter. Officers from across police organisations have a mandate to choose between different courses of action or inaction, including whether they invoke the criminal law and how. Some such as Goldstein (1960) also note that the low visibility of police work on the street means that lower ranking and more junior officers tend to have more discretion and that, moreover, this is an inevitable and necessary feature of police work, albeit this also underplays the significance of the discretion of police managers (Lustgarten, 1986: 20).

In combination, police discretion and the power of the police mean that there is a clear necessity to ensure that the police act in ways which are appropriate to these responsibilities. It is necessary to ensure that they perform their duties in good faith and in accordance with the law and other rule structures and, when they do not, that they can be asked to explain and account for their behaviour. This is also a way of controlling the police so that they do not abuse the powers that are vested in them. This reflects Chan's (1999) two-pronged definition of accountability. On the one hand, accountability is concerned with *control* over the police, in particular, the degree of control over the police by political institutions (e.g. by government and politicians) (see also Lustgarten, 1986: 1). So, accountability thus becomes like a form of regulation. On the other hand, it is said to be fundamentally about "requirements to give accounts" or explanations of conduct. This expresses a more limited sense of control over the police. Giving an explanation is one thing, but the person giving the explanation need not necessarily consider or act on any challenges to this explanation.[19] In reality, as explored in Chapter 2, the police are expected to do both in the cities/jurisdictions of interest in this book with varying levels of effectiveness.

The law and other rule structures including formal police policies and codes of practice, as well as informal rules connected to police occupational cultures, are fundamental influences on the explanations the police give for their (discretionary) decision-making and behaviour.[20] That is, accountability for discretionary decision-making and behaviour cannot just be thought of solely in terms of the legal and administrative rules; rather, it has to also be seen in relation to the informal rules associated with police cultures.[21] This enables us to go beyond false dichotomies about discretion, involving a simple choice between legal rules and unfettered discretion, and takes us into a more subtle, and social science-oriented, conceptualisation of discretion. This entails not just a simple choice between legal rules and discretion, but rather a choice between "different kinds of rules and different degrees of permissible discretion" (Walker, 1993: 20), within different sociocultural contexts. Therefore, how can the relationship between these rules and degrees of discretion be theorised?

A key account of the intertwined relationship between rules and police discretion is offered by Ericson (2007); in particular, he is concerned with the interrelationship between police discretion and a variety of rules, including legal and administrative rules, as well as the informal rules of police cultures.[22] Though he recognises that these rules' structures and the police themselves intersect with social, cultural, political and economic structures, this is not something carefully drawn out in his thesis. He does, however, focus on the following question: "How do criminal law and procedure, as well as other types of rules, relate to police decisions?" Drawing on Anglo-American literature, he then offers five ways of conceptualising the relationship between rule structures and discretionary decision-making: following the rules; using the rules (with the help of the law); beyond the rules; within the rules (as a result of communication formats); without the rules. Details about each of these ideal-types are shown in Table 2.1.

Table 2.1 Ericson's (2007) five-pronged typology of the relationship between discretion and rules structures

Typology	Discretion	Rule structures
Following the rules	• Discretion as a form of deviance. • It is also largely unnecessary and to be curtailed if not eliminated.	• Legal and administrative rules are followed at all times and police powers, specifically, are a set of instructions to be followed. • Rules eliminate discretion. • Rules lead to police reform.
Using the rules	• Discretion is inseparable from the law as "police discretion is part of criminal law" (p. 373).	• The law is inherently permissive and enables the police to pursue their own agenda (e.g. crime control over due process).
Beyond the rules	• Discretionary decisions have a logic of their own that exists beyond the formal legal rules. • This knowledge is embedded in the role and derived from the practice of being a police officer.	• Rule structures are largely superfluous to discretionary decision-making and, at best, in the background.
Within the rules	• Discretion cannot be thought of as deviance per se as is the case for the "following the rules" type. However, not following communication procedures can be regarded as deviant.	• Rules influence discretionary decision-making but only because they are embedded within police communication processes.
Without rules	• Discretion is dispersed through pluralised global policing networks.	• In these global pluralised policing networks, policing agents are able to work without being confined by legal rules as domestic law does not apply or private laws and policies exist instead.

Source: Ericson (2007).

These types coexist rather than being mutually exclusive. Ericson (2007) argues that police officers' orientation to the rules depends on the rules in question and the circumstances faced, meaning that any one of these five orientations to the rules may be possible for any given police officer. For example, when asked to account for their behaviour, the police will demonstrate the rule-following orientation. Yet, in day-to-day policing, they are more likely to sidestep or break the rules or act in ways that are beyond the rules. This is because the rules are only in the background, playing a lesser role against the backdrop of embodied knowledge, which is what actually gives meaning to the rules. Next, I outline in more detail each of these orientations to discretionary decision-making and their relationships with legal, administrative and informal rules associated with police culture. Whilst I use Ericson's conceptual framework (2007) as the basis for the discussion, I also expand it by drawing on additional literature, which falls into each of the rule-following categories, and by considering how Ericson's (2007) framework applies to police detention, bearing in mind that his framework largely focused on street policing.

Following the rules

According to this type, importance is attached to the police following the rules – both legal and administrative – at all times. Discretion is, therefore, perceived as a form of deviance, which can be seen in either benign ways (e.g. getting the job done through liberal interpretation of rules) or less benign ways (in which the police intentionally pursue their own agenda, e.g. crime control justified by a sense of the nobility of their actions). Police powers – as a specific set of legal rules – are seen as a set of instructions to be followed and as something that provides exemptions from civil or legal liability. It also follows, therefore, that within this typology, discretion is regarded as largely unnecessary and as something that has to be curtailed if not eliminated through legal and administrative rules. These rules can also, therefore, act as a powerful way of reforming the police. Together this means that the police are also a barometer for rule-governed order and for the authority of the state in citizens' lives.

Much of the early research on discretion tended to view police decision-making and behaviour in this way. Goldstein (1960), for example, was one of the first to note the centrality of discretion to police decision-making and its contribution to the under-enforcement of the law. He voiced a clear preference for the rule of law, which caused him to view police discretion as deviance in need of eradication through the ramping up of the criminal law. Similarly, Davis saw unnecessary forms of police discretion as deviance, which could have unfair and unjust consequences (1969: 25).[23] For Davis (1969), however, the optimal control of discretion could not come about through the review and revision of the criminal law (as Goldstein suggested). Instead, given his role as the founding father of administrative law, he argued that hope lies "not in better statutory standards, but in earlier and more elaborate administrative rule-making ..." (Davis, 1969: 219), as well as in transparent administrative rules created through transparent processes. Therefore, he was encouraging a need for openness, requiring officials to explain how they planned to make and how they did make decisions, as part of an attempt to create greater openness in government (Dixon, 1997: 300).

As such, Davis (1969) was advocating for wholesale reform of the police institution and its legal context. However, there is little evidence to suggest that these suggested reforms had a direct effect on police practices in the US (Levin, 2005; Dixon, 1997: 305–6). This was partly due to shifts in the prevailing climate of police work; for example, in the US in the 1980s, discretion came to be embraced, not minimised, within community policing and order-maintenance policing, as police officers were required to flexibly adapt to local conditions. However, as noted in Chapter 4, this embracing of police discretion in the 1980s was not just a passing fad, but one deeply rooted in the history and culture of the police in the US (Brodeur, 2010: 71; Scott, 2010; Walker, 2008; Haller, 1976). By contrast, in England, the legitimation of the 'new police' arose in part from the symbolism and emphasis placed on the rule of law (Brodeur, 2010: 72; Dixon, 1997: 121). Therefore, the need to reform the police, based on more extensive legal or administrative rules was less of a "hard sell" to both the police and the citizens.

Hence, when PACE 1984 was introduced in England and Wales,[24] though it met with a range of responses by the police, including resistance, it was fairly readily accepted, with new generations of police officers coming to take it for granted (Skinns, 2011a: 9–10). Therefore, it is likely that in police detention in England, as well as in other countries, such as Ireland and Australia, which have introduced a similarly formalised approach to its regulation (see Chapter 4), one might expect to see greater acceptance and expressions of rule-following behaviour. Just because administrative rules failed to take root in police work in the US, it does not make the failure of rules inevitable elsewhere, albeit there are also limits to the extent to which such rules impact on discretionary police decision-making. This is due to the sometimes ends-focused nature of police work, in which police officers make the rules work for them, something that was not properly acknowledged by Davis (Dixon, 1997: 303–4). As discussed in the following sections, even in the highly regulated confines of police detention in England, these legal and administrative rules are not always strictly followed. They are undermined by ambiguities in the way these rules are written, by informal rules which build up over time and through practice, as well as by the police's pursuit of their own priorities.

Using the rules

"Using the rules" is nearly the opposite of the rule-following type. Within this type, the police use the criminal law to pursue their own agenda (e.g. prioritising crime control over due process) or to engage in deviant activities.

This means that the police might use the criminal law to obtain compliance with a criminal investigation, for example, turning a blind eye to a minor offence, in exchange for important information. Police use of the law to pursue their own agenda is enabled by vague legal terms and the inherently permissive nature of the law, in the ways that McBarnet (1981: 165) highlights. She regards the law as elusive, adaptive and open to interpretation, yet it appears as if it promotes the principles of democratic societies, such as impartiality and equality (McBarnet, 1981: 165). According to Ericson (2007), this using of the law for their own purposes is illustrated by situations in which the police arrest people for obstructing them because the people are being troublesome, not because they are actually obstructing them in their duties. Furthermore, the police use the law to pursue their own agenda, for example, when they arrest someone and then use the law to rationalise their actions post hoc. In such situations, reference to the legal rules helps to legitimise their actions and cover their backs should they be asked to account for them.

This type is illustrated by research on police custody in situations when the police use the law and its associated rules to assert their authority and demonstrate who is in charge, particularly when suspects show "contempt of cop" (Loftus, 2010) by shouting, swearing and generally being non-compliant. For example, legally permissible acts, such as forcibly removing detainees to the cells, strip searching them or using other forms of force or threats of it were, at times, used to cultivate a sense of "total police custody," so that even the most recalcitrant suspect would comply in the end (Skinns et al., 2016: 51). Hence, this police officer said,

> you have got to have a few rules haven't you? ... If they are demanding stuff off you and treating you like complete shit, showing no respect or manners whatsoever and shouting abuse ... if they are up there [in terms of their non-compliance], they have got to come down, or they are never going to be dealt with, so they have got to know who's in charge and it's us.
>
> (MC_CS5)

Beyond the rules

Within this type, discretionary decisions have a logic of their own that exists beyond the formal legal rules. This logic comes from the practice of being a police officer and from knowledge embedded within the role, all of which give meaning to rules and determine discretionary decision-making, rather than the law or policies. Rule structures are, therefore, largely superfluous to discretionary decision-making and at best exist as part of the background and as part of a wider "habitus" of embodied knowledge. In essence, Ericson (2007) argues that there may be formal legal rules, but these are not the rules that police officers use to guide their daily decision-making and behaviour;

rather, they rely on rules which are informal and embedded within their day-to-day knowledge of the job.

This type of beyond-the-rules behaviour has been recently demonstrated in the work of Dehaghani (2016) on vulnerable detainees in police detention in England. Her research shows that the vagueness of concepts, such as mentally vulnerable and mentally disordered, meant that they were variously interpreted by staff, drawing on subjective and culture-laden views of the concept of vulnerability which had been built up over time and through practice. For example, when asked to explain vulnerability, custody officers did not refer to the legal definition set out in the PACE Codes of Practice. Instead, they talked about their working definitions of the term, in which they referred to mental health, poor physical health, addiction, learning difficulties, inexperience of the criminal justice system, the nature of the offence arrested for (e.g. child sex offence), as well as to how detainees were responding to the unpredictability, uncertainty and power dynamics of police custody.

Within the rules

The "within the rules" typology is to some extent a variant of the "following the rules" type. Rules are followed by the police, but only because they are embedded within specific forms of communication. These include incident report forms which are often paperless and involve tick-box, not free-text, boxes; standardised and multiple paper forms used to pass case files to prosecutors; and mass media representations of legal rules (e.g. police procedurals portraying Miranda rules, such as the right to silence).[25] These media representations of the legal rules contribute to the creation of myths, which shape public perceptions and actions in relation to legal rules, as well as those of the police. "The police are compelled to engage in a public 'moral performance' of their conformity to rules, and this performance has a bearing on the achievement of justice …" (Ericson, 2007: 387). Since rules are followed because they are embedded within forms of communication, this means that discretion cannot be thought of as deviance per se, as is the case for the "following the rules" type. However, not following communication procedures (e.g. not filling in the requisite number of forms required for a file to be passed to a prosecutor) can be regarded as deviant.

Drawing on my more recent work on police custody in England, it is evident that within-the-rules behaviour does arise in police custody. As noted by Skinns and Wooff (2017), the construction of risk is partly embedded in risk-assessment tools which are used to ostensibly objectively measure risk, such as on arrival into police detention (the initial risk assessment) and prior to release (the pre-release risk assessment). In some ways these risk-assessment tools are similar to the "communications about risk" that Ericson and Haggerty (1997: 17–19) note, in that assessments of risk were embedded within the paperwork that staff had to fill in about every detainee and in

the technology that they used to do this, as well as in routine police procedures and surveillance. For example, an initial risk assessment was conducted
by staff by going through a series of tick-box questions on their computer
screen. These questions were supposed to be asked to detainees – word for
word and in a set order – about their past and present physical and emotional
well-being, as well as about any learning disability. This risk assessment was
seen by staff as both a proactive tool to prevent risky events from happening
in the first place, as well as a mechanism for covering their backs, if anything
untoward were to happen to detainees in custody. Whilst some staff preferred
to retreat into the comfort and security of abiding by the risk-assessment
rules, others took a more subjective and intuitive approach. Based on their
knowledge and experience of the job, they would, for example, ask the questions in a non-standard order and turn the risk assessment into an informal
conversation. This was an expression of their discretion with regard to the
risk-assessment rules, with transgression being rooted in non-adherence to
the risk-assessment rules rather than in the discretion itself.

Without rules

Within this fifth type, unlike for the "beyond the rules" type, there are limited formal legal rules. However, discretionary decision-making within these
legal rules is dispersed, for instance, through pluralised policing networks, in
which the police work alongside the private sector and other criminal justice actors, sometimes also in global settings (Bowling and Sheptycki, 2012:
53–57, 64–66; Bowling, 2010: 5–11; Walker, 2008; Andreas and Nadelmann,
2006: 59–154). This type is of relevance to police custody, particularly in
England and Wales, where just over a third of police detention facilities are
staffed by non-warranted (non-sworn) civilian detention officers (i.e. with
none or only limited police powers), who are employed either by the police
or the private sector (Skinns et al., 2017b). Though these civilian detention
officers largely perform different roles from those of police officers (e.g. looking after detainees' welfare whilst police officers deal with legal procedures),
there is also some evidence of 'mission creep' and 'power creep', with them
taking on additional roles and powers (Skinns, 2011a: 140–1). This is evident,
for example, in relation to the authorisation of a suspects' detention. By law,
a suspect's detention can only be authorised by a police officer (the custody
officer), who is supposed to check the facts of someone's arrest to ensure their
arrest and detention is lawful. However, since civilian detention officers have
taken on duties, such as booking suspects in on arrival into police custody,
and given that police officers are often simultaneously supervising a number
of civilian detention officers whilst they perform this role, research shows that
the authorisation of someone's detention may only be cursory. In addition,
this authorisation process may not involve a full check of the facts of their
detention by a police officer (Skinns, 2011a: 140). What this means is that

decisions, such as about the authorisation of detention have, in practice, become shared between the police and civilian detention officers and therefore exist in the hinterland beyond the legal and administrative rules.

Conclusion

To conclude, I examine here how the conceptual framework described in the present chapter links to the main purposes of the book, as well as setting out the key arguments of the book and its contributions to the field of comparative police studies.

The conceptual framework

The main purpose of the book is to explore the nature and extent of police powers – and by implication state powers – relative to citizens' rights and the role that discretion plays in *whether* and *how* they use those powers when citizens are arrested and detained in police custody. In the book, I also examine the extent to which the police are held to account for their discretionary decision-making and behaviour in relation to citizens. It goes beyond merely exploring whether or not the police do or do not safeguard suspects' procedural rights and the extent to which these rights are counterbalanced. Hence, notions of legality and Packer's model of crime control and due process are, on their own, insufficient as an explanatory model. Rather, as discussed in the present chapter, the book is situated in three other sets of related theories about, first, *how* the police use their authority, recognising that legitimate forms of citizen compliance coexist alongside coerced, symbolic and induced forms. Second, as discussed in the present chapter, the book is also situated within theories about the role of discretion in police work and its relationship with various kinds of rule structures including the law, police policies and informal rules. Third, as discussed in Chapters 3 and 4, the book is situated within theories about neoliberalism and its impact on criminal justice, as well as in an understanding of the historical and sociopolitical context in which the police and the state regulate and govern citizens (and each other) in the cities/jurisdictions of interest to the research.

Key arguments

My main thesis is that discretion played a role in whether *and* how the police used their authority across the police detention facilities in all of the cities in the research. However, this was particularly the case in the US city, for example, in relation to decisions about the length of police detention. By contrast, in the other cities/jurisdictions of interest, the law seemed to feature more heavily in discretionary decision-making and appeared to have a more central place in the culture of police detention. The exceptionalism of the city in the US and the greater similarity between the cities in England, Ireland and Australia, with regard to the role of discretionary decision-making and the law in police work, is partially explained by the historically localised nature of police work, revolving around close personal ties between the police and citizens, municipal control of the police and, more broadly, the dispersal of power across the federal system (Brodeur, 2010: 71; Scott, 2010; Walker, 2008; Cavadino and Dignan, 2006b: 55; Haller, 1976). Also important in the US is the relative ineffectiveness of the law 'in the books' and the role of the courts in safeguarding suspects' rights, compared to the more robust approach taken in Australia, England and Ireland, where suspects have a broader range of (human) rights consolidated in legislation which is used to preventatively regulate police detention practices (Dixon, 2019; Weisselberg, 2017). However, a further important explanation of the difference between the city in the US and the rest is its exceptionalism when it comes to neoliberalism. In a city/jurisdiction in which neoliberal values, such as individualism, personal responsibility and a limited state, have a particularly prominent place, it is unsurprising, therefore, to find such values embodied in the day-to-day practices of police officers in the American city in the research, namely, in the individualised discretionary decisions taken about citizens in police detention. That is, neoliberalism and its associated values seemed to accentuate historical tendencies towards highly discretionary police practices in the city in the US. This particularly wide discretion, in the American city in the research, provided scope for disparities and unfairness in the way that that the police treated citizens in police detention. This was particularly so for vulnerable detainees, where vague laws combined with discretionary police powers and a particularly individualised way of applying them to detainees. Therefore, discretionary decision-making in relation to (vulnerable) citizens in police detention, especially in the city in the US, perpetuated neoliberal values, whilst also potentially adding to and compounding the inequalities wrought by neoliberalism. Therefore, echoing Kaplan-Lyman (2012), the police can be seen as an important site of neoliberal governance. However, it is not the only site of neoliberal governance, nor are neoliberalism, or the other factors examined in this book, the only explanations for the highly discretionary decision-making in police detention in the city in the US.[26] As Cavadino and Dignan say "individual nations can be just as quirky and esoteric as individual human beings" (2006b: 36). Consequently, just like penality, police practices remain "irreducibly relatively autonomous from any particular factor or combination of factors, however powerful. Particularities of geography, history and even highly specific political circumstances, can all play their part (Cavadino and Dignan, 2006b: 36).

The contribution of the book

This book makes two main contributions to comparative police studies. First, it fills a number of gaps in the existing literature on police custody. These gaps exist across all the cities/jurisdictions of interest, but particularly in Ireland and in the US. In Ireland, this is partly because criminology and police studies, at the time of the research, were nascent disciplines (Manning, 2012: 355), though fast-growing, as indicated by the recent publication of the first *Handbook of Irish Criminology* (Healy et al., 2016). As a result, there is limited empirical scholarship on the police and none on police detention specifically.

In the US, interest in police detention has waxed and waned. For example, there was little research to be drawn on by the *Miranda* court when making its ruling in the 1960s and, though there was a growth in interest in police detention, in the 20 years or so after the introduction of Miranda in 1966, this interest subsequently waned (Cassell and Hayman, 1996; Leo, 1996a). Since then, however, there have been flurries of critical reflection, often marking anniversaries of the Miranda ruling. In a recent special issue celebrating the fiftieth anniversary of Miranda, there was a wealth of papers examining the empirical and legal aspects of the ruling (Cassell and Fowles, 2017; Maclin, 2017; Rossman, 2017; Slobogin, 2017; Weisselberg, 2017). They reveal a curious tendency in American scholarship on police detention to focus almost entirely on police interrogation practices, rather than police detention processes as a whole.[27] In addition, this American police interrogation scholarship also tends to involve laboratory-based psychological experiments, rather than data collection in the field inside police detention (Dixon, 2019). To some extent, police interrogations are understandably given a central place in the American literature, in part, because of their potentially coercive nature and their contribution to false confessions and miscarriages of justice (Guthrie Ferguson and Leo, 2017; Rossman, 2017; Kassin et al., 2010; Leo, 1996a). At the same time, this means that American scholars have failed to consider the broader processes of coercive control in police detention, connected to the conditions of custody and the way that staff use their authority, which also have a bearing on police interrogation practices.[28] This is particularly important given the large proportion of suspects who are not even interviewed by the police, many of whom will subsequently go on to plead guilty. Given its focus on empirical data collected *inside* police detention (see also Appendix 1), which examines police detention, as a whole, and not just police interrogations, the book will thus make an important contribution to Irish and American police studies.

Furthermore, given that comparative police studies is an underdeveloped field (de Maillard and Roché, 2016; Body-Gendrot and de Wenden, 2014: 2, 9–10; Mawby, 1990: 4–5), there are many gaps thus still to be filled. This includes gaps in relation to police detention, where there are few other comparative studies,[29] and none which examine all the cities/jurisdictions that are the focus of the present book. This is no doubt, in part, due to the complexity of the task in which familiarisation with the historical, social, cultural and political context of police work is an immense but essential undertaking. Hence, such contextual matters are examined at length in Chapters 3 and 4.

Second, the book seeks to contribute to prominent debates in police studies about police legitimacy, as well as to discussions about the influence of neoliberalism on criminal justice practices. Though there has been a great deal of interest in recent times in police legitimacy and normative forms of compliance, there has been less interest in the other ways in which police use their authority (coerced, symbolic, induced). The possibility that compliance may be coerced, not just legitimately given, has also been noted by others who argue for the need for more nuanced measures of compliance which examine the possibility of both legitimate and coerced forms of obligation (Bottoms and Tankebe, 2012: 114). More recently, in an attempt to examine the relative influence of these dual mechanisms of legitimate and coerced obligation, Jackson et al. (2015) found that, unlike legitimate obligation, coerced obligation was negatively correlated with experiences of procedural justice and a negative predictor of cooperation. Therefore, the present book develops the limited existing knowledge of the relationship between coerced and legitimate forms of compliance whilst also expanding the even more limited understandings of symbolic and induced forms of compliance. As discussed in Chapter 3, there is a tradition in prison studies of linking penality to neoliberalism and to the wider political economy. However, there have been fewer attempts to explore the consequences of neoliberalism for the police institution, in part because of a tendency to see the prison as the main agency of state-sponsored coercive control. The present book therefore makes what I hope to be a significant contribution in this regard. This is important given that the protections of citizens' rights, in theory, may be difficult to implement, on the ground, "in light of the existing structures of [the State's] criminal justice systems, challenges, and societal and legal cultures" (Weisselberg, 2017: 1281).

Notes

1 In the case of Ireland, and England and Wales, this case law exists not just at the domestic level but also, at the time of writing, at the European level, as a result of the European Court of Human Rights (see Chapter 5 for further details).
2 Crime control and due process are ideal-types in the Weberian sense, in which concrete individual phenomena are arranged logically into a unified analytical construct (Macdonald, 2008). This makes them different from an ideal, which is suggestive of a normative approach, against which empirical reality can be evaluated.
3 This criticism is important to the present book in order to challenge any potential misconceptions that the book's main subject matter, police powers and citizens' rights, is a straightforward dichotomy.
4 In the post-PACE era, there were a number of studies that showed that its introduction served to curtail the discretionary power of the police in police custody. For example, Irving and McKenzie (1989) regarded it as having improved the regulation of police detention and interrogation practices.
5 The research is littered with examples of the ways in which the permissiveness of the law enables the police to make the law 'work for them'. For example, this

permissiveness enables cases to be constructed (McConville et al., 1991); managers to maintain a 'front of legality' (Holdaway, 1980); and judges to elect not to admit evidence (Lustgarten, 1986: 144–5).

6 Though McBarnet is right to identify the permissiveness of the law itself, in so doing, she underplays the role of the police. Certainly, the permissiveness of the law enables the police to make the law work for them by justifying what they do post hoc through a framework of legality. However, police actors also have some degree of 'choice' about such decisions, albeit these decisions are likely shaped – in the same way that human agency is, more generally – by wider sociocultural processes (King, 2010).

7 In the freedom model, Sanders et al. (2010: 47–56) suggest that the maximisation of freedom for all should be the primary purpose of the criminal process, with appropriately weighted human rights and due process considerations being used as a way of achieving this goal. For Ashworth and Redmayne (2014: 48–51), it is *individual* human rights that are key, being used to bring suspected offenders to trial and to produce accurate determinations. They are not suggesting that human rights are an objective of the criminal process, rather, that they are fundamental, where retributive justice is being pursued.

8 Broadly speaking, police legitimacy is defined as the sense of obligation that citizens feel to obey the police and other legal authorities (e.g. Jackson et al., 2013: 7–8). See later in this chapter for a fuller discussion of the meaning of legitimacy.

9 Various research has reached a similar conclusion about the multipronged nature of police authority (Tankebe et al., 2016; Bottoms and Tankebe, 2012; Beetham, 1991: 16).

10 These might be "formal legal enactments or decisions, or established unwritten conventions," according to Bottoms and Tankebe (2012: 137). What this suggests is that these rules reflect largely statewide norms, but what is less clear is how these norms become understood and interpreted within different locales or by different cultural groups.

11 Garland (2001: Chapter 9) similarly identified a relationship between punishment and culture, noting that such culture goes beyond beliefs to lived and felt values, sentiments, and orientations, whilst also recognizing that these are generated through cultural inculcation and socialisation in certain social settings with certain asymmetries of power.

12 Police discretion remains an under-researched topic. According to the US National Research Council Report (2004), police discretion was one of the least researched topics in the field of police studies, along with the use of firearms and deadly force, and criminal investigation (cited in Brodeur, 2010: Chapter 6).

13 Reiner (2010: 243) says that Sir Robert Peel and two successive commissioners (Rowan and Mayne) strove to legitimise the police in a number of ways. They created "a civilian body, minimally armed, relying primarily on the same legal powers to deal with crime as all citizens shared, strictly subject to the rule of law, insulated from governmental control, and drawn from a representative range of working-class backgrounds to facilitate popular identification" (Reiner, 2010: 243).

14 Descriptive legal theory seeks to "identify and explain what law is," developing such explanations "independently of, and prior to, attempting to morally evaluate or justify law" (Dickinson, 2006: 1). That is, theorists attempt to identify and explain law's essential properties, answering questions such as "is coercion an essential feature of law?" (Dickinson, 2006: 1). By contrast, prescriptive theories offer moral and evaluative judgements about the law, which attempt to articulate how the law ought to be, considering questions such as "can the exercise of coercion via law be justified?" (Dickinson, 2006: 1).

15 Kenneth Culp Davis was one of the founding scholars of the sub-discipline of administrative law, who had a profound impact on the field. In the 1940s and 1950s, he provided one of the first systematic expositions of administrative law and established a now much-used distinction between adjudicative and legislative facts (Levin, 2005). His work on discretion was pioneering in that, at the time, it was "unexplored territory" (Levin, 2005: 331), but so too was the application of administrative law to criminal administration (Davis, 1974: 703 cited from Dixon, 1997: 300).

16 Davis (1975: 3–7) also provides 20 quick examples of non-enforcement of criminal statutes and ordinances in Chicago which, even though his book was written some time ago, still resonate today, including possession of marijuana, underage drinking and smoking in places where it is not permitted.

17 Of course, this interplay between agency and social structure is a contentious matter in sociology, sociolegal studies, and criminology, with varying perspectives, for example, by Giddens (1984: 19) vs. Archer (2010 [1982]), Black (1976), and Wikström (2010) vs. Messner (2012).

18 Whilst his account is useful for understanding how the responsibilisation of citizens in a neoliberal climate impacts on the way citizens are seen and policed, he neglects the mechanisms by which neoliberal values, such as personal responsibility, impact on and become reproduced in police work.

19 These two meanings are also reflected in Marshall's (1978) distinction between two styles of accountability: the "subordinate and obedient" model, which seeks political or democratic control over policing, vs. the "explanatory and co-operative" model, which requires decision-makers to provide reasons or information about their decisions without any obligation to take into consideration any challenges to their account.

20 These rule structures exist, beyond the law, meaning that this section is not just about legal fairness, as discussed above, though this is a part of it.

21 These informal rules are, in turn, shaped by a range of other factors. These factors include the cultural context of the neighbourhoods that are being policed; more immediate situational factors (e.g. the race, social class, gender or demeanour of the alleged offender, as well as the reason for their arrest, the number of officers present, the visibility of the arrest); and the outlook, role and rank of officers, as well as police cultures more generally (Buvik, 2016; Skogan and Frydl, 2004; Chan, 1996).

22 Though Ericson's account is helpful in examining the interactive nature of discretion, legal, administrative and informal rules, one area he neglects is the influence of legal and administrative rules on culture. There are good examples of how what begins as externally imposed rules becomes 'the way we do things', such as with regard to the civilising effect of Miranda on police interrogation practices (Dixon, 1997: 307).

23 For Davis, necessary forms of discretion included those that enabled individualised justice, in which police officers were able to tailor "results to the facts and circumstances of particular cases" (1969: 18). However, Dixon (1997), like Campbell (1999), sees the individualising nature of his work as a key problem, as it eclipses the consideration of race and class, also implying therefore a disinterest in social justice.

24 PACE provided enhanced regulation of police detention practices and extensive detail about how police powers should be used via the PACE Codes of Practice (Skinns, 2011a: 34).

25 The *Miranda v. Arizona* (1966) ruling by the US Supreme Court means that confessions made by suspects who have not been informed of their constitutional rights cannot be admitted into evidence. In effect, this means that suspects have to be informed of their right to silence and to defence counsel, which are known as their Miranda rights.

26 Gamble (2001), for example, notes the importance of avoiding the reification of neoliberalism in which it is treated as something that is manifest everywhere and in everything and thus as the only explanation of social actions and institutional practices. He sees such reductionism as not very useful and argues that it is "[f]ar better to deconstruct neoliberalism into the different doctrines and ideas which compose it, and relate them to particular practices and political projects" (Gamble, 2001: 134).

27 There are a few exceptions to this. For example, Primus (2017) examines the benefits of separating the Fifth Amendment right not to incriminate oneself from the Sixth Amendment right to pretrial defence counsel. See also Rossman (2017).

28 I have been unable to locate a single study on this topic in the US or Ireland.

29 Comparative empirical studies of police custody include Vanderhallan et al. (2016), Panzarvolta et al. (2015), Blackstock et al. (2014), and Dixon (1997).

The police in context
Neoliberalism in the selected countries

Introduction

The purpose of this chapter is to put the use of police powers in context, setting out the social, political and economic conditions in each of the common-law countries in which the cities that serve as case studies for the book are located. The focus is on the way that neoliberalism has been made manifest in Australia, England,[1] Ireland and the US in the late 20th and early 21st centuries. The overarching aim of this chapter is to provide a platform for understanding how police powers and the associated discretionary decision-making, explored in the rest of the book, are put into practice in each of the jurisdictions of interest. This chapter is partly theoretical, but also partly descriptive, in order to provide a frame of reference for readers, but also because there are no other systematic comparative examinations of the organisation and context of police work encompassing *all* of the four selected countries within one publication.[2]

Setting out this broad context is important in order to emphasise the symbiotic relationship between police work and its social, political and economic conditions (see Reiner, 1992). Seemingly mundane encounters between the police and citizens are crucial to the formation of social identities, for example, giving citizens a sense of their valued place in society, particularly if they are treated with dignity and respect (Bradford et al., 2014; Lerman and Weaver, 2014: 12–13; Loader and Mulcahy, 2006: 39–40). As a "social litmus paper" for the unfolding dynamics of society (Reiner, 1992: 762), the police and citizens also jointly play a role in creating and maintaining social order, with social changes thus becoming writ large on the police and changes to police policies and practices becoming writ large on the public and on the construction of suspect populations. This suggests that in order to understand the police, we need to also understand their relationship with the conditions under which they operate and vice versa. Such an approach takes us back to the original meaning of the police, which refers to the process by which social order is created and maintained and in which the police institution plays a key role (Brodeur, 2010: 18). In the sections that follow, I therefore examine the context of police work in each of the selected cities. I deliberately move from the broad setting of police work in terms of its political economy and its neoliberal climate, in this chapter, to the narrower context of the way police work is organised and delivered, historically and in the present, in Chapter 4.

Political economy and police studies[3]

There has been no shortage of analysis which has tried to capture variations in penality. This refers to the institutions used to punish those convicted of a crime, their practices and discourses, as well as the social, economic, political and cultural conditions that surround them (Cunneen et al., 2013: 4). There have also been various attempts to theorise about the kind of societal characteristics that determine these variations in penality. Foucault's (1991) *Discipline and Punish*, for example, explores how in Europe and the US, there was a switch from predominantly corporal forms of punishment to disciplinary and carceral forms of punishment between the late 18th and mid-19th century. Similarly, Durkheim's *Two Laws of Penal Evolution* linked forms of penality to different societal types, arguing that the more advanced a society the less intense the punishment and the more reliance there is on imprisonment, as its main mode of punishment (Durkheim, 1973). Both were criticised, however, as their theories did not fit the facts of history (Garland, 1990:48–49). Cavadino and Dignan (2006a, 2006b) further explore these issues, in particular, the links between penality and political economy.

However, when it comes to police studies, there is a more limited and not quite equivalent body of literature examining the mechanisms by which social, political and economic conditions, including neoliberalism, impact on the police institution (Reiner, 2017). This is surprising given the intimate connection between the police and society and given the police's political role in defining "order and ordering" (Manning, 2010: 44). There is also no equivalent term to penality. Though it does capture the interrelationship between the police and the broader social world, the term policing does not capture the role played by social institutions, such as the police, prosecutors and the courts in determining guilt. Were it not so ugly a term, 'prosecutoriality' would capture these ideas better.

Most of the scholarship on neoliberalism and police work tends to treat neoliberalism as a framework for better understanding the organisation of police work. For example, neoliberalism has been seen as an important context for understanding the growth of new public management in police work (Reiner, 2015; Skinns, 2011a: 13–14; Reiner, 2010: 30–31; Jones and Newburn, 2002), as well as for understanding the pluralisation and commodification of police work, in which aspects of police work are outsourced/privatised and in which the police 'brand' is sold for cash (Reiner, 2010: 30–31; Ayling et al., 2009: Chapters 4 and 5; Johnston and Shearing, 2003: Chapter 2; Rigakos, 2002: 154; Forst and Manning, 1999: Part 3). Where the links between neoliberalism and the police have been more directly examined, such as in

Waquant (2009a), the police are generally discussed in relation to the neoliberal state's carceral function. That is, there is a tendency to view the police merely as a "dragnet" or the "long arm" of the penal state (Kaplan-Lyman, 2012: 191). The police have also been used as a vehicle for exploring how neoliberal values have spread across the world embedded in criminal justice practices. For example, Wacquant (2009a: 16–19, 27–38) uses zero-tolerance policing to show how neoliberal ideas became embedded in police practices in New York City (NYC) via think tanks such as the Manhattan Institute and then came to be spread across the world, with London acting as a gateway to the rest of Europe. On the whole, though, the meaning and consequences of neoliberalism for the police institution, for styles of police authority, for policing practices and for policed populations have been given limited consideration in their own right. Yet these neoliberal values are important to how we understand police work, not least because

> how social actors think, talk, write and act in relation to crime and its regulation requires paying careful attention to the ideological positions from within which such activities take place, towards which they contribute, and whose view of social and political arrangements they aim to promulgate and advance.
>
> (Loader and Sparks, 2016: 319)

One exception to this more limited engagement with the mechanisms by which neoliberalism impacts on police work is Kaplan-Lyman (2012). He explores the impact of neoliberalism on the New York Police Department (NYPD). In the context of city-level governmental bankruptcy in the 1980s and 1990s and the rise of public-private partnerships, which were used to regenerate run-down areas of the city, he argues that policing became more accountable to corporate elite institutions and even less accountable to marginalised communities. He also regards the growth in the use of order maintenance policing by the NYPD in the 1990s, as a direct consequence of neoliberalism, with individual citizens' 'poor choices', not poverty, coming to be regarded as the cause of low-level disorder. This low-level disorder was also met with a punitive response in the form of stop-and-frisk ("Terry stops," based on reasonable suspicion),[4] in which citizens suspected of lawbreaking were stopped and their clothes patted down if the police believed them to be carrying an illegal weapon or other contraband. Such stops were justified on the basis of tackling disorder and gun-related crime, even though they had no effect on neighbourhood crime rates, unlike probable cause stops (Fagan, 2016) and also resulted in the expanding of police surveillance, particularly of poor, non-white marginalised communities (see also Eterno and Silverman, 2006). These stop-and-frisks also have the effect of humiliating and punishing these communities and thus keeping them "under control" (Fassin, 2013: 5–6). In essence, Kaplan-Lyman (2012) argues that together these policing strategies became a way of dealing with the fallout of neoliberalism – such as growing social inequalities – making the police, not just the prison, a major site of neoliberal governance. This argument is particularly persuasive given that only a small percentage of police stops resulted in an arrest, let alone a charge or a conviction; for example, contraband was found in only 4% of NYPD's stop-and-frisks between 2003 and 2008. Therefore, "the police may play an important and, as of yet, unrecognised role as part of the neoliberal criminal justice apparatus" (Kaplan-Lyman, 2012: 190–1). Whilst useful in conceptual terms, this study is limited in its generalisability outside NYC and the US. For example, order maintenance policing had a particular resonance in NYC, which has not been seen to the same extent in other parts of the US, nor in other jurisdictions, such as the UK (Newburn, 2010).

Given the limited body of literature in police studies examining the mechanisms by which neoliberal societal characteristics impact on the police institution, in what follows, ideas have been borrowed from the literature on penality. Cavadino and Dignan's (2006a) work is instructive in this regard. They used four types of political economies to explain variations in penality in different countries: neoliberal (e.g. the US, and to a lesser extent, England and Wales, New Zealand and Australia);[5] conservative corporatist welfare state (e.g. Germany but also France, Italy and the Netherlands); social democratic corporatism (e.g. Sweden, but also Finland); and oriental corporatism (e.g. Japan). Of these, the first, neoliberalism, is of most interest, given that the cities of interest in the present book are located in countries, which fall in this category.

Defining neoliberalism and its effects

In simple terms, the economic historian (and barrister) Stedman Jones defines neoliberalism as "a free market ideology based on individual liberty and limited government," which connects "human freedom to the actions of rational, self-interested actors in a competitive market place" (2012: 2). In essence, he defines neoliberalism as meaning less state and more personal responsibility, and he connects these ideas to University of Chicago economists of the 1950s, such as Milton Friedman. Such connections are also made by social scientists. However, they tend to regard neoliberalism as something more complex. According to Cavadino and Dignan (2006a), neoliberalism refers to free-market capitalism and an ethos of individualism in societies in which the welfare state is minimalist and residual through, for example, having means-tested welfare benefits.[6] Though relationships in neoliberal societies are formally egalitarian, extreme income differentials and a lack of access to welfare benefits mean the exclusion of citizens from civil, political and social rights. Wacquant (2009b: 306–7) defines neoliberalism according to four "institutional logics": (1) "economic deregulation," (2) "welfare state devolution, retraction, and recomposition," (3) "the cultural trope of individual responsibility," and additionally (4) "an expansive, intrusive, and proactive penal apparatus." Therefore, Wacquant (2009b) argues that neoliberalism has meant not just the deregulation of economic activity, but also growing state intervention in other areas of society, particularly in relation to punishment. Similarly, Peck and Tickell also note that "whilst rhetorically anti-statist, neoliberals have proved adept at the (mis)use of state power in the pursuit of these goals" (2002: 381). Wacquant, and Peck and Tickell are therefore part of a group of scholars who note that, rather than the state playing a lesser role in the lives of citizens, to some extent, the state has in fact learned to govern 'better' and more adeptly. This is through new sites and modes of governance used to identify, find and contain 'problem' groups. This includes governing through crime (Simon, 2007: 4–5), the penal state (Garland, 2001: 203–4), the penal state / welfare system (Wacquant, 2009b: xvi), cheap credit and debt (Campbell, 2010) and insecurity and surveillance (Lea and Hallsworth, 2013; Hallsworth and Lea, 2011).

It has also been noted that the hegemony of neoliberalism and thus its capacity for providing the means to govern 'better' has arisen, in part, because of its ideological qualities, which means that neoliberalism and the values that it embodies have come to be seen as all-encompassing and taken for granted. Harvey, for example, describes neoliberalism as a hegemonic discourse, which embeds ideas about the centrality of the market into everything we do, such that it "becomes incorporated into the common-sense way many of us interpret, live in, and understand the world" (Harvey, 2005: 3). Similarly, neoliberalism is described by Peck and Tickell as "no longer a dream of Chicago economists or a night-mare in the imaginations of leftist conspiracy theorists; it has become a commonsense of our times" (2002: 381). In Bourdieu and Wacquant's words, it has become a "new planetary vulgate" (2001: 2) or in Beck's terms, an ideological "thought virus" (2000: 122).

These accounts of neoliberalism, as a dominant taken-for-granted and all-encompassing paradigm, therefore, suggest that neoliberalism is constitutive of state-citizen relations. This is particularly the case in *Prisons of Poverty*; as the name of the book suggests, Wacquant (2009a) argues that prisons, but also the welfare state, have jointly been used to criminalise poverty in the post-war period.[7] These organs of the state have been used to tackle the fallout of neoliberalism, which has left those at the bottom of the social structure in a precarious and impoverished position because of the withering of the welfare state and the restructuring of employment (Young, 1999: 8), which in turn has left people either without jobs or in low-paid uncertain jobs. Whilst the social safety net has diminished, paradoxically, the mesh of the police and prison "dragnet" has become ever thinner and stronger, meaning that "the deliberate atrophy of the welfare state corresponds to the dystopic hypertrophy of the penal state …" (Wacquant, 2009a: 58). In the US, this mass incarceration is particularly pronounced for particular groups, largely young black men (Cunneen et al., 2013: 4).

However, this is an overly deterministic way of understanding neoliberalism, which glosses over variations in neoliberal penality within and between nations. For example, Brown (2011: 133) criticises the functionalism of Wacquant's account, in which he "over-eggs" the extent to which neoliberalism is the driver of changes to the penal state, resulting in a failure to grasp the conflict between neoconservatism and neoliberalism, as well as foreclosing the possibility that social actors might rise up and contest neoliberalism and its effects. O'Malley (2014) also takes exception to the determinism in Wacquant's (2009a) thesis, emphasising the varied forms that neoliberal penality takes. He says,

> neoliberalism does not equal punitivism and thus there is no single 'neoliberal penality' – but rather various penalities that are in *varying* degrees and ways influenced by neoliberal rationalities ... there is no monolithic 'neoliberal state' ... Neoliberal rationalities are permeable and labile....
>
> (p. 91)

This means he is critical of the extent to which other countries have adopted the neoliberal penal package and regards the punitive prison, not as a neoliberal phenomenon but as an American one rooted in neoconservative American-Christian morals (see also Tonry, 1999). Even Peck and Tickell point to the tendency to treat neoliberalism as all-encompassing, rather than to see it as a nuanced and contradictory *process*, which is necessarily variegated, albeit the diffusion of these processes may contribute to a pervasive "metalogic" (2002: 383). These critiques are important for the present book as, whilst neoliberalism will be used as an organising framework, I offer a nuanced account of its relevance to police detention. I do this partly by recognising the different ways that neoliberalism has been made manifest in the countries of interest, which is considered next. Throughout the book, I also explore other explanations for the heightened discretionary power of the police in the US, such as the historically localised nature of police work and the dispersal of power through the federal system, and the ineffective control of the police through the courts (see Chapters 4 and 9).

Convergence or divergence? The conditions of neoliberalism in the selected countries

As noted above, there is considerable variation within and between countries in terms of how neoliberalism takes shape. According to Cavadino and Dignan (2006a), the US is the archetypal example of a neoliberal society, in part, because of its more limited social democratic history (see later in this chapter in the section on 'Economic and social policy organisation'). Wilkinson and Pickett (2010: 174) similarly note a clustering of health and social problems in countries with high levels of economic inequality, with the US routinely scoring the worst on most measures.[8] By contrast, the social democratic history of Australia and England mean that, according to Cavadino and Dignan (2006a), they fall short of being described as typically neoliberal. They subsequently argue that, for the most part, countries with neoliberal political economies tend to have the highest rates of imprisonment, which are, in turn, suggestive of more punitive attitudes towards offenders when compared to countries which exemplify other types of political economies. However, this is not because neoliberalism is criminogenic per se. Though this type of political economy is indicative of individualism, inequality and a concomitant lack of social cohesion, all of which are implicated in criminality, it is the attitudes towards deviance and punishment that are important to penal excessiveness. In particular, in neoliberal societies, individuals are blamed for their failures when they commit a crime, and this provides fertile ground for the development of harsh forms of punishment.[9] That said, they hasten to add that the political economy is not the only factor driving differences in penality; also important are penal ideologies and commercial interests. As such, they warn against using political economy in an overly deterministic manner.

This analysis is important for police studies, generally, and for the present book more specifically. It suggests that this approach could be fruitfully applied not just to penality but also to the police institutions and police practices in different jurisdictions. As such, this book is the first step towards an analysis of that kind; in particular, it explores the implications of the neoliberal political economies of Australia, England, Ireland and the US for police powers and citizens' rights in these countries (or the relevant cities/jurisdictions within them). However, in order to do this, it is first necessary to draw out the subtle differences that exist between these countries in terms of the form, extent and reach of neoliberalism. Helpfully, Cavadino and Dignan (2006a) provide relevant socio-economic indicators to help frame such comparisons, some of which are easier to measure across different countries than others. Of particular relevance are *economic and social policy organisation*, which refers to the extent of free market and minimalist or residual welfare state; *income differentials*, which refers to the disparities between the poorest and richest sections of society; *status differentials*, which refers to the extent to which countries are truly egalitarian as opposed to formally egalitarian; and *citizen-state relations*, which refers to the extent to which citizens are regarded as having individual autonomy, free from intervention by the state. After first examining social demographic information about each of the selected countries, each of these socio-economic indicators are examined in turn next.

Social demographics

In the countries in which the chosen cities are located, the total population varies considerably (see Table 3.1). The US was the largest at 317.6 million at the time of the research in 2010, and Ireland was the smallest at 4.6 million. Dublin is the most populous city in Ireland, containing 1.4 million (30%)

Table 3.1 Social demographics of Australia, Ireland, the US and the UK in 1990 and 2010, and projected for 2030

Country	Population						
	Total (millions)			Urban (% of total)		Median age	
	1990	2010	2030	1990	2010	1990	2010
Australia	17.1	21.5	25.7	85.4	89.1	32.2	37.8
Ireland	3.5	4.6	5.6	56.9	61.9	29.1	34.6
UK	57.2	61.9	68	78.1	79.6	35.8	39.9
US	254.9	317.6	370	75.3	82.3	32.8	36.6

Source: United Nations (2015: 184–7).

of the population, whilst London is the most populous city of the UK, containing 7.8 million (13%) in mid-2010 (Office for National Statistics, 2016a). In Australia, the most populous cities are Sydney (4.3 million, amounting to approximately a third of Australia's population in 2011), Melbourne (4.1 million), Perth (1.7 million), Adelaide (1.2 million) and Brisbane (1.08 million) (Australian Bureau of Statistics, 2016a). In the US, in 2010, the most populous cities were NYC (8.2 million), Los Angeles (3.8 million), Chicago (2.7 million), Houston (2.1 million) and Philadelphia (1.5 million) (City Mayors Statistics, 2016). The research informing this book was conducted in populous cities of comparable sizes in all of these countries, though for reasons of anonymity, they cannot be explicitly named. The selected cities/jurisdictions also differ in terms of the proportions of people living in urban areas, with Australia being most urban, followed by the US, the UK and then Ireland. In fact, the proportion of the population of Ireland living in urban areas is 20%–30% less compared to rest.

In terms of the composition of society in each of these countries, there is again immense variation, in part a product of their different geographical locations and histories, including their colonial past. At the same time, there are some similarities between the four countries, in that the police are called on to police an increasingly racially, ethnically and culturally diverse populace.

Though Wacquant (2009a: 88) is somewhat sceptical of the notion of American exceptionalism, the US does appear to be unique. Its legacy of slavery and the racial discrimination that it engendered – including racial restrictions on property ownership and voting, racial segregation in public schools on public buses and public restrooms, and racially discriminatory hiring practices – are only part of this (Weitzer, 2017; Engel and Cohen, 2014; Walker, 2008; Bass, 2001).[10] Another is its religious conservatism and its historically underdeveloped welfare state (O'Malley, 2014). Altogether, these have resulted in a highly unusual, but also volatile set of social conditions, which have served to drive a wedge between black citizens and the state, including the police (O'Malley, 2014; see also Chapter 4). In terms of the racial and ethnic composition of American society, since 2000, the census in the US has distinguished between ethnicity (either Hispanic/Latino or not) and race (including a variety of categories, with respondents being able to classify themselves as belonging to one or more race). As a nation in 2010, 72.4% of the population considered themselves racially white, 12.6% Black or African American, 4.8% Asian, and 1.1% American Indian, Alaskan Native, Native Hawaiian or another kind of Pacific Islander, whilst ethnically speaking, 16.3% regarded themselves as Hispanic or Latino (The US Census Bureau, 2016).[11] In research on the police in the US, the key ethnic groups are deemed to be Black, White and Hispanic, though those of Hispanic origin are not always differentiated from African Americans (Weitzer and Tuch, 2006). Focusing only on these three groups, however, might obscure the experiences of other racial, ethnic and religious groups, particularly Muslim Americans since the terrorist attacks of 9/11.

In Australia, Aboriginal and Torres Strait Islanders are a central part of Australia's non-white citizenry. They comprise 2.5% of the total Australian population. In 2008, there were 520,350 indigenous people (living in private dwellings and thus available to take part in the census), of whom 90% identified as Aboriginal only, 5% identified as Torres Strait Islander only and 5% identified as being of both Aboriginal and Torres Strait Islander origin. In 2008, more than half of the indigenous population lived in either New South Wales (30%) or Queensland (28%), with another quarter living in either Western Australia (13%) or the Northern Territory (12%). In 2008, 40% of indigenous citizens aged 15 years and over spoke fluently or some words of an indigenous language, though there is also much diversity within these groups, who come from different regions and speak different languages.

There are also other ethnic minorities who are distinguished, according to White (2009), from the white Irish and British early settlers in Australia. These ethnic groups emerged following different waves of migration to Australia: in the 1970s, it was Greeks and Italians; in the 1980s, it was Asians (particularly Vietnamese); and by the 1990s, those of Middle Eastern origin (particularly Lebanese) (White, 2009). More recently still, there has been an influx of migrants from Somalia and Sudan (following wars there). The Australian census does not ask questions about ethnicity, but about the birthplace of respondents and their parents and their language (and religion). In the 2011 census, over 300 ancestries were identified. The most commonly reported were English (36%) and Australian (35%). A further six of the leading ten ancestries reflected the European heritage of Australians (Irish, Scottish, Italian, German, Greek and Dutch), with the two remaining ancestries being Chinese (4%) and Indian (2%) (Australian Bureau of Statistics, 2016b).

In Ireland, the population of 4.6 million is comprised of the following groups (with 2011 being only the second census in which information about ethnicity was collected): White Irish (84.5%), Other White (9.1%), Not Stated

(1.6%), Other Asian (1.5%), Black Irish or Black African (1.3%), Other (0.9%), Irish Traveller (0.7%), Chinese (0.4%) and Other Black (0.1%) (Central Statistics Office, 2012: 37). In recent times, Ireland has experienced a wave of migrants looking to prosper from the 'Celtic Tiger'. In 2011, however, the numbers of migrants had slowed down, compared to 2006, which is not surprising given the declining economy. It nonetheless remains a destination of choice for people from Poland, the UK, France, Lithuania, Spain, the US, Germany, Latvia, Romania, Australia and Canada, which are the top ten places where immigrants come from (Central Statistics Office, 2012: 31). In terms of nationality, 88% of the population is made up of Irish nationals, whilst the remaining 12% is made up of nationals from Poland (2.7%), the UK (2.5%), Lithuania (0.8%), Latvia (0.5%), Nigeria (0.4%), Romania (0.4%) and other countries, including India, the Philippines, Germany, the US, China and Slovakia (4.7%). Increases in the number of foreign nationals between 2006 and 2011 in Ireland were largely accounted for by those from Poland (94% increase), as well as those from Latvia (55%), Lithuania (49%), Romania (125%), Brazil (98%) and India (101%) (Central Statistics Office, 2012: 31, 33).

Religion remains an important marker in Ireland. It is a predominantly Catholic country, with 84% of the population declaring themselves Catholic.[12] However, there has been a rise in other faiths over the last five years, including Islam, other forms of Christianity, Orthodox, Apostolic Pentecostal and those with no religion (Central Statistics Office, 2012: 42). The country is also divided by those who speak Irish and those who do not. Whilst 1.8% of the nation speak Irish on a daily basis (outside of school), this rises to 35% in Gaeltacht,[13] such as Donegal and Galway (Central Statistics Office, 2012: 40–41).

Finally, in the UK, successive waves of migration have created a unique context in terms of the origins of migrants, with police forces, particularly in large urban and more ethnically diverse cities, struggling to adapt to the diversity of the citizenry.[14] The late 1950s and early 1960s saw an influx of immigrants from the West Indies, who famously came aboard SS Empire Windrush. Later, in the 1960s, migrant workers came from India, Pakistan and Africa. These pioneers from the Commonwealth answered Britain's call for workers for difficult-to-fill jobs during the rebuilding of Britain following the Second World War (Phillips and Bowling, 2017; Whitfield, 2007). These early migrants from the Commonwealth, and their children, along with the increasing numbers of citizens with a mixed heritage, have come to form the backbone of multi-ethnic Britain. In the 2011 census, data for England and Wales showed that White was the majority ethnic group at 48.2 million in 2011 (86%),[15] though this had declined by nearly 8% compared to 1991 − the first time when questions about ethnicity were asked − when the White ethnic group accounted for 94.1% of the population (Office for National Statistics, 2016b). The remainder of the British population is comprised of Asian / British Asian (7.5%), Black/ African / Caribbean / Black British (3.3%), Mixed/Multiple ethnic groups (2.2%) and other (1%).

Economic and social policy organisation

By the 1950s, there was a degree of convergence between the UK and the US in terms of the growing influence of social democratic principles, albeit they were not translated into policy and practice to the same extent. Born out of the Great Depression and the electorate's desire that "never again" would citizens suffer the indignities and degradations of market failure (Stedman Jones, 2012: 21), Roosevelt's mid-1930s New Deal proposals encompassed the right to work, earn enough to eat, trade in conditions of fair competition, a decent home, adequate medical care, and economic protection from old age, sickness and unemployment (Harcourt, 2010; Cavadino and Dignan, 2006b: 52). Around the same time, Nye Bevan, the Secretary of State for Health under Labour's Atlee government, drafted the 1942 Beveridge report. It recommended a cradle-to-grave welfare state and was the basis for the creation of the UK's National Health Service (Humpage, 2015: 20; Cavadino and Dignan, 2006b: 73). These developments were important not only with regard to the development of the welfare state, but also because they conveyed clear messages to citizens about the "tasks of government and the meaning of political responsibility" (Loader and Mulcahy, 2006: 7–8). In practice, however, provisions in the US never went as far as in the UK. For example, universal healthcare remained elusive in the US, in part, because it was viewed as going against American cultural ideals of "individual initiative and liberty" (Stedman Jones, 2012: 26).

From the late 1960s to the late 1970s, the US and the UK continued to converge, but this time towards neoliberalism. Using Peck and Tickell's (2002: 388) terms, this was the "bedding in phase" of neoliberalism, albeit this was in differing degrees in the US and the UK. Particularly in the US, social democratic ideals increasingly came under sustained critique, with American economists – such as Hayek, Friedman and Stigler – being particularly vocal in their support for a new and more radical version of liberalism (Stedman Jones, 2012: 125; Harvey, 2005: 20–30; Peck and Tickell, 2002). This resulted in a greater focus in the US on the need for individualism and less of a willingness to compromise with New Deal liberals or social democrats than had hitherto been the case. According to Stedman Jones, these more extreme views in the US were in part borne out of the different historical, cultural and geographic traits of the US, especially its "deep-rooted cultural obsession with the rugged individualism of the frontier" (2012: 125). They were also rooted in perceived threats to individual liberty, associated with communism and the Cold War. Chicago School economists, such as Hayek, Friedman and Stigler, therefore saw themselves as fighting against the threat of collectivism, which they saw as undermining a vital part of American culture, namely, individual liberty and autonomy (Peck and Tickell, 2002).

After bedding in from the late 1970s into the 1990s, neoliberalism increasingly "came in from the wilderness" (Stedman Jones, 2012: 6–9). Using Peck and Tickell's (2002) terminology, neoliberalism "rolled back," in the UK and the US in this period, in the sense that the state was shrunk and retracted. At the forefront of this second phase of neoliberalism were Thatcher and Regan, who respectively took office in 1979 and 1980. According to Peck and Tickell (2002), this was an era, in both countries, in which state power mobilised in favour of marketisation and deregulation, which meant also the dismantling of the Keynesian welfare settlement. This occurred against the backdrop of the 1970s recession, with the blame for this being apportioned to the Keynesian financial system (e.g. strong unions, state ownership of public assets and regulated labour markets), which was therefore dismantled in both countries. This transatlantic convergence of neoliberal policies and practices was facilitated by think tanks (e.g. the Centre for Policy Studies and the Adam Smith Institute in the UK and the Heritage Foundation and the Cato Institute in the US) and politicians (e.g. Thatcher and Reagan), drawing also on the ideas of Hayek, Friedman and Stigler (Stedman Jones, 2012: 161–73; Harvey, 2005: 20–30).

Further convergence between the US and UK can also be seen in the "roll out" phase of neoliberalism (Peck and Tickell, 2002: 389). From the early to the mid-1990s until the late 2000s, on the surface, some politicians began to acknowledge the limitations and contradictions of neoliberalism, including high levels of private debt, growing social inequalities and child poverty (Humpage, 2015: Peck and Tickell, 2002). However, in this third phase of neoliberalism, it did not implode as might have been expected; rather, it was reconstituted via the Third Way politics of Blair and Clinton in ways which masked the effects of neoliberalism. Humpage notes, for example, that

> attempts to reduce the threat that roll-back reforms represented for 'social inclusion' were driven less by genuine political concern about social inequalities and more by an interest in running the market economy more effectively.... As such, they had the effect of embedding, legitimating and securing neoliberalism.
>
> (2015: 32)

Following the financial crisis of 2008, there has possibly been a fourth phase of neoliberalism referred to as "roll-over" (Humpage, 2015: 30–31), which has further entrenched neoliberalism. Whilst the financial crisis revealed more doubts about neoliberalism, it also paved the way for a conservative resurgence in the US and the UK, based on their policies of slashing public spending. Humpage concludes that, in spite of resistance to neoliberalism in the form of anti-austerity protests, such as the Occupy movement, on the whole, the public have rolled over, either endorsing neoliberal values or, at least, accepting their inevitability (2015: 34).

In sum, over the course of 50–60 years, there has been a reasonable degree of convergence between the US and the UK with regard to the different phases of neoliberalism, as well as the embracing of neoliberal policies and practices. Moreover, this zeal for neoliberalism spread beyond the UK and the US to other countries, as well as to global institutions. For example, think tanks, such as the Atlas Economic Research Foundation, had worldwide influence, supporting the development of neoliberal thought in 80 countries around the world, including in Australia (http://atlasnetwork.org/). Furthermore, neoliberalism began to gather momentum and to percolate into policy and practice at a time when globalisation simultaneously began to gain pace (Beck, 1981: 7). Indeed, neoliberalism has been seen as one of the motors of globalisation (Aas, 2013: 9). As such, it is logical to conclude that neoliberal tendencies, such as the espousing of the importance of individualism and the minimal state came to influence global institutions. For example, the market liberalisation introduced into fiscal policy in North America and Western Europe eventually spread to global institutions like the International Monetary Fund, the World Bank and the World Trade Organisation,[16] as well as to European financial institutions such as the European Central Bank (Peck and Tickell, 2002).

This global climate of neoliberalism has impacted on Australia, but particularly on Ireland. The neoliberal stance of Ireland is evident in the rise of the 'Celtic Tiger' from the 1990s onwards,[17] with the economic boom that the Irish experienced being driven, in part, by financial deregulation, the pioneering of low taxation for corporations and an expectation that the market would regulate itself, which are all hallmarks of neoliberalism. These neoliberal policies and practices were further consolidated following the Celtic Tiger's fall from grace. Allen (2012), for example, argues that Ireland rejected any Keynesian-type solutions to the economic crisis in 2008 and focused instead on cutting public spending and on regaining competitiveness in the marketplace, such as by cutting public sector pay, rather than the pay of private sector bankers. Such strategies were an attempt to increase the confidence of foreign investors in Ireland and to make Ireland appear as a "model pupil" willing to be tutored by the European Union (EU) (Allen, 2012: 423), in terms of how it handled the aftermath of the economic crisis, unlike Greece, for example. According to Allen (2012), these strategies to regain its competitive edge have not yet boosted the Irish economy and have had the simultaneous effect of intensifying the impact of neoliberalism on its citizens by increasing things like social deprivation and inequality.

As for the method by which these neoliberal ideas spread, as noted above, though think tanks and policy entrepreneurs were key in America and Britain, in Ireland, Manning (2012: 350) points to the historically frugal nature of the country and its tendency towards limited government. Phelan (2007), however, notes the central role that the media played. He argues that the more ideologically infused variant of neoliberal discourse associated with Third Way politicians was constituted and reproduced through a variety of discourses, but in particular through the way they were represented in the media.

By contrast, Australia has not seemingly demonstrated the same level of zeal for neoliberalism as Ireland, England or the US, with regard to economic, social or penal policies (Humpage, 2015: 62; O'Malley, 2014). Nonetheless, neoliberalism started to intensify in the 1980s, following the election of the first Labour government (led by Hawke). According to Western et al. (2007), from this point onwards, governments began to eschew Keynesian macroeconomic approaches, such as using fiscal policy to smooth the business cycle. Centrally regulated industrial relations were also dismantled and replaced by negotiations between individual employees and employers and trade unions no longer had to be involved in pay-setting for ordinary employees. Educational policy was also subject to neoliberal pressures, with universities, for example, receiving decreasing amounts of state funding, having to compete for research funding,[18] and having to increasingly compete for but also rely on fees from international and postgraduate students. As for social policy, welfare payments have become increasingly conditional on satisfying certain criteria, such as the completion of work activity tests (Humpage, 2015: 63). Rather than these changes to economic, industrial relations, education and social policies being solely about deregulation and state withdrawal, they have also encouraged state agencies to mimic market principles and to enable markets to flourish, such that neoliberalism has continued alongside and within the project of state-sponsored 'nation-building' by providing the institutional conditions for marketisation.

Whilst neoliberalism may have intensified in Australia since the 1980s, the effects of this were not as sharp here, as compared to the UK (Humpage, 2015: 80–81),[19] and neither did neoliberalism impact on all areas of social policy. O'Malley (2014: 92–93) argues that Australia lacks the kind of neoliberal penality that Wacquant (2009b) describes in relation to the US. He attributes this to the fact that Australia and other Commonwealth countries, who Wacquant (2009b) claims are strongly influenced by American neoliberalism, have only a weak neoconservative tradition, which is required to support the wholesale adoption of a neoliberal penality.[20] Moreover, this wholesale adoption of American neoliberal values has simply not happened. He says:

> Despite Wacquant [in *Prisons of Poverty*] pointing to the Commonwealth countries as being strongly influenced by the American 'Leviathan', Canada, Australia and New Zealand represent three examples in the Anglophone world which have not gone very far down the American track, while the Scandinavian countries provide another even more prominent instance of refusal. In all of these countries, social democratic or labour-oriented parties have been at the forefront of the economic transformations associated with neoliberalism while maintaining strong elements of social welfare.
>
> (O'Malley, 2014)

Income differentials

In sum, in terms of economic and social policy organisation, there appears to be divergence but also a degree of convergence in terms of the emphasis placed on individualism, the free market and the role of the state in the US compared to the UK, Ireland, and to a lesser extent, Australia. Another way of examining this debate is to look at income differentials in these countries; one might expect that countries which show the greatest zeal for neoliberalism also have the highest levels of income inequality. Indeed, this is broadly what the research suggests. Data collected as part of the *UN Human Development Report 2015* show,[21] firstly, that the US is the richest of the four countries. The gross domestic product (GDP) per capita in 2013 was the highest in the US (see Table 3.2), followed by Ireland, Australia and the UK. Secondly, across all measures of income inequality shown in the report, the US was the most unequal of all of the four countries, followed by the UK, Australia and Ireland. For example, the respective Gini coefficients for these countries between 2005 and 2013 were 41.1, 38, 34 and 32.1.[22] This pattern of income inequality fits with the idea that the US is the archetypal neoliberal political economy, with neoliberal political economies in Australia, Ireland and the UK being tempered, for instance, by their social democratic histories (Wilkinson and Pickett, 2010: 174; Cavadino and Dignan, 2006a). This is particularly interesting, as given that Ireland seems the most similar to the UK and US in terms of its tendency to adopt neoliberal economic and social policies, it has less income inequality than Australia, which has ostensibly shown less favour towards neoliberal economic and social policies (O'Malley, 2014; Wilkinson and Pickett, 2010: 174).

Status differentials

All the cities/jurisdictions of interest to this book are democratic, and thus ostensibly and politically, even if not socially, egalitarian. However, this egalitarian

Table 3.2 Data on income differentials in Australia, Ireland, the US and the UK

Country	GDP per capita 2013 ($)	Gini coefficient (2005–2013)
Australia	42,831	34
Ireland	44,931	32.1
UK	51,340	38
US	37,017	41.1

Source: United Nations (2015: 216–9).

ethos is sharply undermined by neoliberal tendencies, for example, the declining availability of social support through the welfare state and as result of welfare conditionality, and increased control of the poor through a range of mediums such as prisons, crime and the benefits system. That is, in practice, the four cities/jurisdictions of interest may not be truly egalitarian, and the purpose of this section is to assess some of the evidence in this regard. Again, the data collected as part of the UN's report on *Human Development in 2015* is instructive. There are a range of measures in this report which give an idea of egalitarianism in practice across Australia, Ireland, the UK and the US. First, there is the human development index (HDI) which

is a composite index focusing on three basic dimensions of human development: to lead a long and healthy life, measured by life expectancy at birth; the ability to acquire knowledge, measured by mean years of schooling and expected years of schooling; and the ability to achieve a decent standard of living, measured by gross national income per capita.

(United Nations, 2015: 3)

Countries can score up to 1 on this index, and the higher the score, the higher the level of human development. According to the 2015 UN report, Australia, Ireland, the US and the UK fall in the group of countries which are regarded as having very high levels of human development, being ranked, respectively, 2, 6, 8 and 14 in the world (see Table 3.3). However, this HDI score decreases when measures of inequality, connected to life expectancy, education and income, are taken into account. This is the inequality-adjusted HDI. Though it does not affect each country's rank, the decrease in this index is particularly pronounced in the US; as shown in Table 3.3, the HDI decreases by 17% in the US compared to 8%–9% in Australia, Ireland and the UK, once levels of inequality are taken into account, thereby suggesting a greater gulf in the US between the ethos and practice of egalitarianism. These data are in keeping with the overall thesis that Australia has engaged to a lesser extent in neoliberal economic and social policy formation, compared to Ireland, but especially compared to the UK and the US.

This is further supported by data collected as part of the gender inequality index, which combines data on the maternal mortality ratio, the adolescent birth rate, the sharing of seats in parliament, the proportion of the population with some secondary education and labour force participation rates. For this index, a lower score indicates a lower level of gender inequality. As shown in Table 3.3, the US demonstrates the highest level of gender inequality, followed by the UK, Ireland and Australia. The US is the only country of the four not to have ratified important equality and anti-discrimination conventions, including the C100 Equal Remuneration Convention 1951 and the C110 Discrimination (Employment and Occupation) Convention 1958

Table 3.3 Data on status differentials in Australia, Ireland, the US and UK

Country	Human development index (HDI)				Status differentials			
	HDI rank 2014	HDI score 2010	HDI score 2014	Rank change 2009–2014	Inequality-adjusted HDI score 2014	Inequality-adjusted HDI 2014 – overall loss (%)	Gender inequality index 2014	Gender inequality rank
Australia	2	0.927	0.933	0	0.858	8.2	0.110	19
Ireland	6	0.908	0.916	−2	0.836	8.6	0.113	21
United States	8	0.909	0.915	−3	0.76	17	0.280	55
United Kingdom	14	0.906	0.907	−2	0.829	8.6	0.177	39

Source: United Nations (2015: 208–12).

(United Nations, 2015).[23] Furthermore, though data are not presented in the UN report for all countries of interest, in the US

> racial discrimination is the most frequently reported form of discrimination at work, accounting for 35 percent of charges presented to the US Equal Employment Opportunity Commission. In the United Kingdom 22 percent of poll respondents had witnessed racism in the workplace, and 34 percent of Black people and 29 percent of Asian people reported first-hand experience of racial or religious discrimination at work.
>
> (United Nations, 2015: 37)

As with income differentials, the data presented here on status differentials fits with the overall picture of the US as an archetypal neoliberal political economy, followed by the UK, Ireland and Australia.

Citizen-state relations

As for citizen–state relations, these are more difficult to quantify, though some of the UN data on taxation in the four countries of interest provide a proxy for understanding them. Taxation levels demonstrate the extent of a country's commitment to social democratic principles, as well as providing a measure of the extent of involvement of the state in the lives of citizens and also the extent of individual autonomy. Again, the US is an outlier. Total tax revenue as a proportion of GDP between 2005 and 2013 was 10.6% in the US, whilst for Australia, Ireland and the UK, this figure was 21.4%, 22% and 25.3%, respectively. This suggests that there are fewer resources available to fund a welfare state and that, by implication, there is an expectation that citizens are responsible for themselves, irrespective of their personal circumstances.

Therefore, this helps further corroborate ideas about the potency of rugged individualism and freedom from intrusion by the state in American culture (Stedman Jones, 2012: 125; Peck and Tickell, 2002), but also in the fabric of its taxation policies and in its state institutions.

As argued in this book, the centrality of these ideas to citizen-state relations in the US also spills over to affect police-citizen relations. As Wacquant (2009a: 173–4) notes, in relation to Europe, the US is unique, amongst other things, because of its "strength of moral individualism supporting the mantric principle of individual responsibility." The value placed on individual autonomy and freedom from the state may help to explain the personal and individualised nature of police-citizen relations in the US, characterised also by the use of discretion (Brodeur, 2010: 71; Scott, 2010; Walker, 2008; Haller, 1976). Such police-citizen relations are discussed in more detail in the section 'Relations with citizens' in Chapter 4.

Conclusion

This chapter has examined the neoliberal context of the selected countries, focusing on the four countries in which the cities that are of interest to the book are located. For the purposes of the book, neoliberalism is understood in a nuanced way, recognising its variegated character both within and between countries. It is defined as values, practices, discourses, policies and power struggles that coalesce around a series of interlinked ideas, including free-market fundamentalism and the idea that the state should play a more limited role in the lives of citizens, for example, through the rolling back of the welfare state, the deregulation of markets (e.g. for banks or stock markets) or through outsourcing (e.g. of police duties). In addition, and of particular importance here, is the growing emphasis placed on individualism and the personal responsibility of free-willed 'rational' social actors under conditions of neoliberalism, who can be held responsible for their perceived failings, including personal difficulties or allegations of lawbreaking. Moreover, neoliberalism is also understood as involving a growing grip on *certain* citizens by the state, in particular, those engaged in the criminal justice process, including as suspects in police detention, who tend to be disproportionately young black men from deprived communities (Lerman and Weaver, 2014: 181; O'Neill and Loftus, 2013). As argued in Chapter 8, police custody acts as a conduit for neoliberal values and expectations, such as about personal responsibility, as well as helping to address the fallout from neoliberalism by ushering 'problem' citizens into police custody as the gateway of the criminal justice process. This transforms police custody into a potential site of neoliberal governance. By focusing on neoliberalism, this book is an attempt to buck a trend in police studies, in which there have been limited attempts to *explicitly* link police work with political economy (Reiner, 2017). The comparative nature of this book lends itself well to such an undertaking.

Drawing on the literature on penality, particularly the work of Cavadino and Dignan (2006a), it is argued that although there is a need to be wary about regarding the US as an exceptional case, in many areas of policy and practice it *is* exceptional. It is set apart from most other countries in terms of the extent to which it has adopted the principles of neoliberalism into social and economic policies. As a result, it also stands out in terms of its levels of income inequality and the extent to which it scores highly on measures of human development (United Nations, 2015; Wilkinson and Pickett, 2010: 174). In spite of it being one of the wealthiest nations in the world, it has one of the highest levels of income inequality and is ranked lower than the other selected countries on measures of human development. The UK also displays distinctly neoliberal characteristics based on the UN human development measures, though not to the same extent as the US. Its more deep-rooted social democratic history also partially moderates the effects of neoliberalism. As a result, the UK is the second-most neoliberal nation of the four of interest to the book. Whether Ireland or Australia follows next is contentious. On the one hand, O'Malley (2014) argues that Australia has avoided the neoliberal tendencies seen in the US and the UK because of its lack of neoconservatism. Yet Australia has higher levels of income inequality than Ireland. On the other hand, Ireland's levels of income inequality are smaller than Australia's, yet it is more avowedly neoliberal in terms of its economic and social policies, as indicated all too well by the fall of the Celtic Tiger.

As is argued in the remainder of the book, the fact that the US is exceptional, in terms of its embracing of neoliberalism, may be *one* of the reasons why police officers seemed to value discretion to the extent that they did in the detention facilities in the American city in the research. Such individual autonomy – as exhibited in the discretionary decision-making and behaviour of police officers – appeared therefore to be part of a broader mindset amongst the public, policymakers and politicians. That is, it may have been an expression of the "rugged individualism" characteristic of the days of the frontiers in the US (Stedman Jones, 2012: 125) and, more importantly, characteristic of the personal responsibility discourse associated with neoliberalism. At the same time, as considered next in Chapter 4, the emphasis on discretionary police decision-making in the US, is also rooted in the way the police developed there, as a localised municipally-controlled form of governance, in keeping with the diffusion of power across the federal system (Walker, 2008).

Notes

1 Though England is of primary interest in this chapter, occasionally, reference is also made to England and Wales or to the UK due to limitations in the available evidence.
2 Comparative research on the police and on police detention is still relatively limited. There are important exceptions, such as Bayley (1996) and Blackstock et al. (2014), but neither explore all of the countries of interest to the present book.
3 Political economy can be broadly conceived as an appreciation of the "interdependence of macro, meso and micro processes, and of the different dimensions of social existence" (Reiner, 2017: 117), including the economic, political, cultural, social, and psychological. He also notes that such understandings have

commonly been drawn on to explain penality, but less so to explain crime and criminal justice institutions such as the police.

4 Fagan and Geller (2015) note that reasonable suspicion has been subject to capacious interpretation both in the post-Terry Fourth Amendment jurisprudence and also, in practice, with police officers tending to focus on neighbourhood factors and suspects' race.

5 Newburn (2010) cautions against treating the US as uniform in its approach to punishment, identifying a number of variations between states which belie the overall tendency towards growing incarceration. By implication then, it is difficult to treat any of the countries/jurisdictions, which are of interest to the present book, as being uniform in terms of the effects of neoliberalism.

6 Individualism refers to the idea that social actors operate in their own interests rather than collectively for the greater good in society. Driven by capitalist markets, scholars have also noted a growing culture of moral individualism in the post-war period (Giddens, 1991: 197), with the 1980s being particularly noted for breeding the "me generation" (Loader and Mulcahy, 2006: 15). This culture of individualism is what supports the mantra of "individual responsibility" under conditions of neoliberalism (Wacquant, 2009a: 173–4). However, individualism also seems to vary in the form it takes. As noted throughout this book, in the US, there is a more extreme and "rugged" version of individualism, rooted for example, in life on the frontiers and the dispersed and federal nature of state power (Stedman Jones, 2012: 125). As such, individualism in the US is an expression of the need for liberty and freedom from governmental interference (not just the need for personal responsibility).

7 O'Malley (2014) observes that the connection Wacquant (2009a) makes is familiar to critical criminologists and is, in essence, a revival of Marx's argument about the penal and welfare sector pushing its clientele into deskilled job markets so that there is a reserve of labour that can be exploited at will.

8 Wilkinson and Pickett (2010) show that economic inequality is linked to a wide range of social problems, including less trust between members of the public (pp. 52–53); a greater prevalence of mental illness (p. 67); greater illegal drug use, addiction, and deaths from drug use (p. 70); worse physical health and life expectancy (p. 81); greater prevalence of obesity (p. 92); worse educational attainment (p. 105); higher teenage birth rates (p. 123); and less social mobility (p. 168). Though the US fares the worst on these measures, other countries are not far behind, including Portugal, the UK, New Zealand, Australia, Greece and Ireland (Wilkinson and Pickett, 2010: 174).

9 There has been a similar hardening of attitudes towards welfare recipients, accompanied by similarly harsh sanctions. Welfare recipients may have money deducted or their payment rescinded entirely if they do not comply with particular conditions, such as to look for work, irrespective of the reasons for their non-compliance (Lister, 2012).

10 Such overt and legally permissible forms of racial discrimination lasted until the Civil Rights Act 1964, though the effects of this legacy continue to be felt into the present day. This is seen for example, in the segregated nature of American cities in which African Americans tend to live in the most deprived neighbourhoods and tend to be the most over-represented in the criminal justice process, with Wacquant (2009a: 76) wryly referring to this as carceral affirmative action.

11 These figures do not add up to 100% given that they represent data collected on two different topics: race and ethnicity. This is important given that someone may be black but also Hispanic/Latino.

12 This predominance of Catholicism in Ireland is mirrored by the predominance of Protestantism in Northern Ireland due to the partitioning of the two jurisdictions from 1921 (Mulcahy, 2013: 3–5). See also Chapter 4 in the section on 'A brief history of police work'.

13 This refers to Irish-speaking areas, which were designated as such after the creation of the Irish Free State to encourage the revival of the Irish language.

14 The increasingly strained relationship between the police and the black community eventually resulted in race-related rioting in the 1980s in Brixton, London, followed by Manchester, Liverpool, and Birmingham (Bowling et al., 2008).

15 Of this 86%, the vast majority identifies as white British (80.5%), but 5.5% identify as either Irish, Gypsy or Irish Traveller or White Other, with this latter category being comprised of migrants from other, largely Eastern European countries, such as Poland, who came to work in the UK following accession to the EU (Office for National Statistics, 2015).

16 For example, Stedman Jones notes that in the US, these ideas were slipped in under the banner of individualism (one of the traditions and myths of America) and libertarianism, as well as being combined with social and cultural conservatism (2012: 9).

17 Phelan (2007: 43) says that the "Celtic tiger" is an (over)used metaphor for describing the Irish economic "miracle" of the early 1990s. This revolved around "consistent macro-economic management of the economy, investment in education, social partnership, EU structural funds combined with the fiscal discipline imposed by the Maastricht criteria and, of course, very high levels of US investment" (Kirby, 2001: para 3 cited in Phelan, 2007: 29).

18 The government share of funding for universities declined from 91% in 1983 to just over 60% in 1994 (Western et al., 2007).

19 Humpage (2015: 63) notes, for example, that social security changes, in the UK in the 1980s, became hinged on notions of personal responsibility and reciprocal obligations, whilst in Australia there was also talk of the right to employment and that the welfare state should be redistributive to lower income earners.

20 This is part of a broader critique of Wacquant (2009a), in which O'Malley (2014) argues that Wacquant underplays the importance of the alliance between neoliberalism and neoconservatism in the US and the UK, the like of which has not been seen in other countries.

21 The data collated and presented in this report come from a variety of sources and collaborators. See here for a full list: http://hdr.undp.org/en/statistics/understanding/sources [last accessed 15 December 2015].

22 The Gini coefficient is a statistical measure of income inequality, which is usually a value between 0 and 1, in which the higher the coefficient, the higher the level of inequality. However, some such as Piketty are critical of the Gini coefficient, for example, for attempting to "summarize a multidimensional reality with a unidimensional index," the result of which is oversimplification (2014: 266). The Gini coefficient, so Piketty argues, also "tends to confuse inequality in regard to labour with inequality with regard to capital" (2014: 266). Unusually, the Gini coefficient in this report is displayed so that a value of 0 represents absolute equality and a value of 100 represents absolute inequality (United Nations, 2015: 219).

23 These were respectively ratified in 1974 and 1973 in Australia, in 1974 and 1999 in Ireland, and in 1971 and 1999 in the UK.

The police in context
Patterns of policing in the selected countries

In this chapter, I critically examine patterns of policing in the countries where the cities of interest to the book are located. In particular, I focus on the historical origins of police work, focusing on the lasting legacy of colonialism, but also the centrality of discretion to police work in the US from a historical perspective; the contemporary organisation of police work, in particular, the tensions between centralised or localised provision; accountability mechanisms, particularly the legal frameworks of relevance to police detention; and the ebbs and flows in police–citizen relations and their implications for detainees. Though necessarily descriptive, this provides further vital contextual material that can be used to make sense of findings from the empirical research, which are presented in later chapters of the book.

A brief history of police work

An important part of the history of the police in the four countries of interest is that Australia, Ireland and the US are all former British colonies, admittedly of different sizes and with differing histories and trajectories, in terms of their relationships with their former colonial rulers. The US became fully acknowledged as a self-governing nation in 1783, following seven years of civil war after the formal declaration of independence in 1776. Ireland became independent of British rule, as a result of the Anglo-Irish Treaty in 1921, though it remained a part of the Commonwealth until 1949. This Treaty followed prolonged resistance to British rule, which the police and army were called on to quell. This Treaty also partitioned Northern Ireland from the Republic of Ireland, a contentious decision, which initially provoked a civil war, the effects of which are felt into the present day, but particularly during the height of 'The Troubles',[1] in which the Irish Republican Army (IRA) led a series of bombing campaigns, including against the then-ruling Conservative government.[2] Australia is also a former British colony, which simultaneously gained independence and became a part of the Commonwealth in 1901, its membership of which has continued into the present day. Born out of the British Empire, the British Commonwealth of Nations was created in 1931.

However, it was in 1949 that the word 'British' was dropped and the modern meaning of the Commonwealth – involving self-governing nations with shared interests and shared values (e.g. about democracy) who retain the British monarch as the symbolic head of state – came into being.[3] Leaders of Commonwealth nations agreed at this time that their countries would be "free and equal members of the Commonwealth of Nations, freely co-operating in the pursuit of peace, liberty and progress" (thecommonwealth. org). It also serves a multitude of purposes acting as a network which provides self-help and support, as well as being a value-based association which shares common-law roots, common values and a common language, all of which are also viewed as enabling trade links. Hence, it is described as a "radiating influence not a hard power" (Letts, 2016).[4] During the 1999 referendum, Australian citizens voted against becoming a republic, meaning therefore that Australia continues to be a part of the Commonwealth.

The colonial past has left a lasting legacy on the police in all four countries, and this is no doubt part of the reason why there are similarities between them, though also some important differences. As Brodeur (2010: 43–44) argues, North American policing is essentially a derivative of the British model, as are the Irish and Australian models of policing. It is argued, in this brief history of the police in the 18th and 19th centuries in Australia, England, Ireland and the US, that the concept of the 'police' originated in France. It was then borrowed and reinterpreted by the English, most notably, by police reformer Sir Robert Peel, who was central to the creation of the London Metropolitan Police in 1829. However, the idea that a police force could be hierarchically-organised and paid for by the state had, in fact, emerged 45 years earlier in Dublin in 1786. This model of police work in England was exported but also reinterpreted in the US and Australia to meet with contextual exigencies, such as indigenous opposition to British rule in Australia and the large, diverse and more difficult-to-govern nature of the US. With regard to the latter, this required a more localised, but more importantly – for the purposes of the book – a highly discretionary approach to police work in the US. Though there were certain factors that encouraged a similarly personalised approach to police authority in England (e.g. localised policing structures) and in Ireland (e.g. Irish informalism), they were overridden by the desire for the police to be answerable to the law in England and by the national, centralised structure of the police in Ireland. This was not the case for Australia, which quickly established a centralised approach to police work controlled by government officials at the centre of each state, suggesting more of a top-down impersonal approach to police authority, than in the US.

The police in England

In England, the term police came to have a different and more specific meaning than that ascribed to it in France, where it originated from, and where it was understood to mean "order and the power to establish it" (Brodeur,

2010: 47–48). Driven by a similar set of concerns to those in France, namely, the belief that social disorder and crime were growing, particularly in metropolises like London, and that this was a threat to social order (Elmsley, 1996: 16), as well as by the broader processes of modernisation, over the course of the mid- to late 18th and early 19th century, the early institutions of policing began to change, becoming more like the police institution, as it is understood today. These early institutions of policing included parish constables, who were volunteers appointed from within the communities where they lived and who were only paid when they executed warrants or attended court; night watch, who were local unpaid citizens mandated to carry out night-time patrols in urban areas; and justices of the peace, who gave orders to parish constables and were involved in the local administration of justice. They were replaced by paid policing agents, such as the professional 'thief takers', the Bow Street Runners (who were established by Henry Fielding at Bow Street Magistrates' Court in London in 1749 to assist with the detection and apprehension of offenders), and formalised patrol and watchmen, for instance, as a result of the Westminster Watch Act 1735 (Rawlings 2002: 32–37; Elmsley, 1996: 8–15; Lustgarten, 1986: 25–27).

The biggest shift came, however, with the introduction of the Metropolitan Police in London in 1829 (henceforth referred to as the Met). 'The Peelers', as they were also known, which is a reference to Sir Robert Peel – who was Home Secretary of the Conservative government of the time, and who was instrumental in persuading government of the need for the Met[5] – were the first formalised, uniformed and hierarchically-organised police force in England who were also paid for by central government through tax income. From this point onwards, the word 'police', also took on a narrower meaning than that ascribed to it in France in the 17th century.[6] In particular, the police came to be understood as an instrument for preventing crime and disorder. For example, the instructions to the 'new police' were that they were about "*the prevention of crime … the protection of life and property, the preservation of public tranquillity*" (from Sir Richard Mayne's instructions to the 'New Police of the Metropolis' in 1829 cited in Scarman, 1981: 62). Peel also expressed a desire to retain the police as part of the communities that they policed. He famously said, "the police are the public and the public are the police," thus implying a need for accountability to the public if the police are to secure their cooperation with them (Loader, 2016). Even though it is unclear whether they originated from Peel, these and other 'Peelian principles' are regarded as central to self-understandings of Anglo-American policing, thereby having a material and structuring effect on the aspirations of police institutions (Loader, 2016).[7]

The introduction of the Met was not without criticism and resistance. One of the primary concerns about this 'new police' was that, even though they deliberately wore a uniform in a different colour and cut to that of the military, they were seen as a paramilitary force (Elmsley, 1996: 25). This was because they engaged in tasks associated with the military, such as the quelling of disorder. A former colonel in the military, Charles Rowan, was also installed as one of the first two commissioners of the Met. The police were also hierarchical, like the military, and engaged in military-style training (e.g. drills). Hence, the public saw them as "soldiers" irrespective of the colour of their uniforms, denouncing them as "the blue army" (Rawlings, 2002: 120; Storch, 1975: 66). There were also serious concerns that the police would become like the gendarmerie in France, acting as spies for an authoritarian state. That is, there were concerns that the police would infringe on citizens' liberties, particularly on those of the working classes (Storch, 1975). Indeed, the public colloquially called them 'the Jenny Darbies' which was a corruption of the French 'Gens d'Armes', i.e. they were seen as a symbol of potential English despotism (Rawlings, 2002: 120). Other concerns about the Met and other new police organisations related to cost-effectiveness and accountability (Rawlings, 2002: 72; Elmsley, 1996: 25), as they were seen as more expensive and less locally accountable to taxpayers, as well as like a plague of "'blue locusts' who devoured tax money and produced nothing of use in return" (Storch, 1975: 84). In spite of these concerns, with the exception of some areas of London (e.g., Marylebone), a decade after its establishment, the Met was growing in acceptance; property owners perceived it as effective in preventing crime, and 'respectable' inhabitants were pleased by the policing of drunkenness, riots and debauchery (Rawlings, 2002: 123; Elmsley, 1996: 29).

These deep-rooted concerns about the 'new police' were overcome in two main ways. First, the Met were deliberately unarmed, in that they did not carry swords or pistols, though they did carry a truncheon and a rattle, which were hidden from view. Though the police did have ready access to weapons at police stations, the overt appearance to the people of London was as unarmed (Waddington, 1999a). This use of unarmed officers by the Met was thus symbolic, putting into practice Peelian principles about the importance of policing by consent.[8] Second, attempts to create a single national police force, such as by Lord Palmerston, were rejected in favour of localised police forces. These arrangements were established through the County and Borough Police Act 1856, which created an expectation that a body of constables from a defined local area would act under the direction and control of a chief constable. (Elmsley, 1996: 47). As such, this preserved the ancient office of the constable. Though localised policing arrangements were retained in England both then and now (as discussed later in this section), unlike in the US, which took a similarly localised approached to police work, police authority came to have an impersonal, not discretionary, character, founded on a Peelian principle that the police should be answerable to the law and to the law alone (Brodeur, 2010: 71).

The Garda Síochána: back to the future?

This was not the first time that such policing arrangements – including a hierarchically-organised publicly-funded and, eventually, unarmed police force – had come to pass. In fact, policing arrangements of this kind first appeared about 45 years earlier in Dublin (Walsh, 1998: 6), with some of these developments being overseen by Sir Robert Peel. As noted above, the history of the police in Ireland must be seen within the broader context of British rule in Ireland, followed by civil war from 1919 to 1921 and Irish independence in 1921 and the creation of the Irish Free State (which became the Republic of Ireland). Prior to Irish independence, the colonial model of policing was implicitly about protecting the English elite and controlling rebellious populations, thereby making it similar in character to the police in London (Manning, 2012), albeit there was a more obviously coercive overtone to such attempts at control in Ireland (Reiner, 2010: 7), given the colonial context of policing. Subsequently, postcolonial policing in the form of the Garda Síochána was intimately connected to the quest for Irish independence.

It was in 1786 that an organised police force first made an appearance in Ireland. This police force, the Dublin Metropolitan Police (DMP), was confined to the capital city, Dublin. It functioned in a crime prevention role and retained the constable as the basic unit. It differed from policing in London in two ways, however. First, it was subject to close control by the central government at Dublin Castle, which represented English interests in Ireland. Second, the force was armed and specifically structured and trained to respond with force to breakdowns in public order (Manning, 2012; Waddington, 1999a; Walsh, 1998: 6–7). The Royal Irish Constabulary (RIC) was subsequently established in 1814 to perform a similar role to the DMP, though in the policing of unruly populations in the regions, rather than in Dublin, eventually becoming established as a nationwide permanent police force in 1836 (Finnane, 1994: 11). Sir Robert Peel was intimately connected with the development of the RIC during his time as Chief Secretary for Ireland from 1812 to 1818 and remained in contact with the incumbent Chief Secretary about the reform of the RIC. In fact, aspects of the model of policing developed in Ireland in this period were imported into England, including the wearing of a uniform, discipline and hierarchy, as well as the role of the police in controlling riots (Conway, 2010; Wilson, 2009).

From the last decade of the 19th century and with growing nationalist sentiments, the RIC became increasingly hated as a symbol of British oppression. As a result, the RIC and the DMP faced sustained ostracism from the community and armed attack by the IRA. Conway (2014: 19) says that between 1919 and 1922, there were over 1,000 attacks on RIC members, of which 493 involved RIC officers being killed. Following the signing of the Anglo-Irish Treaty, the DMP survived as a separate force until 1925 (when it was merged with the Garda Síochána), though the RIC was disbanded in 1922 as part of the terms of the Treaty. The perceived lawlessness and social upheaval in this period meant there was a rush to establish a police force which could protect life and property, apprehend criminals, restore law and order and instil a sense of security and stability to the fledgling Irish State (Walsh, 1998: 8). The first attempt at this, in the form of the Civic Guards, failed. This was in part because of internal tensions between those for and against the Anglo-Irish Treaty, which were exacerbated by the recruitment of a large number of ex-RIC officers to the force, all of which contributed to the Kildare Mutiny in which new recruits stopped pledging their allegiance to the Commissioner (Conway, 2014: 33). However, what the Civic Guards did establish was the importance of having an unarmed police force (Conway, 2014: 46), an idea which lived on into the force's next incarnation, in 1923, as the Garda Síochána (Conway, 2014: 30). At the same time, the Garda Síochána also inherited other aspects of the RIC, including its "centralised command structure, barracks-based distribution of personnel, broad administrative-regulative functions as well as a national security riot control remit" (Manning, 2012: 352). Therefore, it largely lacked the localised and personal character of police work in the US and England, albeit the centralised command structure was somewhat tempered by "Irish informalism," that is, the cultural preference in Ireland for resolving criminal justice matters informally (Hamilton, 2013: 161–2).

The US: imperfect importation of the British model

Thus far, it has been argued that the form that policing took in England during the emergence of the 'new police' borrowed ideas – such as about the need for a hierarchically-organised force – from colonial policing in Ireland. Postcolonial policing in Ireland, in turn, borrowed ideas from the English, such as about the symbolic value of unarmed officers, as a means of convincing the populace of policing by consent. Moreover, in both jurisdictions, the form that this policing took grew out of a perception of rising crime, lawlessness, as well as disorder, which in the case of Ireland was also an expression of resistance to British rule. The conditions under which police forces began to emerge in 19th-century US were not dissimilar to this, though the form that this policing took differed. This was partly a product of the large immigrant population, the hard-to-govern nature of such a large country, and also the desire to draw a line under the colonial past. Hence, Brodeur (2010: 70–72) describes the importation of the British model of policing as both reluctant and flawed.

In the colonial era in the 17th and 18th century, the burden of policing in the US rested on the shoulders of local community volunteers, who were banded together for the purposes of investigation, trial and sentencing, and were often free from formal procedures or rules. They included "constables, sheriffs, marshals, and various auxiliaries, such as thief-takers and bounty hunters" (Brodeur, 2010: 69). Following the American revolution (1775–1783), community control of policing continued as citizens called for the dissolution of the military and local sheriffs were converted from agents of the British Crown to democratically elected public servants. These sheriffs had wide discretionary powers and duties, including running jails, serving subpoenas and apprehending offenders. "In fact, due to their democratically elected status, sheriffs served, in large part, as little more than armed agents of local majority control" (Walker, 1983, cited in Walker, 2008: 328).

In the postcolonial period of the late 18th and early 19th century, these existing policing arrangements came to be seen as insufficient, as a result of perceived growing urban unrest, social disorder and rioting, as well as felonious and spectacular crimes, such as the murder of Marie Rogers in New York City (NYC) in 1841 (Brodeur, 2010: 69).[9] Hence, elected officials in NYC, Philadelphia, Boston and other major cities began to look abroad for ideas, the most appealing of which came from England (Walker, 2008). Following the birth of the Met in London in 1829, police forces also began to be established in major American cities, such as Boston in 1838, NYC in 1844 and Philadelphia in 1854. As in England, to begin with, officers did not carry firearms, at least not officially. However, from 1895, officers, such as in the New York Police Department (NYPD), began to be systematically issued with revolvers (Brodeur, 2010: 69).

Curiously, however, as Walker (2008) notes, there was little attempt in these American cities to link local policing arrangements to federal control – quite the reverse, as 1820–1840 was a period when American politics moved away from federal control. Consequently, police departments retained close ties with local elected officials, particularly mayors, who encouraged the police to be responsive to the demands of the electorate, as they regarded policing as a way of placating them. Not surprisingly then, progressive police reformers of the 1880s and 1890s, such as Theodore Roosevelt, took an interest in breaking such close ties between local politics and policing, such as by introducing federal-level police organisations like the Federal Bureau of Investigation (FBI). This was not altogether successful, though, as evidenced by the refusal of working-class police officers in working class industrial areas, such as Pennsylvania, to police disputes with big businesses, meaning that private detective agencies like the Pinkerton agency were paid to do the work instead (Walker, 2008).

Though some of the social conditions in which the police institutions were introduced in the US in the 19th century were similar to those in England (e.g. as a response to perceived social disorder), Brodeur (2010: 70) argues that the importation of the model was both resisted but also flawed in its realisation. These flaws largely stemmed from the way that the police came to use and understand their authority. Police authority in England, so Brodeur (2010: 70) argues, was connected to institutions and the law, i.e. it was impersonal and institutional. For example, British police commissioners sought to cultivate an image of the police as answerable to the law and the law alone – hence the Peelian principle that the police were "to seek and preserve public favour not by pandering to public opinion, rather by demonstrating impartial service to the law" (Loader, 2016). By contrast, in the US, policing was personal, not institutional. It depended on closeness to citizens and on their informal expectations of individual officers, rather than on formal or legal standards (Brodeur, 2010: 70; Scott, 2010; Walker, 2008; Haller, 1976). This personal and localised nature of policing was rooted in the American constitutional structure and the diffusion of power across the federal system, which had the effect of limiting centralised power and preserving local municipal control over the police in America (Walker, 2008).

This personal and localised nature of police-citizen relations had a particular impact on police work, which is of special relevance here. Brodeur says "[t]he immediate consequence of this emergence of personal authority is the incomparable extent of police discretion that is the hallmark of US policing" (2010: 71). Similarly, Walker says that, over time, there was a "perpetuation of a highly decentralised, remarkably discretionary, and fundamentally democratic American police" (2008: 326). Whether this amounts to a flawed importation of the British model is an empirical question. Another way of looking at this is to say that police authority in the US was adapted to suit the context in which it was deployed, namely, a large, diverse and hard-to-govern country. Under these circumstances, perhaps such impersonal and discretionary authority was a necessity. These ideas all have a particular salience for the present book: they provide a way of making sense of the looseness with which the law and police policies seemed to be put into practice in the present day, in the American jurisdiction in the research, as explained at the start of the book. As argued above, this has been further aided by neoliberal discourses about the need for personal responsibility and for responsibilised citizens, which are also particularly prevalent in the US.

Australia

It has been argued thus far that there was a certain amount of borrowing and sharing of ideas from within the British model of policing by police reformers in England, Ireland and the US, but that the British model of policing was interpreted in a way that suited the context in which it was deployed. In the US, this led police authority to have a personalised character, the result of which was to create an important role for discretionary decision-making in American police work (Brodeur, 2010: 70; Scott, 2010; Walker, 2008; Haller, 1976). It is similarly the case that the British model of policing was interpreted in a particular way in Australia, in the 18th and 19th centuries. This was in order to meet the demands of the context in which it was deployed (Finnane, 1994: 9–30), albeit this resulted in a more top-down impersonal kind of police authority, of the kind seen in Ireland. Of particular note was the fact that for some 80 years it was a penal colony and a place to which prisoners were transported, resulting in a large convict population (Bronitt and Finnane, 2012). Even after transportation ended, it was a place of migration for people from England and Ireland. Indeed, these migrants swelled the ranks of the police. In the 18th and 19th century, Australia was also a place of economic turbulence and social dislocation, brought about by the gold rushes. Of great importance during the birth of the Australian nation, however, was the dislocation, oppression and sometimes near extermination of Indigenous Australians, which has left a lasting mark on Australian society including in the relations between indigenous groups and the police (Nettelbeck and Ryan, 2018; Finnane, 1994: 25–26).

In the 1770s, early settlements, such as Botany Bay, were protected by the military, but it was not long before there were proposals to appoint constables in Sydney, in order to prevent theft and assault (Wilson, 2009; Finnane, 1994: 11). These constables were often drawn from the "better behaved convicts" (Bronitt and Finnane, 2012: 19). By the late 18th century, this was followed by calls for paid and permanent police forces to replace the voluntary and locally-organised English type of constable, who were directed by justices of the peace (Finnane, 1994: 11). However, rather than such paid forms of policing mimicking the British model of locally-focused police organisations, a more centralised approach was taken, albeit at the state-level, being shaped by the also centralised approach to government in the new Australian colonies (Bronitt and Finnane, 2012). These state-wide police forces covered vast territories, from coastal cities to frontier settlements, and were modelled on forces such as the Metropolitan Police and the RIC (Bronitt and Finnane, 2012). This centralised approach was a key point of variation in Australia compared to England or the US, but not Ireland (Nettelbeck and Ryan, 2018; Bronitt and Finnane, 2012; Finnane, 1994: 9). Thus, from the mid-1850s, the police were controlled from the centre of political power in each colony (which became the Australian states of the present day), rather than by local authorities within them (Nettelbeck and Ryan, 2018; Bronitt and Finnane, 2012). Putting this centralised control over policing into practice required the elimination of existing municipal forces, even in places such as Tasmania, where there was initial resistance to such an approach (Finnane, 1994: 18). The vesting of authority in a single police commissioner answerable to the colonial secretary also excluded other important players like the magistracy, judiciary or locally elected officials from taking an overview of policing practices (Finnane, 1994: 15–16).

The centralised control of policing in Australia was partly shaped by a similarly centralised approach to government. However, it was also seen as an effective way of dealing with the perceived social problems of the 19th century, thereby enabling the police to control crime but also act as "the ultimate guarantors of social and political order" (Finnane, 1994: 13). First, centralisation was seen as a way of dealing with convicts, escaped convicts and emancipated convicts, for whom there was a perceived need to monitor and control their movements across the country as a means of reassuring citizens and being seen to act to create and secure order (Finnane, 1994: 24–25). Second, the gold rushes, such as in Victoria and New South Wales (NSW) in the 1850s, created an itinerant, rootless and thus volatile and hard-to-regulate population, who were seen as a threat to the social order (Finnane, 1994: 27–28). Centralised police forces were thus seen as the only way to deal with such a transitory group for whom local police forces would have been an irrelevance. Third, indigenous people were seen as another 'troublesome' group, whose actions on the frontiers could only be effectively controlled by a state-wide police force (Nettelbeck and Ryan, 2018; Finnane, 1994: 25–26). As newly arrived settlers and emancipated convicts moved westwards from the early settlements in NSW, Indigenous Australians were "increasingly displaced from their own lands, pressed into confined territories and placed under the authority of the 'protectorates'" (Bronitt and Finnane, 2012: 19). State-wide police forces played a role in these processes, for example, bringing 'order' to the frontiers by suppressing indigenous dissent and enabling indigenous land to be given to white settlers. In the mid-19th century, this often happened by force, with the help of 'native troopers',[10] but later in the 19th century, land dispossession was enabled by laws, which permitted monitoring, surveillance and the criminalisation of indigenous groups (Cunneen, 2001: 24; Finnane, 1994: 24). In this context, "multiply dispossessed indigenous people, who were ruthlessly expropriated, exploited, disenfranchised and discounted by the white settlers and their descendants" (Cavadino and Dignan, 2006b: 81), subsequently formed intensely problematic relationships with the police, which continue to the present day.

The contemporary organisation of police work

The foregoing discussion illuminates the historic tensions between centralisation and localisation in England, Ireland, America and Australia, the legacy of which has infused the contemporary organisation of police work. In England and Wales,[11] police work remains a largely localised matter, though only just, as a result of national bodies, such as the National Police Chiefs Council (formerly the Association of Chief Police Officers), chipping away at the independent identity and power of individual forces. Currently, there are 41 county or area forces, as well as the City of London Police and the Met (who police the rest of London), making in total 43 police forces in England and Wales, which are funded by the Home Office. In contrast to the predominantly localised form that police work takes in England and Wales, the police in Ireland, the Garda Síochána, the Gardaí or the Guards, as they are referred to colloquially, continue to be a centralised national police organisation, albeit they are organised around six regions which are in turn broken down into divisions and districts. In Australia, there is a clear emphasis on a centralised model of policing, albeit at the state-level, which is complemented by national-level police organisations. The policing system is comprised of one federal, six state and two territory police forces. Showing greater similarity to the English model, police forces in the US are comprised of federal police organisations and a dizzyingly large number of local police departments.

Table 4.1 Total police personnel at the national level

Country	2009		2012	
	Count	Rate per 100,000	Count	Rate per 100,000
Australia	54,193	245.9	60,364	261.9
Ireland	14,547	329.8	13,424	293.4
UK (England and Wales)	143,734	260.2	129,584	229.1
US	706,886	228.4	670,439	211.2

Source: UNODC (2016).

These local forces include State Police, both State Bureaux of Investigation (equivalent to the FBI but at the state level) and State Highway Patrol; City Police Departments in large cities, one of which was used as a case study in the present research; Municipal Police, i.e. police departments in small towns; and County Sheriff Departments (Peak, 2009: 59). Altogether, there are close to 18,000 police forces in the US, most of which are municipally-based and some of which are overlapping in their remits, powers and jurisdictions, creating battles over jurisdictional responsibility and hindering cooperation (Brodeur, 2010: 10). As shown in Table 4.1,[12] at the time of the research, each of the jurisdictions had roughly comparable police officer levels per 100,000 of the population, with the exception of Ireland, which was much higher in 2009.

Accountability arrangements

Bearing in mind the role historically ascribed to discretion in police work in the US, it becomes important to also consider the corollary to this: accountability arrangements. As noted in Chapter 2, Chan (1999) argues that accountability can be seen in terms of what it tries to achieve i.e. whether it controls the police and/or whether it invites explanations or accounts of their action. We might also think of accountability in terms of the structures and institutions that it is connected to. As such, there are three kinds of accountability: democratic, organisational and legal. Given that one of the purposes of this book is to explore the relative influence of discretion, the law and other rules structures on police practices in police detention, I focus on the last of these here. Legal forms of accountability emphasise the links between the police and the law and legal institutions like the courts and sentencers. However, to appreciate these links, it is necessary to first understand the wider and somewhat complex legal context in which they rest and which will be briefly summarised here. All four jurisdictions that are of interest to the book were chosen because of their common-law context, meaning there is a greater emphasis on judge-made law, that is, on customs and practices being determined by court rulings rather than by statutes, as is more commonplace in parts of continental Europe.[13] At the same time, these judge-made laws can be expanded or reduced by laws passed by parliament (Australian Human Rights Commission, 2016).

Whilst the four countries share similar common-law roots, they also have important differences, which affect how citizens' rights are understood, including by the police. First, Australia and the US are different from England and Ireland because they are both federal countries, meaning that, though together they each form a single nation, each state within both of these nations are separately governed and have their own legal systems. This makes for a complex legal context, especially in the US, where federal laws and legal decision-making at the federal level (such as by the Supreme Court in the US) come to be interpreted at the state-level, such as by state courts, sometimes in different ways, as well as Supreme Court judgements being put into practice in different ways on a state-by-state basis (Mulroy, 2013). For example, the Supreme Court case *California v. Beheler* 463 US 1121 (1983) resulted in only 33 of 50 states adopting Beheler-type warnings so that suspects who come voluntarily to the police station with the police (but who are not under arrest) must be told that they are free to leave (Weisselberg, 2008: 1545).[14]

At the same time, England and Ireland also have supra-state forms of accountability. This is through the European Convention on Human Rights (ECHR), as well as the Council of the European Union (EU) Directives on Procedural Rights, which have developed in tandem to the ECHR, including the right to interpretation, the right to information, the right of access to a lawyer and the presumption of innocence. With regard to the ECHR, cases pursued under it or its domestic legal equivalent may be heard at the European Court of Human Rights (ECtHR), which is the last stop for appeal cases that have already been heard by all relevant domestic appeal courts. This means that rulings made by the ECtHR apply across the 47 European countries signed up to the ECHR,[15] including in England and Ireland.[16] For example, *Salduz v. Turkey* 2008 required suspects arrested by the police anywhere in Council of Europe member states to be given access to a lawyer prior to their first interrogation. Nonetheless, European countries have been slow to take up this requirement in law and in practice. Some jurisdictions – Scotland, Belgium, France and the Netherlands – altered their laws and policies to take account of this ruling, but change in practice was slow and difficult (e.g. restrictions were placed on the number of and length of consultations in France and the Netherlands) (Blackstock et al., 2014: 353–4). This variation in interpretation and practical application of ECtHR rulings is not dissimilar to the variation seen in relation to Supreme Court rulings in the US, though Weisselberg (2017) argues that it is even more complex in Europe, given the distinct legal and societal cultures of each of the countries that are signed up to the ECHR. Nonetheless, Weisselberg (2017) still regards the ECHR and the EU Directives on Procedural Rights as offering more robust 'on the books' protections for suspects, than those existing under the Miranda doctrine in the US (as explained later in this section).

The existence of the ECHR points to a second important distinction between the US, England and Ireland, at least. The human rights discourse, which underpins it, simply does not exist in the US. Fineman (2010) notes that the US has not ratified conventions on human rights, for example, connected to economic rights or the rights of women or children. She goes on to say that, in fact, attempts to apply human rights to American practices and laws "have been met with resistance, if not outright rejection," such as by several justices of the Supreme Court, who regard human rights principles as "foreign fads" which should not be used, given the superiority of American constitutional provisions (Fineman, 2010: 255).[17] The absence of a human rights discourse in the US speaks to a further distinction worth noting, at this point, about the higher degree of tolerance in the US for miscarriages of justice / wrongful convictions. This is evident, for example, in the greater emphasis placed on ex post facto judicial interventions (by not admitting confessions or admissions) rather than on ex ante regulation of police detention practices through legislation (Dixon, 2019). It is also evident in the limited structures in place to investigate and review wrongful convictions. In the US, there are only 11 states which have innocence commissions or a law reform commission which perform this role, and there is no federal-level agency (Huff and Naughton, 2017). This contrasts with England, for example, where, since 1995, there is a national Criminal Cases Review Commission, which performs this role, albeit imperfectly (Elks, 2008: 42). This absence of human rights and the higher degree of tolerance for miscarriages of justice in the US are also inherently racialised: they heap further injustices and inequalities on African Americans who are particularly over-represented throughout the criminal justice process (Walker et al., 2012: 2–3). Though offering an individualised approach to what are largely institutional and structural problems, the #BlackLivesMatter movement can be seen as an attempt to challenge this tolerance of racialised miscarriages of justice in the US. This can be seen as part of the growth of a "new visibility" with regard to police accountability, in which police misconduct is revealed to mass audiences via social media (Brown, 2016; Goldsmith, 2010: 915).

Aside from the issue of federalism and the absence of human rights in the US, a third key difference that exists between the four countries is the way police powers are codified and, linked to this, whether these countries have formal constitutions, which more broadly set out citizens' rights and clarify the nature of the relationship between the state and its citizens. England is the one country of the four not to have a formal constitution. Though the Magna Carta – which is regarded as the basis of the constitutions of some of the jurisdictions/countries of interest – is an important part of the history of citizens' rights in England, governments have largely shied away from creating a formal constitution or a Bill of Rights.[18] This is because citizens' rights are, in part, determined through the common-law process as well as being set out in a range of statutes; citizens' rights exist, but they are not codified in a single constitution.

At the time of writing, police powers and citizens' rights are largely enacted through the Police and Criminal Evidence Act 1984 (PACE), which covers stop-and-search, arrest, detention in the police station, investigation, identification and interviewing of detainees.[19] PACE is also accompanied by the PACE Codes of Practice, which provide further guidance about rights and entitlements under PACE, both for staff and those arrested and detained by the police. Indeed, a key right of detainees in the police station is that they may read a copy of these Codes of Practice. The introduction of PACE involved enhanced powers and authority for the police to intervene in the lives of citizens through stops, arrests and detention, but it also imposed limits on the use of these powers. For example, the police were authorised to detain citizens, but limits were imposed on how long they detained them. Hence, Dixon (2008: 30) describes PACE as an "authorise and regulate" strategy rooted in increasing recorded crime and fear of crime, as well as the power of liberal elites in the Home Office and in the Royal Commission on Criminal Procedure 1981 (RCCP) who saw having a rule-bound state as a primary way of protecting individual freedoms. PACE therefore cannot be seen as straightforwardly neoliberal or as encouraging neoliberal values amongst police officers, in spite of the fact that it was enacted in a period when neoliberalism ascended to prominence under the Thatcher government (1979–1990).

On the surface, therefore, the compromise struck in PACE between giving the police more authority to use their discretion, whilst also regulating this authority to a greater extent, may appear incongruent with aspects of the present book. After all, a key argument of the book is that neoliberalism partially explains heightened discretionary police power (particularly in the US), not heightened regulation of police powers, or a compromise between the two. However, the fact that PACE cannot be seen as straightforwardly neoliberal might be explained by the fact that PACE was set in motion by the RCCP 1981 (see also Chapter 8), which had itself been set in motion under Thatcher's predecessor, the Labour leader James Callaghan (1976–1979), hearing evidence between 1977 and 1981. As such, PACE cannot necessarily be viewed as an intended part of Thatcher's neoliberal policies. Once in power, the law and order politics of the era would have also made it politically unpopular for Thatcher to have changed the course of an already established review of criminal procedure, particularly at a time when there was growing concern about miscarriages of justice, as well as rising crime and fear of crime. Moreover, PACE might also be seen as an example of the "quirky" and uneven development of neoliberalism (Humpage, 2015: 243–4; Cavadino and Dignan, 2006a: 452). For example, social, economic and structural forces may have been contested on the ground (Brown, 2011), including by Home Office officials who saw the need for a rule-bound state (Dixon, 2008), suggesting that criminal justice actors are able to maintain some degree of autonomy during periods of neoliberal dominance. This argument about the uneven effects of neoliberalism is particularly compelling, given the far from avowedly neoliberal nature of Thatcher's penal policies. This was contrary to what might have been expected, given Thatcher's status as a believer in harsh penal policies and as a pioneer in introducing neoliberalism into the UK in the 1980s. In fact, although there were some manifestly harsh penal policies such as 'short, sharp shock' detention centres, under the direction of Douglas Hurd as Home Secretary (1985–1989) – which includes the period when PACE was implemented, i.e. in 1986 – he steered the criminal justice system away from a harsh penal culture (Cavadino and Dignan, 2006b: 74). This did not last though, with the murder of the toddler, James Bulger, in 1993 by two ten-year-old boys, provoking a return to a harsher penal rhetoric and set of practices (Green, 2009).

In addition to PACE, there is also the Human Rights Act (HRA) 1998, which translated the ECHR into domestic legislation and thus provides an additional layer of accountability, as well as covering a wider range of matters beyond police powers. It concerns mainly civil and political rights. Its main articles include rights to: life, freedom from torture or inhuman or degrading treatment, freedom from slavery or forced labour, personal freedom, fair trials, no punishment without law, private life and family, freedom of belief, free expression, free assembly and association, marriage and freedom from discrimination (Gearty, 2007: 24–25). The main thrust of the HRA is that the courts should be mindful of it when interpreting existing laws. At the same time, the human rights contained in the act can be "restricted or truncated where the interests of the democratic system itself demand" (Gearty, 2007: 27). Nevertheless, the HRA offers some protection against authoritarianism; it provides the means for individuals to challenge what they regard as unacceptable infringements of their human rights by the state after the event. In practice and in relation to police custody, this means that cases involving unsatisfactory police practices may ultimately be heard in the ECtHR, having progressed through all of the relevant domestic courts.[20]

Although Australia has a constitution, unusually, it does not have a Bill of Rights, and nor does it have many individual rights set out within the constitution (Saunders, 2011: 257), which focuses more on the institutions of the state. There are only five explicit individual rights in the Constitution. These are the right to vote (Section 41), protection against acquisition of property on unjust terms (Section 51 [xxxi]), the right to a trial by jury (Section 80), freedom of religion (Section 116) and prohibition of discrimination on the basis of state of residency (Section 117) (Australian Human Rights Commission, 2016). Following *Dietrich v. The Queen* in 1992, the High Court of Australia has interpreted the Constitution as *implying* human rights, in particular, the right to a fair trial, including the provision of legal counsel in serious cases.[21] Nonetheless, Bronitt and Finnane are right to remark that "Australia lacks an entrenched constitutional Bill of Rights" (2012: 21). Instead, Australia has taken a hybridised approach to rights protection, with these rights being variously protected by legislation passed by the Commonwealth Parliament (i.e. its parliament), by the courts involved in administering the common law and through the application of international human rights law (Saunders, 2011: 258, 262, 267, 270). By and large, individual human rights, in relation to the police, are determined by state laws (Bronitt and Finnane, 2012; Saunders, 2011: 279). For example, in NSW, one of the key legal frameworks setting out police powers and citizens' rights, which is derived indirectly from PACE (Dixon and Travis, 2007: 52–53), is the Law Enforcement Powers and Responsibilities Act 2002 (LEPRA). It covers police powers in relation to entry, requirements about the disclosure of identity, search and seizure with and without a warrant, and in cases of domestic violence, emergency powers in public order situations, crimes scenes, arrest, use of police in-car video equipment, investigation and questioning, other powers relating to detainees in police custody (e.g. relating to identification procedures such as fingerprints and photographs), drug detection, powers relating to vehicles and traffic, powers to give directions, powers relating to intoxicated detainees, property in police custody and the use of force. LEPRA 2005 updated and extended the 2002 Act to include sections on vulnerable detainees, custody records and the role of custody manager. In many respects then, Australian jurisdictions, such as NSW, are similar to England and Wales in terms of how police powers and citizens' rights in police custody are codified and thus regulated.

By contrast, in the US, the American Constitution and its ten amendments, known as the Bill of Rights, provide a single repository for the rights of individual citizens across the nation, with the Supreme Court playing a significant role in how these rights are interpreted and put into practice. From the mid-20th century, the Supreme Court's interpretation of the Constitution came to take normative priority such that "what the Court said the Constitution meant *was* what the Constitution meant" (Tushnet, 2015: 139). As a result, though individual states have jurisdiction over state law-only issues, such as through their interpretation of state law rules and local ordinances, where those state laws implicate constitutional rights and protections, these cases are heard by the Supreme Court. Moreover, state courts have limited recourse to challenge Supreme Court rulings, as they apply to their particular state (Bronitt and Finnane, 2012).[22] Of particular importance to the regulation of the police are the Fourth, Fifth and Sixth Amendments to the Constitution and the ever-expanding body of case law that has built up around them to clarify and further interpret them. The Fourth Amendment encompasses the 'probable cause' required by the police to search someone, make an arrest, take someone into police custody and to the police station for interrogation, and also to exclude evidence if obtained by improper means. The Fifth Amendment protects citizens from self-incrimination. In essence, this means that no one has to answer questions which might incriminate them, either in the police station or at court, although some may interpret 'pleading the fifth' as an indication of guilt. This Amendment also encompasses the right that citizens have to be informed of their rights, such as to silence and to defence counsel. The Sixth Amendment relates to the right that the accused has to a speedy, public and fair trial in which they are provided with the assistance of a defence counsel.

Since their inception, these constitutional rights have been continuously clarified and, to some extent, undermined (see Weisselberg, 2008), such as by the Supreme Court and other federal courts, as well as by state courts and legislatures responsible for applying the laws at the local level.[23] For example, with regard to the Fifth Amendment right that citizens have to be informed of their rights, the Supreme Court rulings *Escobedo v. Illinois* (1964) and *Miranda v. Arizona* (1966),[24] meant that confessions made by suspects who had not been informed of their constitutional rights cannot be admitted into evidence. These Supreme Court rulings mean that suspects have to be informed of their right to silence and to defence counsel, which are known as Miranda rights. Once "Mirandarised," and once a suspect has exercised their right to silence, in theory, the police cannot try to interrogate them again unless their lawyer is present.

The Miranda ruling was supposed to afford custodial suspects the right to silence and prevent them from making involuntary statements to the police. However, aside from the fact that there was never any evidence to show that the system of warnings and waivers introduced by Miranda would protect Fifth Amendment rights, since its introduction, Miranda has been struck a number of blows over the years, both in terms of the law 'in the books' and the law 'in practice' (Rossman, 2017; Weisselberg, 2017; Weisselberg, 2008). In terms of the 'law in the books', Weisselberg (2008: 1521) notes the gutting of the Miranda safeguards to the extent that, as a protective device, Miranda is "largely dead." For example,

> officers need not advise a suspect of the subject matter of the interrogation or that a lawyer is trying to see him; police are not required to obtain a waiver before beginning to interrogate; the physical fruit of a statement taken in violation of Miranda is not excluded and the statement itself can be used to impeach the defendant at trial; … the right to remain silent (like the right to counsel) must be asserted affirmatively and unequivocally.
>
> (Weisselberg, 2017: 1248–9; see also Rossman, 2017)

In terms of Miranda, 'in practice', the picture is similarly gloomy. For example, the social science literature shows that suspects, particularly vulnerable ones, tend not to understand the Miranda warnings; as a result, they cannot meaningfully assert their Fifth Amendment rights and Miranda has had little effect on reducing false confessions (Rossman, 2017; Weisselberg, 2017, 2008). Weisselberg (2017) also notes how the police have been trained to create situations which the courts will find "'noncustodial', such as by inviting suspects to the police station and telling them they are not under arrest so that Miranda warnings need not be given. This advice to suspects, that they are not under arrest, often termed a 'Beheler warning', is a deliberate tactic to avoid giving Miranda warnings" (p. 1249). He furthermore notes that Miranda was introduced without altering the basic structures of the criminal process (e.g. there is a continued absence of lawyers, in practice). The effect of this is that the police play a dual and contradictory role in which, on the one hand, they have to secure a confession, which continues to be a highly valued aspect of the criminal process and, on the other hand, they seek to advise suspects about whether to talk to them. Hence, the World Justice Project (2016) ranked the US 22nd when compared to 36 equally wealthy (high-income) nations.[25] It was also found to be below the mean of these high-income nations with regard to key criminal justice measures, including "due process of law," "effective correctional systems," and "no corruption," as well as being substantially below the mean for "no discrimination" (World Justice Project, 2016: 153).

Regardless, this dynamic and constantly changing nature of legal rights, which are set down in the constitution and reinterpreted, as a result of the common-law process, means that it is imperative for police officers to keep abreast of legal changes and for police agencies to have a formal mechanism for imparting these changes to their staff. This is often done through police training manuals and police directives (Moskos, 2008: Chapter 2),[26] which are largely unavailable to the public.[27] As Weisselberg notes, "[b]ecause most police officers are not lawyers and do not read judicial decisions, training is the link between the Supreme Court's pronouncements and the way in which interrogations" and probably other police practices "are conducted every day in police stations" (2008: 1521). Though this imperative also exists in England and Australia, it is not quite as strong as in the US as any key changes, as a result of the common-law process, are often eventually adopted into statute.[28] As shown in Chapter 6, these complexities and ambiguities in the laws on police powers seemed to affect how the police put them into practice, particularly with regard to the length of detention, though police discretion played a role too.

Like the US, Ireland has a constitution which was adopted in 1937 and which, through its 50 articles, sets out the fundamental rights of Irish citizens, as well as the main institutions of the state. It includes principles such as the right to fair procedures used by the courts or other bodies making decisions about citizens and the right to equality before the law. Any amendments to the constitution have to be agreed by referendum. However, not all human rights are encompassed by the Irish Constitution, with some human rights also being enacted through Ireland's signatory of the ECHR, which was translated into domestic law through the ECHR Act 2003 (see Walsh [2009] for further information about its application to police procedures). Furthermore, key police powers are also enacted through the Criminal Justice Act 1984,[29] setting out police powers and citizens' rights in relation to the detention of arrested people in Garda custody in certain circumstances (e.g., non-terrorist related offences), offences committed on bail and other offences, inferences from the accused's failure to account for certain matters, trial procedures and miscellaneous matters, including proceedings after arrest and the electronic recording of questioning.

In spite of Ireland's status as a signatory to the ECHR and in spite of things like the Criminal Justice Act 1984, Manning (2012) argues that the written Constitution of Ireland places limited legal constraints on policing, which are more similar to the US than other common law countries. This, he argues, is because of the "loose configuration of legislation and common law traditions" and the hitherto relatively undeveloped organisational policies (2012: 356). However, a more important explanation is "Irish informalism," which refers to the cultural preference in Ireland for resolving matters informally without the involvement of the criminal justice system (Hamilton, 2013: 161–2). Hamilton (2013) found that this informalism was seen by the criminal justice policymakers in her research as having a continued influence on criminal justice practice.

Relations with citizens: public attitudes towards the police

This final section of the chapter examines public attitudes towards the police because they provide a useful frame of reference for understanding suspect responses to police detention. In England, there has been a decline in trust in the police since the heyday of the English bobby in the 1950s, but particularly since the 1970s (Bradford et al., 2009; Reiner, 1995), which is referred to by Reiner (1995) as desacralisation. Though this decline has more recently begun to reverse and may also not be as stark as Reiner (1995) suggested,[30] these findings, in combination with the increasingly less deferential attitude of the public towards the police, suggest that the police–detainee relationship may be subject to a particular kind of dynamic. In theory, detainees may feel more emboldened than they did 40–50 years ago to scrutinise and question their treatment, notwithstanding any sense of disempowerment they feel by dint of their detention. Therefore, how do the different jurisdictions compare with regard to how they regard the police? What are the implications of this for police–detainee relationships in police custody? The International Crime Victims Survey (ICVS) can help to answer the first of these questions.[31] The ICVS uses three measures of public perceptions of the police, which are highly interrelated and are thus combined to produce an overall measure of police performance.[32] For the countries/jurisdictions of interest to the book, Australia had the highest rating according to this single measure of police performance at 84%, followed by England and Wales (82%), Ireland (73%) and the US (72%) (van Dijk et al., 2007). This could be broadly interpreted as implying that detainee trust and cooperation with the police may be greater inside police detention in the Australian and English cities in the research and lower in the cities in the US and in Ireland. However, this glosses over some important nuances connected, for example, to the historical development of the culture of policing and differences in opinions based on race.

Even though Ireland is lower ranking in terms of this overall measure of police performance compared to other countries, Irish scholars nonetheless note their revered status. Conway (2010), for example, says that the positive image of the police was seemingly unassailable, as was the public's confidence in them, even following revelations of brutality used by a group of officers known as the "heavy gang" to secure confessions from terrorist suspects in the late 1970s. For example, Bohan and Yorke (1987 cited in Conway, 2010) found in a survey of the public that 56% believed the police abused suspects physically or mentally, 40% believed that the police lied in court, yet 62% expressed satisfaction with the police and 70% believed they did not get enough recognition for risking their lives. This may be because, as Mulcahy (2007: 25) argues, confidence and satisfaction in the police "does not always equate with belief in their professionalism or propriety and can co-exist with bleaker assessments of police behaviour." More fundamentally, as Manning (2012) says, this semi-sacred position of the Guards, which leaves them seemingly impervious to criticism, is linked to their symbolic role in Irish society. They represent citizens' collective obligations and are closely connected to the origins of the state, which differentiates them from the police in other secular countries which have not experienced a revolution (e.g. Britain, Canada, Australia) or where the revolution is long forgotten (e.g. the US). This suggests that the favourableness of public attitudes towards the police in the Irish city, including amongst detainees, may not be as low as the ICVS results suggest.

When discussing public perceptions of the police, it is difficult to ignore their racialised character, none more so than in the US. A wealth of studies have shown that young minority men often feel "harassed, belittled and disrespected by the police" (Eterno and Barrow, 2018: 47), largely as a result of stop-and-frisk, racial profiling and zero tolerance policing practices. Together these practices contribute to the over-representation of non-white Americans at all stages of the criminal justice process (Engel and Cohen, 2014; Brunson and Miller, 2006). At the time of writing, there was also growing public concern about the disproportionate use of (lethal) force.[33] These concerns came to a head after the shooting of an unarmed 18-year-old African American, Michael Brown, in Ferguson, Missouri, on 9 August 2014. His death was preceded, only weeks earlier, by the death of 43-year-old Eric Garner, who died after being arrested for allegedly selling loose cigarettes and being placed in a chokehold by the NYPD on 18 July 2016. During his arrest, he repeatedly said, "I can't breathe," but to no avail. These were only two of a number of high-profile deaths of black Americans killed by police officers in 2014. Michael Brown's death was followed by civil unrest in Ferguson and nationwide, as well as prompting high-level debate and discussion about the policing of people of colour in the US. Growing concern about racialised police practices in the US has also galvanised protest movements, such as Black Lives Matter, which was set up following the death of unarmed 17-year-old African American Trayvon Martin shot by a white man, George Zimmerman, who was acquitted of his murder in 2012. Subsequently, the Presidential Task Force was set up by President Obama, in 2014, as part of a broader set of discussions about how to create a police institution befitting the 21st century in which there are concerns about its racialised and possibly racist character; the report of this task force focused specifically on providing a pathway forward.

Such police practices have to be understood as historically, socially and politically situated (Eterno and Barrow, 2018; Engel and Cohen, 2014; Bass, 2001). In many ways, they can be seen as a reflection of the legacy of the long history of racism, discrimination and exclusion experienced by non-white Americans. For example, both during and immediately after the end of slavery, police organisations were implicated in enacting state-sanctioned discrimination through slave patrols, as well as through the upholding of the Black Codes in 1865 and subsequently the Jim Crow laws (Bass, 2001). Not only did these police practices reinforce the view that African Americans were inferior to whites, they also encouraged the view that African Americans should be subject to law enforcement, including authoritarian police practices, a view which has seemingly continued into the present and is manifest in racial profiling, zero tolerance policing and gang profiling (Bass, 2001). These narratives were also encouraged by the long-standing history of linking blackness to criminality, in which African Americans were pathologised for their supposed innate wickedness and degeneracy (Muhammad, 2010: 5). These links proved persuasive from the late 19th century onwards, even in the face of counter-factual evidence; they were dressed up in the pseudoscientific language of statistics and promulgated by largely white scholars in respected universities (Muhammad, 2010: 52). Not only did this pathologising of African American criminality add to their over-policing, it also encouraged the view that African Americans were deserving of harsh treatment – and under protection – by the police (Muhammad, 2010: 225).

Therefore, what distinguishes the US is the significance of race, it being considered a "master status" such is its influence on police-citizen relations (Skogan, 2006: 101). The Presidential Task Force found, for example, that 60% of white Americans were confident in the ability of the police to protect them from violent crime, compared to only 49% of non-white Americans (United States Department of Justice, 2015: 9). This pronounced lack of confidence in the police amongst black people exists, in part, because of long accumulated negative experiences of the police/courts over time, in the context of racism and exclusion, which can be direct and vicarious (Bradford et al., 2009: 202–3; Brunson and Miller, 2006). Taken altogether, this suggests that non-white citizens' relationships with the police, including in police detention, especially in the US city in the research, may be particularly tense, emotionally charged and thus highly problematic. Indeed, given the over-representation of non-white citizens amongst policed and other criminal justice populations (Walker et al., 2012: 2–3), this may partially explain the lower levels of overall satisfaction with the police in the US in the ICVS results.

Conclusion

Building on the material presented in Chapter 3 on neoliberalism and its effects in the selected countries, the aim of the present chapter has been to place the police institution in Australia, England, Ireland and the US in the context of the historical development of the police, the way that contemporary police work is organised, and the relationship between the police and legal accountability mechanisms and the police and the citizenry. These two chapters are necessarily descriptive in order to provide a solid foundation for understanding and explaining the material presented in subsequent chapters.

The overall argument thus far is that discretion is more widespread in police work in the US, it being the "hallmark" of American policing, according to Brodeur (2010: 71). As examined in Chapter 3, this is a consequence of the atypically neoliberal climate in the US, compared to the other places of interest, and the emphasis placed therefore on personal responsibility and individualism and minimal intervention by the state. As discussed in the present chapter, it is also rooted in the historically personal and localised nature of American police work, which grew out of the difficulties of governing such a large and populous country and which continues into the present. The diffusion of power across the federal system also had the effect of limiting centralised power and preserving local municipal control over the police in America (Walker, 2008).

Also important in the US is the relative ineffectiveness of the law 'in the books' and the courts in safeguarding suspects' rights, compared to the more robust approach taken in Australia, England and Ireland (Dixon, 2019; Weisselberg, 2017). This is partly due to measures, such as the ECHR and EU Directives on the procedural rights of suspects in England and Ireland, which set out a broader range of rights than are available under Miranda and its associated jurisprudence (Weisselberg, 2017). They also convey the importance attached to human rights in Europe, a discourse which is absent from the US (Fineman, 2010). The ineffectiveness of the law is also partly because, in the US, greater emphasis is placed on ex post facto judicial interventions (by not admitting confessions or admissions), rather than on ex ante regulation of police detention practices through legislation (Dixon, 2019). As such, the rules of police detention in the US are part of an ever-changing legal terrain, which is never meaningfully consolidated into legislation, which could be used to prevent malpractice from happening in the first place. Moreover, in a large and legally complex country, such as the US, it is difficult to see how the continual shifts in the interpretation of legal rules of police detention could be relayed to and implemented by front-line officers in police detention.

Chapters 6–8 examine how such discretionary decision-making plays out, in the present day, in relation to whether and how the police use their authority, particularly in relation to vulnerable suspects who have been arrested and detained by the police. Before delving into these matters, however, Chapter 5 examines the conditions of the police detention facilities in each of the four jurisdictions. Chapters 5–8 draw on empirical evidence collected in five cities in four jurisdictions. Further information about how, when and why these data were collected, as well as about the challenges involved, can be found in Appendix 1 and Skinns (forthcoming).

Notes

1   The partitioning of Ireland on religious grounds increasingly became a source of conflict, resulting in deep divisions and 'The Troubles' (from the late 1960s to the mid-1990s), which were policed by forces on both sides of the border (Mulcahy, 2013: 3–9).
2   The IRA bombed the Conservative party conference in Brighton in 1984, with the then leader of the party, Margaret Thatcher, narrowly escaping death.
3   Critics of the Commonwealth have argued that it is a relic of colonialism, which symbolises Britain taking from, but not necessarily giving back to those in Commonwealth countries (Letts, 2016).
4   In recent times some have asked, however, what is the point of the Commonwealth (Letts, 2016)? In its heyday in the 1980s, it served a political purpose; for example, it was used to campaign for the end of apartheid in South Africa. However, more recently, it has been superseded by other supra-state governmental structures such as the United Nations, the G7, G8, G20 and by the EU. However, in the future it may be reinvigorated, in part, under the leadership of a new Secretary General, Lady Scotland (appointed in 2015), but also post-Brexit it may offer alternative markets for the UK.
5   Peel claimed that crime in London had increased by 55% whilst the population had increased by only 19%. He also managed to sidestep conflict with the City of London by omitting them from the jurisdiction of the Met (Elmsley, 1996: 24).
6   Brodeur (2010: 47–48) notes that when the term 'police' arrived in the English language in the mid-18th century, it carried both the broad meaning of the regulating of public peace, security, morals, the economy and the environment. However, it was about this time that in Paris, the meaning of the word police began to contract. The Parisian Guard, for example, devoted the bulk of their time to preventative patrolling, the maintenance of peace and public order, the investigation of crime and intelligence-gathering. Therefore, the word police became associated with a body of officers charged with a narrower set of responsibilities than originally conveyed by the term in the mid-17th century. This refinement soon crossed the English Channel.
7   Loader (2016) goes on to argue that these principles are deficient and need to be recast in light of the notion of "civic policing" in which the police materially and symbolically mediate belonging, educating the populace, for example, about what it means to be a citizen.

8 Unarmed policing put into practice Peelian ideas that the police should recognise that their power to fulfil their duties and functions rests on public approval and respect; cooperation is undermined by the use of physical force and compulsion (See Loader, 2016 for a full list of the Peelian principles).

9 Mary Rogers, a clerk in a tobacconist, was murdered in 1841 and her body was found floating in the Hudson River. Her murder attracted national attention, appearing in the national press, in part because it exposed the inadequacies of policing in NYC at the time (Lankevich, 1998: 84–85).

10 Indigenous groups were not involved in policing white settlers (as was the case for Maori constables in New Zealand in the 1840s, who had significant powers in relation to settlers); rather, they were involved in the process of securing land for the settlers (Finnane, 1994: 25–26). 'Native troopers', as they were known, were paramilitary units used to combat Aboriginal resistance on the frontier. They were established in Port Phillip in 1842, NSW in 1848 and Queensland in 1859 (Nettelbeck and Ryan, 2018; Finnane, 1994: 23). In some cases, they were deliberately repressive, driving people from pastoral and mining areas. For example, in Central Australia and Queensland they were known as "killing machines" due to their violent strategies, often involving indigenous people from tribes in neighbouring areas, who were in conflict with those in Queensland (Nettelbeck and Ryan, 2018; Wilson, 2009; Finnane, 1994: 25–26). Hence, Nettelbeck and Ryan conclude that, though imagined as a peacekeeping force, which might help "civilise" indigenous Australians, they eventually became "an arm of legalised violence in Colonial Australia" (2018: 49).

11 As in Chapter 3, though England is of primary interest in this chapter, occasionally reference is also made to England and Wales or to the UK due to limitations in the available evidence.

12 According to UNODC (2016), "Police Personnel" refers to personnel in public agencies, whose principal functions are the prevention, detection and investigation of crime and the apprehension of alleged offenders. Data concerning support staff (secretaries, clerks, etc.) were excluded.

13 Other accountability mechanisms can also be determinative of police practices, and to a greater extent than the common law, given that a case must first arrive at court before the issues it raises can be considered. For example, in relation to Australia, Clark (2014) argues that growing scrutiny of the police has not happened through the courts, rather through police complaint mechanisms and anti-corruption agencies.

14 In this case, the defendant voluntarily went with the police to the police station, where officers told him he was not under arrest and did not give him his Miranda rights. He was allowed to leave, but was arrested a few days later, based on what he told the police whilst at the police station. The supreme court ruled in favour of the police, in this case, arguing that Beheler was not legally in police custody and so his Miranda warnings were not required. Following this case, some police departments encouraged their officers to use such warnings strategically, so that they could turn their meeting with a suspect into a "non-custodial" one (Weisselberg, 2008). For example, the police might invite a suspect to the police station telling them that they are not under arrest, so that Miranda warnings need not be given (Weisselberg, 2017).

15 The 47 members of the Council of Europe who are signed up to the ECHR outnumber the 28 countries in the EU who are also subject to the EU Directives on Procedural Rights for suspects.

16 Indeed, the applicability of such rulings by the ECtHR have enraged some members of the Conservative party during their time in office. For example, the ECtHR has been seen as eroding the sovereignty of the UK in determining its own laws to such an extent that some Conservative politicians have long had

their sights set on withdrawing from the HRA, if not the ECHR (Conservative Party, 2014: 5; BBC, 2012). Now that the UK is set to leave the EU (following the Brexit referendum result on 23 June 2016), Conservative MPs may no longer deem this withdrawal from the ECHR necessary.

17 Indeed, Fineman (2010) began to develop the concept of vulnerability, as a stealthily disguised attempt at a human rights discourse for an American audience. Such a concept is also aimed at challenging the individualising effects of identity politics, which have grown in importance in the absence of a human rights discourse. See Chapter 8 for a fuller discussion.

18 The Conservative party has recently bucked this trend. For example, on 3 October 2014, the Conservative Party set out plans to repeal the Human Rights Act 1998 and to replace it with a Bill of Rights.

19 In addition, the Regulation of Investigatory Powers Act 2000 (RIPA) covers the way that the police may use communication information acquired through interception, the use of surveillance and covert policing agents, the investigation of electronic data protected by encryption, etc., which is thus of less relevance to the present book.

20 For example, in *S and Marper v. United Kingdom* the ECtHR ruled in 2008 that keeping the DNA of the innocent constitutes an infringement of their right to respect for private and family life, under the ECHR. In the cases of these two men, both provided the police with a DNA sample after being arrested and detained by the police, though charges against them were subsequently dropped. As a result, both requested that South Yorkshire Police remove their DNA from the police database and, when the police refused, their cases were eventually heard in the ECtHR, which ruled in their favour.

21 There is also an argument that this interpretation of the Constitution should also restrict the changes to the right to silence that have been implemented, such as in New South Wales (see Dixon and Cowdery, 2013).

22 In relation to the laws about unlawful detention, for example, Weisselberg (2008: 1592–3) argues that the reach of federal *habeas corpus* – that is, the laws relating to the lawfulness of someone's detention – is such that the state courts cannot play a meaningful role in reviewing the application of Supreme Court rulings like *Miranda v. Arizona 1966* in state courts. For example, they cannot establish that state court rulings are contrary to or are unreasonable applications of Supreme Court judgements. That said, on application at the state level, Supreme Court rulings can lose their intended meaning. For example, *County of Riverside v. McLaughlin 1991*, which established the use of 48-hour holds of suspects without charge, was applied in a variety of ways nationwide which, in Tennessee, included "somehow morphing into an incorrect understanding that the police could hold someone for 48-hours, even if they did not have probable cause" (Mulroy, 2013: 848).

23 This has resulted in a constitutional criminal procedure doctrine which is "byzantine" in character, which has furthermore been enabled by "shifting ideological majorities on the Supreme Court and the Court's reluctance to overrule precedents, rather than distinguish them to death" (Mulroy, 2013: 866).

24 There was a racial dimension to these Supreme Court cases in that the plaintiffs belonged to racial minorities (Walker, 2008: 334).

25 Australia and the UK were respectively ranked 12th and 10th amongst the 36 high-income nations (World Justice Project, 2016: 51, 152). Ireland was not included in the study.

26 Whilst in training as a police officer for Baltimore Police Department, Moskos (2008: Chapter 2) notes that normal rules about police work were codified in great and verbose detail in the Department's book of General Orders, the violation of which, recruits were told, could lead to disciplinary action.

27 Some police departments have bucked the trend of secrecy about their policies and procedures. For example, the Philadelphia Police Department recently published most of its directives online (www.phillypolice.com/accountability/).
28 For example, in relation to the treatment of 17-year-olds as children in police custody, a High Court case brought by the Howard League and the Coram Children's Legal Centre in February 2013 led to a revision of the PACE Codes of Practice in October 2013, which extended the provision of appropriate adults to 17-year-olds. This change was made legally binding as a result of Section 73 of the Policing and Crime Act 2017. An anomaly in the law meant that, up to this point, 17-year-olds were classified as adults in the police station, unlike in other parts of the criminal justice system.
29 This 1984 Act was accompanied by regulations in 1987 but amended in 2006 arising from Superior Court Judgements (i.e. from the High Court or the Supreme Courts).
30 Recent analysis shows a modest increase in the favourableness of attitudes towards the police since the early 2000s (Office for National Statistics, 2015). Loader and Mulcahy (2006: 32–36) also found, for example, that support for the police remained high amongst certain sections of the population, but not others, which they explain with reference to three sets of dispositions towards English policing – dominant, residual, and emergent – which reveal a complex mixture of sacred and profane world views of policing. The coexistence of these different dispositions towards English policing explain why it is that, in spite of the general decline in trust in the police in the post-war period, some parts of the public – in particular, those who express the residual world view – continue to express a commitment to English policing, e.g. by routinely demanding more bobbies on the beat.
31 The ICVS became operational in 1989, surveying people across 78 different countries in 1992, 1996, 2000, and 2005. The main object was to seek advancement in international comparative criminological research, beyond the constraints of officially recorded crime data.
32 These three ICVS measures are the percentage of those victimised who report their victimisation experience to their local police; victim satisfaction with their treatment by the police when they reported a crime to the police; victim satisfaction with the effectiveness of the police in controlling crime.
33 Campaigning organisations have long expressed disquiet about the lack of routine monitoring of people killed by the police and the lack of independent investigation of these deaths, with such investigations typically being carried out in-house and then being passed to prosecutors if deemed necessary (Amnesty International, 2016). As there were no available figures, The Guardian newspaper began to collate statistics on people killed by the police in the US in 2015 and 2016, finding that Native American, African American and Latino/Hispanic citizens are over-represented in these figures, including in police detention (The Guardian, 2016). On 8 August 2016, it was announced that all police departments will be required to provide the Department of Justice with full details of lethal arrest-related incidents (Swaine, 2016).

Inside police detention
Conditions, routines, rituals and rules

Having explored the socio-political context of police detention in Chapter 3 and the organisation and history of police work in Australia, England, Ireland and the US in Chapter 4, in the present chapter, the focus is narrowed even further. The aim is to explore how police detention was organised and delivered in the cities in the research, exploring first of all the meaning of police custody and how it was described and talked about. This is important given what Nelken (2010: 86) says about the possibility that the same terms can mean different things in different countries.[1] Second, I examine the conditions of the police detention facilities in the research and, third, the key processes that suspects were subject to during their time in police detention, as well as fourthly considering how police officers and staff perceived their discretion and the legal rules and police policies that surrounded it. As well as describing the conditions, routines, rituals and rules of police detention in the cities in the research, I also reflect on how they may have affected detainees. This is because, as shown in the prison studies literature, these features of police detention may impact on inmates' state of mind, identities and behaviours, as well as on how they come to understand their relationship with criminal justice institutions and the state (Hancock and Jewkes, 2011; Sykes, 2007: 8). For example, "cage-like interiors and heavy, vandal-resistant furnishings" may communicate to inmates that "'you are animals' and 'you are potential vandals'" (Hancock and Jewkes, 2011: 62).

It is argued in the present chapter that the conditions and procedures of contemporary police detention conveyed to detainees a sense of coercive control by the police. This was particularly so in some of the more run-down detention facilities which were dirty, damp, cold and unpleasant and in facilities where the routinised nature of police procedures, such as booking-in, fingerprinting and photographing were dehumanising. Such detention facilities and procedures existed in all of the cities where the research was conducted, but there seemed to be a preponderance of them in the American city, suggesting a higher degree of coercive control of detainees therein, a matter which will be explored in more detail in Chapter 7. Suffice to say, particularly in the American city, there was little need for the police to engage in overt forms of coercive authority. Their mere presence and what this represented – i.e. their symbolic coercive authority – combined with the coercive conditions and dehumanising procedures were enough to ensure a certain kind of meekness and docility amongst most detainees, which was not seen to the same extent in any of the other cities in the research. In combination with the language used and the conditions and procedures of the police detention facilities, this encouraged detainees to believe that they had next to no control over what happened to them and when, and that they were, therefore, at the mercy of the police who presumed them guilty and expected them to do the 'right' thing. These perceptions were also further rooted in the political socialisation of detainees – that is, of "custodial citizens" – who through their multiple contacts with the criminal justice system have learned to accept their lot and not make demands of the police or other state institutions (Lerman and Weaver, 2014: 10, 200).

The language of police custody

In the American city, police detention facilities were referred to as 'Booking Centers' in police directives,[2] though they were colloquially referred to as 'CCTV.' 'CCTV' was a reference to the fact that there were video links between the police detention facilities and the courts where decisions were made in preliminary arraignment hearings, such as about bail, whilst 'booking' was a reference to the fact that police detention was a place where people went to get 'booked,' i.e. when an official record was made of their arrest and the charges against them. Similar video links and virtual decision-making about bail also existed in the Australian city and in the English cities in the research, though not in the facilities visited as part of the research. Nonetheless, police detention facilities were not referred to as 'CCTV' in these two jurisdictions. In the cities in England, Australia and Ireland, the terms 'police custody,' 'custody suite,'[3] 'custody area,' 'custody facility' or simply 'custody' were all used interchangeably to refer to the place where someone was taken whilst their case was investigated and whilst a decision was taken about whether to charge them or not. However, such terms meant little to research participants in the American city; whenever I used these terms, they drew blank looks and questions about whether I meant local jails where remand prisoners were taken or perhaps prisons. Hence, in the American city, I adopted research participants' language of 'CCTV' or 'booking' or sometimes the more explicit term police detention, whilst sticking to the terms 'police custody,' 'custody area,' or just 'custody,' as well as, occasionally, 'police detention,' in the other cities. For the purposes of the book, I largely use the term 'police detention,' given that it was understandable by research participants across all the cities, meaning that it should also, therefore, be more intelligible to those who may be reading this book. For linguistic convenience, I also sometimes use the term 'police custody.'

Not only did the name given to police detention facilities vary across the cities in the research, so too did the names given to the broadly similar roles of staff who worked in these facilities. In what follows, I name the main roles in police detention and provide a brief description of them:

- Custody assistant (Australian city), detention officer, civilian detention officer, or designated detention officer (English cities), jailor (Irish city), turnkey or cell attendant (American city). Staff in this role looked after detainees' welfare in police detention (e.g. through cell checks, responding to detainee requests and by providing food and drinks) and also helped to administer police procedures (e.g. fingerprints and photographs).
- Custody manager (Australian city), custody officer (English city) and member in charge (Irish city). Their role was largely connected to the legality of someone's detention (e.g. authorising someone's detention, sometimes charging and bailing them, as well as ensuring that they were detained only for the permitted period). There was no equivalent role in the American city.
- Duty officers (English and Australian Cities), duty officers or senior house officers (Irish city), or operations supervisors (American city) were normally higher ranking officers overseeing custody and other operational matters relating to the local policing area.

What was curiously commonplace across all cities in the research was the word 'prisoner.'[4] This was the term that was routinely used to refer to those detained by the police, even though it was rarely the case that they were actually a remanded or sentenced prisoner.[5] To an extent, this term was used in an unthinking way, with little consideration given to its meaning or connotations. However, it was also symbolic of how the police saw those in their custody and some of their attitudes towards them as a result, i.e. as already guilty rather than innocent until proven guilty. The symbolism of the term was recognised by detainees, though; it spoke to the concerns they expressed (see later in this chapter in the section on 'Prosecutorial mindset') about being judged by the police as guilty, irrespective of what stage their case was at in the investigatory process, which they found humiliating and lacking in humanity. In what follows, I opt for the more neutral and factually accurate terms, detainee or suspect, which I use interchangeably.

The physical conditions

The following description illustrates how poor some police detention facilities were:

> When the Lieutenant opened the door to CCTV, the smell hit me. Maybe it seemed particularly strong as it was a week since my last trip to a custody area or maybe it was just strong. The custody area was old and any

tiles were cracked, faded or dirty. The concrete floor in the main cell-block was bare. There were two wings with eight cells on each, meaning that there were 16 in total. All the cells had the usual stainless steel toilets and sinks. Four of them were 'suicide cells' which had Perspex walls, rather than the usual bars, and they had call buttons in them. However, I was later told by one of the turnkeys that these call buttons did not work properly. They had one larger cell on each side, which they used for women. They said to me that, initially, they had housed the women on the far wing, but because it was cold back there and because there was no heating at all in the custody area, they had stopped doing that. At this far end of the custody area there was a television, a number of fridges, property lockers (that were supposed to be for suspects' things, but were in fact used by staff) and, randomly, a disused cooker. In practice, all suspects were put in the cells nearest to the room used for finger-printing and photographing suspects. There were no emergency call buttons in CCTV, although it was not far to the operations room.... Whilst one of the turnkeys showed me around the custody area, he opened a door which revealed the pipes and plumbing between the two wings. He said that in the summer, this was full of cockroaches and mice and that they would scatter when the door was opened.... Later, one of the detectives told me that the building was condemned.

(AMEPO7)

In fact, this and IREPO4 were the worst police detention facilities I have ever visited in ten years of conducting research on police custody. Though they were not representative of the range of police detention facilities seen in the research in these cities or elsewhere, they serve to illustrate how depressing, oppressive and consequently coercive the physical conditions of police detention can be, affecting both staff morale but also detainees. It is these matters that this section seeks to address.

As noted in the methodology section, data were collected in two police detention facilities in two English cities, in four facilities in the Australian city, in six in the Irish city and in seven in the American city. Though they may not have been fully representative of all police detention facilities across each of these cities, they provided a flavour of what they were like inside. What was common to all was their coercive atmosphere, as a result of the physical conditions, though this was in different ways and to differing degrees. Here, I explore the design and layout, cleanliness and quality, as well as the way that the space was used.

The design and layout of police detention

This coercive atmosphere was first of all connected to the subterranean feel of the facilities, with limited natural light and inadequate ventilation. ENGPO2 was on the ground floor of a fully operational police station. Whilst the custody area was not underground, it felt as if it was, as there were no windows letting in natural light. The custody area was also poorly ventilated with a few air conditioning units being used to improve working conditions for staff during the warm summer months when the data were collected. Similarly, ENGPO1 had a subterranean feel to it, although there was more natural light than in ENGPO1, as a result of two windows in one corner of the custody area. The ventilation of the custody area was also better, as the whole custody area was air-conditioned. This coercive atmosphere was added to in some detention facilities by the cramped conditions; two facilities in the Irish city (IREPO5 and IREPO), for example, were noted for their long narrow corridors which penned staff and detainees into a confined space and likely only served to ex-acerbate tensions between them, especially when emotions were running high.

This coercive atmosphere was also evident in the prison-like architectural design connected to the hub-and-spoke layout, heavy doors, jail bars and the sparseness of the cells. Most of the police detention facilities in all of the cities could be loosely described as having a hub-and-spoke layout. They had a central area where detainees were booked-in, off which a number of corri-dors protruded, often containing different wings to separate different kinds of detainees, e.g. women from men or children from adults, though these wings were not always used in this way. For example, in ENGPO2, the booking-in area was the hub, which was connected to three corridors as the spokes, whereas in ENGPO1, the booking-in area was connected to eight corridors. For the most part, these corridors led to the cell-block areas.

In addition, the cells themselves were sparse, with most having nothing other than a call bell/intercom – though this often did not work or could be switched off if detainees were perceived as too demanding – a bench, as well as, in some cases, a mattress, blankets, toilet and a sink. The cells in the English, Australian and Irish cities tended to have most of these things as standard. In the American city, however, mattresses and blankets were never provided, not even on request:

> [t]here were no blankets for suspects, even though it was cold in the cells. Suspects were only allowed one item of clothing to prevent them using things to hurt themselves, so I was told. Consequently, suspects were huddled into their t-shirt or sweater, using their shoes as a pillow.
>
> (AMEPO1)

What was also striking was the lack of screening of the toilet area in the American, Australian and Irish cities, where multiple occupancy of cells was commonplace. In effect, detainees were expected to relieve themselves in front of their cellmates, or, if they were lucky, they might be able to per-suade a member of staff to take them to a more private toilet elsewhere. Such practices were degrading and dehumanising for detainees. Whilst detainees in the American police detention facilities had next to nothing, staff had TVs to watch. TVs were ubiquitous in CCTV and detective divisions, being used by staff to help pass the time and to alleviate their boredom and dissatisfaction with the work. Yet, it was made clear to me that such small pleasures were not available to detainees. In AMEPO5, for example, I noted down that one cell was out of service, in part, because the door was broken but also because detainees would be able to watch the staff's TV if they were placed in it.

There were further aspects of the design of the police detention facilities which were either prison-like or conveyed to detainees the coercive control of the police. In the English, Irish and Australian cities, cell doors were solid, heavy and metal, creating a solid clank and a thump when they were shut. These doors also had a hatch in them, known as the wicket in the English cities, which could be opened allowing staff to observe or speak to the detainee. In the Australian jurisdiction, this hatch/wicket was lower down than in the English and Irish facilities, serving both as a meal hatch but also as a place through which someone's hands could be handcuffed prior to the police escorting them out of their cell, if this was deemed necessary, for instance, because they were non-compliant (AUSPO1). As for the cells themselves, the walls between all cells in the English, Irish and Australian cities were solid and without metal bars, giving a more enclosed feel and no doubt contributing to a sense of isolation for detainees, especially if they were detained there alone. By contrast, in the detention facilities in the American city, most cells were divided by metal bars approximately 30 cm apart, going from ceiling to floor, out of which detainees could reach towards staff or other detainees for that matter. This was a source of concern for some staff, who feared for their safety if a detainee were to grab them as they walked past. However, whether detainees were confined within four walls or by jail bars, the message was the same about the disempowered status of detainees relative to the police.

Cleanliness and quality

The coercive atmosphere was also evident in the cleanliness and quality of the cells. In all cities in the research, at least some of the detention facilities were dirty, decrepit and of a poor quality in terms of the physical conditions and the equipment available. However, this tendency was particularly pronounced in the American city and, to a lesser extent, in the Irish city. These matters have the potential to shape detainee and staff experiences and interactions. Aside from the message conveyed about the oppressive and coercive nature of police custody, they also contributed to detainees' sense of stress and unfairness, bearing in mind that they are only suspects, as well as sending detainees clear messages about their status in society. That is, the physical conditions, just like the way that staff used their authority (see Chapter 7), conveyed to them something about the extent to which they felt respected by the police and, by implication, the state.

In the English cities, one of the detention facilities, ENGPO1, was a new purpose-built facility with new equipment which, with the exception of the blankets, was generally clean. The second, ENGPO2, was to a large extent the opposite of this. In 2007, when the data were collected, it was described by detainees as dirty, having blood, dirt and worse on the walls and having unclean and pungent toilets. Staff in this custody area, who were not permanently based in the custody area, also considered it to be dirty; for example, a doctor complained that cleaners only mopped the custody area but never hoovered or power cleaned it so that the dirt dried as dust, causing allergic reactions amongst staff.

In the Australian city, one of the three detention facilities visited was of a much poorer quality than the rest. It was a

> smaller and grotty custody area in need of refurbishment, a matter which was commented on by an arresting officer, who happened to be in the custody area when I was present. When I told her that I was a researcher, she instantly launched into an attack on the custody area and how it was in need of refurbishment. The Custody Manager said to her that this was going to happen in the coming months, and then a debate ensued about whether this was going to happen at all, given that similar promises had been made about a neighbouring police custody area.
>
> (AUSPO3)

This discussion demonstrates how the physical conditions impacted on staff and most probably on detainees too. By contrast, AUSPO4 had been relatively recently refurbished and purpose-built. Hence, the layout was much better than in AUSPO3, as well as being a newer and more pleasant custody area.

Virtually all of the seven facilities in the American city were unclean and decrepit. AMEPO4 and AMEPO5 were the exceptions to this, as they were new or new-ish purpose-built facilities. With the rest, they were invariably dirty and often with peeling paint and crumbling plaster. In one detention facility, the floor tiles were coming up all over the facility to the extent that some staff worried about pieces of tiles being used as a weapon against them (AMEI3). What was also common to these facilities was that they were strewn with leftover food and drinks, which would have remained there unless staff or sometimes detainees cleared them up, which for detainees probably brought them some welcome relief from sitting doing nothing in a cramped cell (AMEPO6).

What was also apparent was the lack of cleaners in the US city. None were seen in any of the detention facilities, bar AMEPO5 and staff said that there were none, even when specialist cleaning was required, for example, if cells were used by detainees with infectious diseases or if one of the few suicide cells became smeared with excrement. In fact, staff in AMEPO2 said that such "dirty protestors" were made to clean up the excrement themselves.

Not only were the facilities in this American city old and decrepit, they also contained semi-functioning equipment, which made staff and detainees' lives difficult. This was most evident with regard to the fingerprinting machines, which were described by staff as "crap." In order for them to work well enough to take the necessary fingerprints, staff had to spray large amounts of water on to the machine and on to detainees' hands, as well as sometimes making multiple attempts at this, much to the chagrin of staff who complained about it being time-consuming.

Aside from IREPO4 mentioned at the start of this section, three of the other facilities where I conducted research in the Irish city, were also unclean and poor in quality. They were dirty, had crumbling paint and/or plaster, as well as having problems with things like escape routes and ligature points in the cells and furniture, which were therefore unfit for purpose. What was also a surprise was to find was that in 2009, when the data were collected, the police were still using videotapes and VHS recorders to record police interviews and, furthermore, not all detention facilities had computer-based fingerprint technology, meaning that staff were observed taking fingerprints using ink (e.g. in IREPO4).[6] In one facility, a member in charge described the paucity of the conditions, some of which I noted in my field notes:

> Only three of the four cells were operating here because the first cell had a ligature point as there was a gap between the doorframe and the wall which could be used by suspects. The Member in Charge said that they never put anyone in that cell. He also said that there was a passcode for the door that "prisoners" came in through. However, the back entrance did not require a passcode, meaning that suspects had to be watched at all times as they could simply walk out. The booking-in desk was wobbly and could be easily pushed over, if suspects were violent. Consequently, he said that he booked-in detainees in the medical room, simply because there were fewer risks there.
>
> (IREPO3)

By the same token, there were also a number of new purpose-built facilities in this Irish city (e.g. IREPO6), which had a clean, bright and airy feel and had modern technology, such as automated fingerprint identification machines, which were similar in character to ENGPO1. Unlike in the US city where detention facilities were, in the main, poor in quality, there was more of a contrast in the Irish city between those of a higher and lower quality in terms of the physical conditions.

The use of space

Beyond the physical conditions of the facilities, the coercive atmosphere was also evoked by the way that the detention facilities were used; the prolonged detention of detainees in small and overcrowded cells, particularly in the American and Australian city was one aspect of this. In addition, in the American city, the unique way in which cells in the detective division were used – to hold people without formally arresting them – could also be construed as coercive and oppressive. These cells were quite separate from the cells in CCTV.

Multiple occupancy of cells

In the English cities, indeed, in England as a whole, it is a rarity for detainees to be placed in cells together (Skinns et al., 2017b). Though this enhanced detainees' sense of isolation, it was also seen by staff as a way of protecting detainees from each other, thereby covering the police's backs. In the detention facilities in the other cities, the police largely took the opposite view. They saw the multiple occupancy of cells as a way of protecting detainees and themselves; it was seen as a strategy to alleviate boredom and feelings of isolation in detainees, as well as meaning that other detainees could alert staff if detainees were to engage in self-harm. AUSI1 noted that, given the sparseness of the cells, a cellmate provided detainees with the necessary stimulation and might also reduce the possibility of self-harm, which was of particular concern for indigenous detainees. AMEI5 felt that the multiple occupancy of cells was particularly important as, in spite of its name, CCTV cameras were only used to link to court rather than to monitor cells or the corridors of the facility in which he worked. This cell-block attendant also saw the cell allocation process as an opportunity to let detainees know who was in charge. Here he describes how he handled any objections to the cells to which detainees were allocated:

> [Y]ou will go in the cell that we designate, now if there's someone in the cell that says, "look man, I'd appreciate it if you don't put anybody in this cell with me, I want to be in this cell by myself" … Well, we tend not to let them dictate that to us, because if you start doing that then before long we'll run out of cells to put people in, we'll be stacking other people on top of each other, so we don't allow that to happen. My answer to him would be, "look bro, if I have to put somebody in here I will, but if you want to be comfortable and have your freedom to move around while you're in this cell, then if you do anything or threaten to do anything to a person that I put in this cell, then I'm going to cuff you to the cell, I will put shackles on you and cuffs".… We dictate the person that goes in the cell.
>
> (AMEI5)

As this quotation also demonstrates, concerns that detainees might harm each other were quickly dismissed by this interviewee. Staff would simply threaten to handcuff and shackle detainees to prevent this from happening.

A further difference in the Australian and American cities, compared to the Irish and the English, was the overcrowding of cells and secure waiting areas. Some cells would have so many detainees in them that there was no longer space to sit or lie down. Such was the overcrowding that they would also become unbearably hot and stuffy. In AMEPO4, there were "large numbers of detainees in custody awaiting virtual court and who had all been placed in a cell together (9 in a cell made for 3)." The cell-block attendant said that you could "feel the heat coming off them." Whilst this was only a temporary measure, how long they would have been in the cell together was unpredictable, given that staff in the detention facility had no control over when detainees would be seen by the court. This placing of large numbers of detainees in a cell together simply suited the staff so that they had all the detainees in the right place at the right time, so that when the court called them, they would be ready. The inhumanity of the situation was seemingly lost on them.

The inhumanity of overcrowded cells often for long periods was also seemingly lost on staff in the Australian city. Multiple detainees would be held in what were known as 'docks,' which were temporary see-through Perspex holding cells in the main custody area in which detainees were, in effect, on constant watch. There were usually two to four docks in each detention facility, and each dock was only a couple of metres square and would contain nothing other than a bench. These docks were used for detainees until they were charged and their bail was refused, after which they would be taken to the cell block even if this meant multiple detainees sitting in overcrowded conditions overnight. Such was the overcrowding in the docks that, at one point, "a Lebanese suspect fell off the bench whilst he slept" in AUSPO4. When I asked staff about this, their views suggested that they unthinkingly accepted this situation as the norm, without considering the impact on detainees, such as on their fitness for interview, if they had been deprived of sleep having been sat in the dock all night. As in the American city, this overcrowding of the docks also arose because it suited the police. One custody manager said that though custody managers did have the discretion to move detainees from the docks to the cell blocks, they left suspects in the docks, as they wanted to give the impression to incoming police officers that the detention facility was busy and that they could therefore justify not accepting any more detainees.

Detainees understandably detested these conditions, both because of their overcrowded and claustrophobic nature but also because of the lack of privacy afforded to them. In the American city, for example, there were no opportunities for them to use the toilet unless of course they were willing to relieve themselves in front of their cellmates on the unscreened in-cell toilet. One detainee that I spoke to in AMEPO3 said that

> the worst thing about being there was waiting and not knowing why she was waiting. She was also sick, suffering with a cold and anemia. She said

that she was also freezing cold. She also complained at the lack of privacy of the toilets in the cells, where anyone could see her using it.

A number of detainees spoken to in AMEPO6 whilst they awaited virtual court

> said that they had been in custody for around 24 hours. I asked them what it was like in the cells and they said that it was freezing, and that all you were allowed in the cells were the clothes that you wearing on arrival, even if you were arrested only in your pants. They said that they hated sharing cells, as they did not know what the other person was like and they might be crazy. They also said that it was filthy in the cells and that they threw out their clothes, after they left custody, rather than wear them again.

Upstairs vs. downstairs in the American city

In the American city, what was unique about the way police detention was physically organised was that, generally speaking, in CCTV/booking, there were cells but no interview rooms for detectives to interview suspects about allegations made against them. These interview rooms were upstairs in the detective division, along with more cells in which to hold people. According to the relevant police directive, these temporary holding areas, which had to be designated as such by senior officers, were supposed to be used for a short period of time whilst someone was questioned, interviewed, tested (e.g. for DNA or using a breathalyser) or processed. According to research participants, the holding facilities upstairs were mostly, but not always, used for these reasons. For example, I was told that they were used to hold people whilst detectives were in the process of interviewing them. In some cases, if the police knew that they were going to want to interview someone that they had arrested, they would be taken directly to the detective division. This was because it was "too complicated for them [the detectives] to take people to and from CCTV and the interview rooms in the detective division" (AMEPO3). The cells upstairs were also used to separate suspects from each other in order to prevent them from conferring or when a suspect was worried that they would be seen as "snitching." However, what also became apparent was that the cells in the detective division were also used in a more coercive manner. They were used as somewhere to hold people who had been detained but not formally arrested and who were therefore not considered to require their Miranda rights (see also Chapter 6). For example, this detective said that the cells in the detective divisions were used in the following circumstances:

> Well it goes like this, let's say we have a shooting and there's a couple of people on the street, like it gets really hectic, and they bring in people

who they know are involved, but they don't know how, so we end up
with cells that are filled, and then through the investigation we find
out who did what, who's a witness, who had something to do with it,
who knew the shooter, and before you know it, somebody who was
brought up here and detained is arrested, then their name does go in
a book. And the detective does the paperwork, then their name goes
to the district where they were arrested, and their name is put on
the books, then they're charged with whatever they're charged with,
shooting, aggravated assault, then they go downstairs, that's how that
works....

(AMEI1)

In short, the holding cells in the detective division were used in a variety of
ways. What was also curious was the difficulties that the staff had in explaining how the detective division cells were used. It was perhaps because there
was no single and straightforward answer, highlighting the discretionary nature of the world in which the police operated in this American city, which
was aided, in part, by the permissive and distant nature of the law from police
practices. What this discretionary power of the police meant, though, was
that the physical space of CCTV/booking and the detective division could be
used in ways which were coercive and oppressive and thus further eroded the
power of citizens against the police and, by implication, the state. The use of
the cells in the detective division was just one example of the particularly coercive and discretionary nature of police work in this American city, relative
to the other cities in the research.

Routines and rituals in police detention

In all cities in the research, there were particular procedures and processes
that each detainee went through on arrival into police detention. These included things like being booked-in, being risk-assessed, having their rights
read, fingerprints and photographs taken, and having cell checks completed,
as well as having a custody record opened and information regularly placed
in it about detainees. These processes and procedures had a routinised and
ritualised feel to them, in part, because most staff had performed them so
many times before. This meant that when it came to how detainees' rights
were read to them, for example, this could be done in a mechanistic way,
perhaps using a monotone voice and paying little attention to whether detainees actually understood these rights. The point was to have been seen to
have completed the task and to be able to record this task as completed on the
custody record. That is, there was a certain degree of performance to these
processes and procedures, many of which took place in full view of anyone
who was in the main custody area. Whilst police detention facilities were
largely 'backstage' areas, hidden from view from the public, these processes

and procedures were performed on the 'frontstage' of this 'backstage' area, in the main charge room at the booking-in desk. Like the conditions of custody, these processes and procedures could also become coercive and oppressive as a result of the routinised and mechanised way in which they were performed. As this interviewee noted, this emphasis on the processes and procedures of police detention tended to override consideration of detainees' feelings and their well-being. She said:

> look at the attitudes in a police station, you've got police officers, the custody staff's attitude which is, this is a process we've got to deal with, a, b, c, d, and get this done, get that done, fill this in, fill that in, and it doesn't really look at it from the point of view of the detainees ... because if there was more explanation, and more information given [to detainees], then the stress levels would be lower and everything would work much more easily.
>
> (ENG2S11)

In this section, these matters are explored in relation to the booking-in of detainees, risk assessments and custody records. What was striking was the similarity of some of these processes across the cities in the research, in terms of how they were performed and the purposes they served. Though these processes were lawful, they were nonetheless oppressive, expressing something of the perils of bureaucracy/rationalisation in democratic societies in which means come to be prioritised over ends.

Booking-in

Booking-in was a relatively similar affair across the detention facilities in the cities in the research. Staff would try to establish basic information from detainees about their name and date of birth, and from arresting officers about the grounds for their arrest. Staff would also remove most of detainees' property, log it and store it and, furthermore, search detainees, which mostly entailed either pat-downs and/or the use of metal detector wands. These procedures mostly took place in the main custody area at a charge desk or hatch, often in view and earshot of anyone else in the vicinity at the time of the detainees' booking-in. In the Australian, English and Irish cities, booking-in was also the point when most detainees would,[7] in theory, be reminded of their main legal rights in police detention, including to silence, legal counsel and intimation (see Chapter 6). However, the giving of this information could be delayed, or omitted entirely, if, for example, a detainee was intoxicated (Skinns, 2011a: 105–6). This giving of information on rights and entitlements on booking-in was not the case in the American city, where detainees – i.e., those formally arrested by the police – were only informed of these rights if they were to be interviewed by the police, usually immediately prior to the interview. The routinised nature of this process is evident in the following descriptions, which are typical examples of the booking-in process:

> [S]o they're [arrestees] brought into the custody area where they meet the jailors, so the arresting member stays with them outside, and then the jailor then goes through the custody record and asks them all the questions, and reads out their entitlements, and they go through all that, which takes about five or seven minutes to do it. And then, the prisoner is asked then if he wishes to sign to acknowledge that he got receipt of his notices [of rights and entitlements].
>
> (IREI2)

> [T]hey [arrestees] are brought in by the arresting police, they'd be searched, all their property would be entered up into the computer, our custody management system … all the questions would be asked, talk to them about their health, look at their wrists, and all those sort of things to basically determine what sort of risks there will be while they're in custody, and obviously that will depend on whether they're intoxicated, or drug affected, and whether there's warnings on the system saying that they've threatened harm before, or they've committed, tried to commit suicide before, and all those sort of things. And, then at that stage, if they weren't intoxicated and they were ready to go for interview, then the custody manager would read them their rights and entitlements, and obviously if they wanted to speak to a solicitor or something like that, or have support people here, or whatever it is, if they're a juvenile, we'd organise that, and then basically they'd get sat in the dock and secured in there.
>
> (AUSI5)

Risk assessments

As this last quotation illustrates, part of this booking-in process would involve often quite personal questions being asked of detainees about their health and well-being, as part of a risk assessment process. This was less formulaic than the booking-in process as a whole, with some important differences to this process being evident between the cities in the research. In the English cities, suspects were questioned in a structured and formal way about their physical and mental health, including drug problems, previous suicide attempts and whether they had trouble reading or writing or any other learning difficulties. At this stage, the booking-in officer sometimes decided whether or not they needed a doctor and/or an appropriate adult if they were a child or a vulnerable adult. They were also asked whether they would like to see a drug worker. There were a fairly standard set of questions asked by custody officers, although staff also varied in how they asked them, the order they were asked in, as well as perhaps asking some questions of their own, based on their intuition.

By contrast, in the Irish and Australian cities, the risk assessment was a less in-depth and a less structured affair. In the Irish city, there were a few risk-assessment-type questions asked when a custody record was opened for a detainee, which focused on their physical and mental health, medication and intoxication, but this was not a rigid checklist, and instead, staff acted based on their intuition. For example, this police interviewee explained that

> [T]he new custody record now has a series of questions you ask them in relation to, have you taken medication, have you been to a hospital.... So there's kind of a risk assessment built into that, but there's no separate form ... they're [staff] go through this risk assessment in their head, they just don't realise they're doing this risk assessment, and it's like the instinct ... they don't do it in that structured checklist type approach, which is why we don't have very many serious incidents.
>
> (IR.EI1)

Other interviewees were more critical of the reliance on intuition, which, in one interviewee's opinion, had resulted in vulnerable people being put in cells on their own when other courses of action would have been more appropriate.

There was a similar approach in the Australian city to the risk assessment process in that a series of fairly basic questions were asked whilst the custody record was being opened for a detainee, focusing on "symptoms of pain, intoxication, illness or injury, or self-harm" (AUSI1). The questions asked included the following: "Are you currently taking any tablets, drugs, insulin, medication? Have you ever been treated for heart disease, asthma, diabetes, epilepsy? Do you have any serious medical or mental problems? Are you currently receiving any treatment? Is this the first time you've been arrested? Have you ever tried to kill yourself?" As in the Irish cities, any more in-depth information – such as about communication barriers or learning difficulties – was gleaned by the custody manager using their intuition. All of this information fed into custody manager's decisions about whether a detainee was fit for detention and interview. Unlike in the English cities, medical staff were rarely asked to provide information to assist with these decisions.

The approach to risk assessing detainees, like other aspects of the police custody process, was more fluid in the American city. Staff in CCTV/booking went through a basic medical checklist with detainees, which asked about whether they had any injuries and about any medical problems. In particular, they were keen to know whether detainees were epileptic or diabetic. If they were, then they were sent to a different booking facility, where there were nurses on-site. If detainees did not admit they had medical/mental health conditions to staff, then nothing would be done about this. Even if such conditions became apparent later in their detention, they would simply be logged on the system, as this interviewee explained:

> [O]f course there's things that are not on that sheet that we never ask, and unless you volunteer it we don't ask you specifically … so when we ask, 'do you have any medical problems?', then, it's up to you to say, yes, I've got so on and so forth, I'm bipolar, whatever. If you're honest with us … we put it in the computer so that it travels with you everywhere you go, so everybody will have an idea of what they're dealing with.
>
> (AMEI5)

Other than this medical checklist, the only other point that detainees were asked anything of relevance to assess the risk they posed was prior to a formal police interview, the purpose of which was to ensure that the police had a watertight case and that the interview evidence would not be rendered inadmissible at court. A detective, AMEI2, explained that they would ask suspects if they had been confined to a mental institution – though if they had, this did not preclude them from being interrogated by the police – as well as about whether they understood where they were. He went on to note that collecting this information was optional and they did it in order to "anticipate what may be argued in court."

Custody records

Police detention was the point at which a paper trail was set in motion, which, in some cases, logged nearly every aspect of a detainee's time spent therein. Across all the cities, this logging of information was seen as a necessary bureaucratic procedure, to some extent reminiscent of the "knowledge workers" observed by Ericson and Haggerty (1997: 8), who seemed to believe that "the world can be made more secure by ever more perfect knowledge of risk" (p. 8). However, it was not just information about risk that was logged on the custody records.

In the English cities, a detailed record of detainees' time in custody was kept by staff for each detainee in the facility. It contained things like socio-demographic information; details of their arrest and the investigatory process, including fingerprinting, photographing, visits by detectives and time out of the cell for interviews; details of when, whether and how often they had spoken to legal advisers, medical staff, appropriate adults, drug workers and family members; a log of what detainees were doing during cell checks; food and drinks provided; showers; and spells in the exercise yard. In theory, no details were spared from being logged in the custody record. Were anyone to complain about their treatment, then their custody record could be used to explore the veracity of these complaints, as well as to thus determine whether any evidence could be rendered inadmissible in court. In one of the English cities (ENGPO2), at the time of the research in 2007, these records were still paper-based, and in the other (ENGPO1), they were electronic. Paradoxically, these electronic records encouraged a more bureaucratic approach to logging information about detainees; this was partly because the electronic system flagged when cell checks were needed or were overdue. One of the unintended consequences of this was that after doing the cell checks, staff prioritised logging that they had performed the cell check rather than responding to suspects' requests made during the cell checks, such as for water or for a legal adviser. This was also not altogether surprising, given that the private security company who provided the staff in ENGPO1 were fined, as part of their contract with the police, if these cell checks were late (Skinns, 2011a: 155). Moreover, random 'dip checks' of the electronic custody record system in ENGPO2 were also used by managers to monitor the performance of individual staff members. That is, the custody record system in ENGPO2 was used to monitor and surveil staff, not just detainees.

Unlike in ENGPO1, custody records in the other cities were primarily used for the monitoring and surveillance of detainees (not staff), recording similar information as described above about each detainee. As in ENGPO2, these records were all paper-based, and they were seen as a log of everything that happened to someone whilst in police detention. For example, IREI1 described the custody record as a legal requirement as part of the Treatment of Persons in Custody regulations, which recorded the grounds for arrest, details of searches, whether guardians had been contacted etc., which served as an important official record that may eventually be carefully scrutinised at court. Therefore, as in the English cities, this interviewee emphasised the legal significance of the custody record as a way of ensuring and showing adherence to the law. The custody record was similarly viewed in the Australian city.

By contrast, in the American city, the log of a detainees' experience of police detention was seen as of less importance than the information logged about their whereabouts in the criminal process through the Preliminary Arraignment System (PARS). AMEI2 described how information would only become logged on this system once someone was arrested and charged, after which staff in CCTV could fingerprint them and verify their identity, with their details eventually being passed to the courts. PARS was, in effect, a system for 'booking' detainees, the bureaucratic nature of which has been described by Moskos in relation to Baltimore Police (2008: 125–6).[8] PARS was entirely separate from the paper log-book held in CCTV. The latter was used to collect basic information, including detainees' name, dates of birth, what they had been arrested for, and cell checks, of which there was limited evidence. In only one detention facility did it include information about when a detainee left, and it did not contain information about visits by detectives or interviews (AMEPO1). There was little sense of it being a document of significance to subsequent legal proceedings, as was emphasised by IREI1. This contrast in record-keeping between the American city and the rest is revealing about the priority accorded to detainees' rights relative to police requirements to process cases and pass them on to court. There was limited interest in what happened to detainees prior to charge, at which point information about a detainee was logged on PARS. In effect, detainees did not exist prior to this point and presumably neither did their rights.

Discretionary decision-making in context

Across all of the police detention facilities in the research, there were plenty of examples of staff acting in discretionary ways, that is, making choices about different courses of action or inaction, based on their perceptions of the quantity and quality of their authorised capacity to do so (see Chapter 2 for the full definition of discretion used in the present book). For example, this custody manager talked about using his discretion to determine what constituted a time out to the detention clock, bearing in mind in this Australian city that there were a number of possible time outs available. (See Chapter 6 for further details about these time outs and how they affected the length of detention).

> Now, I make a point of not introducing myself to the detained person prior to whenever I'm ready, for the simple reason that I can then put it down as a timeout because facilities aren't available … it's a time out in regards to specialist resources, I suppose, which is the custody manager, if that person is not available due to more pressing matters, then I would read into it that it's a timeout.
>
> (AUSI4)

This cell-block attendant talked about using his discretion to give extra food and drinks to detainees, if he could, even if this was more than was permitted.

> Now with me, I will feed you. If you're thirsty, if you want more water I will give it to you. I've got enough stuff to give it to you more than one time…. I will give them water in the cells more than once, it's only mandatory once in an eight-hour period, sometimes I may give two or three sandwiches, two or three waters, and say that's it for the night…. I go through [the cell block], if you ask me I'll go get you something, give me the trash, and you can have a fresh water.
>
> (AMEI5)

Further examples of discretionary decision-making are littered across the present and subsequent empirical chapters; it was evident with regard to how

the detective division cells were used, the reading of rights, the length of detention, and also the way that staff used their authority. To some extent, many
of the decisions that staff took were discretionary – they had some leeway,
no matter how small, to do things as they chose – even if they did not fully
recognise this as such. This raises questions about some of the factors that
impacted on these decision-making processes.

The purpose of this final section in this chapter is therefore to examine
the immediate context of these discretionary decisions in police detention.
In particular, I first examine staff perceptions of the formal and more explicit rules of police detention, that is, the law and police policies and how
this impacted on police decision-making about detainees. Second, I examine
the more informal and implicit rules, that is, some of the beliefs, values and
norms about how police detention work should be performed. It is argued
that though the formal, legal rules were a source of criticism from time to
time, in the Irish, Australian and English cities, staff worked with a profound
sense of their importance to what they did and how they did it. By contrast, in the American city, the law seemed particularly distant from everyday
police detention work; it was not as common a feature of their everyday
decision-making in police detention. With regard to the more informal rules
of police detention, there were more similarities across all the jurisdictions.
Across all the cities, staff expressed a sense of suspiciousness towards detainees
and those who helped them, such as lawyers. However, this served a purpose.
Along with the use of humour (in which staff on occasions laughed at rather
than with detainees), this helped to reinforce solidarity amongst staff. Staff
also seemed to share a prosecutorial and somewhat punitive mindset, though
this was particularly marked in the American city. Even more unpleasant and
pernicious, though, was the casual bigotry that existed in police detention,
which was directed at women and ethnic minorities, for example. This was
most pronounced in the Australian city.

Legal rules

The codification of case law into statutes in the English, Irish and Australian
cities meant that this was a topic that was readily and frequently discussed
with research participants, with reference to the relevant legislation. Some of
these participants in all of these cities viewed the law as "their bible" and as
something to be strictly adhered to:

> [T]hat's our Bible, the Treatment of Persons in Custody Act. That's what
> we have to do, and that's what we do. It says all the entitlements and
> all that, and what they need, and that's our Bible, that's our legislation,
> that's certainly followed ... 110 percent of the time that we're working
> anyway.
>
> (IREI2)

> Well it's the Police and Criminal Evidence Act, it's the codes of practice, it's code C, the detention, questioning and treatment of prisoners, that's the Bible of the custody officer, you've got to do what it says in the book, and if you don't do what it says in the book you can be held to account ... it's as simple as that.
>
> (ENG1I8)

Consequently, interviewees saw the role of the custody manager / member in charge as needing to stick to the 'letter of the law,' even if this flew in the face of what other police officers wanted, including senior ones. For example, AUSI1 said, "noone can order me to do anything that's not lawful. It doesn't matter if they're the Commissioner of Police, they can't come in here and direct me to do something that is unlawful." Using remarkably similar language, IREI3 said,

> the legislation and the regulations, such as they are, leave the ultimate decision to the member in charge who is responsible, full stop ... the commissioner himself could come in and say, I want this person detained, and I can turn round and say, well, I hear what you're saying but I'm not going to detain this person, there's no grounds to detain them.

Together this suggests a strong sense of needing to adhere to formal legal rules, particularly by custody staff, with such stances being partially enabled by the clarity of legal provisions in the Irish and Australian cities (see Chapter 4). These quotations also illustrate, however, that the police are far from monolithic in their beliefs and actions, with differences manifesting themselves *within* police organisations, in this case, between custody staff, arresting officers and their managers. This was partly rooted in the ostensibly independent role of the custody officer. Such tensions have long been noted in research on police detention in England, with custody officers immediately post-PACE being found to sometimes take the same side as arresting officers (Dixon et al., 1990), but also more recently taking the opposing side (Skinns and Rice, 2016).

There were, however, some more complex and sometimes critical views of the role of the law inside police detention. It was seen as either too permissive, by a small number of lawyers interviewed in the research, but also as a hindrance by police officers. Part of the permissiveness of the law was seen as stemming from its inadequacies at holding the police to account. For instance, a lawyer in one of the English cities said that only the most flagrant abuses of PACE – involving things like violence or unlawful arrest – were challenged by detainees, lawyers and the courts. This permissiveness was also seen by lawyers in the Irish city as rooted in the less structured or less institutionalised nature of police detention rules compared to those in England; they felt there was a greater certainty with regard to almost all detainee rights and entitlements in England. Furthermore, one of these lawyers also attributed the permissiveness with which the law was viewed as attributable to the way police were trained on the job. He said that as soon as new recruits left the police academy, they were told to leave the legal rulebook there and that this is how things are done in the "real" world, as "this is the way you get results" irrespective of whether it was "unwise or downright illegal" (IREI7). This perception of the permissiveness of the law fitted with what a member in charge told me in IREPO3, in which he tried to prevent rule-breaking, by only allowing known and trusted Gardaí to use the interview room furthest from his desk. He said that this was because

> some Gardaí from other areas had bad practices and might try to slip into the room, without it being noted on the custody record and so he wanted to avoid this happening. As a member in charge, he felt this was his duty.

As this last quotation hints, whilst lawyers, in the main, saw legal rules as too permissive, by contrast, some police officers tended to view them as too much of a hindrance and thus as something which needed bending from time to time to suit their own purposes. Taken together, the findings from the present research on Garda perceptions of legal rules chime with the conclusion of Charman and Corcoran (2015). They note that within the occupational culture of the Garda Síochána, there is a tendency to see such formal rules as "self-serving" (Charman and Corcoran, 2015: 497), by which they mean that there seemed to be a strong sense of the importance and necessity of adhering to legal rules, which Gardaí thus saw as legitimate, but that they also made these rules work for them. Similarly complex views about the importance of legal rules – but at the same time the need for rules to be made to work for them – were also expressed by police officers in the Australian and English cities in the research.

In the American city, there were no equivalent views to these, at least not in relation to police detention. Discussions about the role of the law in police detention were met with blank looks and uncertain and varied responses, even when it came to seemingly basic questions about the maximum permissible length of detention (see Chapter 1, but also Chapter 6). There was, however, more certainty when it came to powers of arrest, with staff sometimes going to great lengths to explain things like reasonable suspicion and probable cause. This revealed that even though, at times, the law may have been seen as overly permissive or as too much of a hindrance, in the Irish, English and Australian cities, there was also a profound sense that it mattered to the day-to-day operation of police detention facilities and to the way staff treated detainees, in a way that was simply not the case in the American city. This suggested that, at least inside police detention, police officers in the US city had greater leeway than in the other cities, in terms of enabling access to rights and entitlements and in terms of how they used their authority, both of which are examined in more detailed in Chapters 6 and 7.

Informal rules

With regard to some of the informal rules about police detention work, there were three main themes in the data, each of which are examined next: suspiciousness (which also helped cultivate a sense of solidarity), a prosecutorial and punitive mindset, and casual bigotry manifest in sexist and racist attitudes. Perhaps with the exception of the prosecutorial mindset, these have all been found to have a central place in the occupational culture of other front-line officers (Loftus, 2010; Reiner, 2010: 118–32; Westmarland, 2008; Skolnick, 2005; Foster, 2003).[9] That said, as argued below, this prosecutorial mindset can also be seen as a derivative of a more general crime control orientation of the police, which is regarded as commonplace in the existing research (Reiner, 2010: 244; Loftus, 2009: 189; Waddington, 1999b: 117–8; Chan, 1997: 76; Reiner, 1992; Holdaway, 1983: 20; Ericson, 1982: 198). The findings presented next offer an exploratory insight into the occupational culture of staff in police detention in the cities in the research. What was curious about this cultural landscape were the similarities across the cities in the research, though there were also a few subtle distinctions. For example, as argued next, the prosecutorial- and punitive-mindedness of the staff was particularly prevalent in the American city. This fits with the general conclusion within the police culture(s) literature that, though there may be commonalities of outlook rooted in the common difficulties that the police face, these core characteristics are manifest in different ways, depending, for example, on rank, role, police organisations and the wider context of policing (Reiner, 1992).

Suspiciousness linked to solidarity

As noted by Skolnick (2005), the potential for danger in the world of front-line police officers breeds in them a near perpetual sense of suspiciousness, in an attempt to always be on the lookout for potential trouble. Suspiciousness was a routine feature of police detention in all of the cities in the present research, where staff were suspicious of detainees and those who represented them, such as their lawyers. On occasions, staff in the Irish city seemed to believe neither the detainee nor their lawyer about the detainees' well-being.

> Male one – He was suspected of hijacking a car and robbery. Whilst I was sitting in the main custody area the suspect's solicitor came in and said to staff that she had concerns about her client, given the apparent recent

attempt on his own life (he had clear signs of having self-harmed on his arms) and that she would like this to be borne in mind and that she would like the doctor to assess him. This was eventually recorded on the custody record as her having said that she had concerns about his well-being. One of the Gardaí said that it was probably a ploy for ensuring that he was treated more leniently.

(IREPO1)

Similarly, in ENGPO2 – in an incident which had racist elements to it, given that decision-making seemed to rest on stereotypes – staff were suspicious about whether certain detainees, largely Chinese immigrants, were feigning illness because they believed that this would result in more favourable treatment. As a result, these detainees were given short shrift. In one case, a man complaining of stomach pains was treated with derision by staff:

> He was slouched on the custody desk and intermittently he would be hauled to his feet by the staff on the other side of the desk. The custody officer kept telling him to stand up and was very impatient with him. She also said "I don't want him slobbering all over my custody desk."

(ENPO2)

There were similar racist aspects to incidents in the Australian city. There, staff were observed to be suspicious about whether a lawyer who called the detention facility to talk to their Lebanese-Australian client was a bona fide lawyer rather than an accomplice. Hence, they insisted that detainees always had to speak in English whilst talking to their lawyer in earshot of staff in the facility, which, combined with the fact, that the telephone was in the main custody area, would seem to breach any requirements about lawyer-client confidentiality (Pattenden and Skinns, 2010). This decision seemed also to be based on a stereotype; it was reported to me that in a recent murder investigation, a Lebanese-Australian detainees' family member had pretended to be their lawyer so that they could speak to them.

The corollary to the suspiciousness that police officers showed towards detainees and those who helped them, was a sense of solidarity amongst staff. This solidarity enabled and emboldened them to be suspicious of detainees, those who helped them, and indeed anyone else from outside of the police. That is, there was a dialogic relationship between staff suspiciousness and solidarity; staff suspiciousness of detainees and lawyers rested on a broader sense of suspicion towards outsiders, an 'out group,' which concomitantly encouraged the sense of solidarity that the police felt towards each other, 'the in group,' and vice versa. This chimes with existing research on police cultures. Skolnick (2005), for example, notes that dangerous situations do not only prompt a sense of suspiciousness and stereotyping, as noted above. This sense of imminent danger also encourages isolation from those outside the police and solidarity amongst those inside the police, as officers come to rely on each other to address the dangerous situations that they face. In the present research, this interviewee described a similar sense of solidarity, noting its roots in the dangers the police face, meaning that they had to rely on each other:

> [I]f you're out there and you're being attacked it's your colleagues that have to come along and support you, so you have to gel as a group because all you've got out there if your life's at risk in the future, is each other....
>
> (ENG2S4)

Not only was this sense of solidarity reinforced through a suspiciousness of others, it was also reinforced through cop humour. For example, they would, on occasion, join together in mocking and belittling detainees, sometimes in the presence of other detainees, which, as discussed in Chapter 7, was indicative of a lack of respect. In this case, out of earshot of detainees, a detective showed me a computer system used to compile images of suspects to show to witnesses:

> Whilst we were doing this, his colleague came along and said, "oh, show her the guess the offender game." He then pulled up the pictures of people who had recently been arrested and then they took it in turns to try to guess what each had done.
>
> (AMEPO7)

There were also other instances of such gallows humour,[10] such as when staff would laugh at pictures of detainees that showed a deterioration in their physical well-being over time or about the use of force. In ENG1PO3, whilst forcibly searching a detainee in his cell, staff found a small amount of cannabis, at which point he was informed of his arrest for possession of the drug.

> There was a real camaraderie (all the boys together) in the restraining of this man. When they left him in his cell, they laughed and joked down the corridor, saying 'that was the smallest bit of cannabis I have ever seen', although they shushed when they realised I was listening.

Prosecutorial mindset

To some extent, staff across all four cities exhibited something of a prosecutorial mindset, with this being particularly pronounced amongst the detectives in the American city, where it was also often accompanied by punitive attitudes about what should happen to detainees, if indeed they were found guilty. This prosecutorial mindset encompassed things like a belief that most suspects were guilty and, as a consequence, that they were not deserving of any rights and entitlements in police detention and that what the police needed to do was to make them confess. Furthermore, there was a belief that suspects should also be punished harshly, using corporal forms of punishment and the death penalty. This set of beliefs was captured during conversations with police officers and detectives in the American city:

> Once in the custody area, a police officer showed me around. He implied that he was a firm believer in capital punishment, saying that as soon as people came into police custody then that should be it. He never expressly used the words death penalty or capital punishment, choosing to gesticulate or make a sound to convey what he meant. Later, however, he did say that he would prefer a return to the old-fashioned method of a rope over a tree. He said that he was not sympathetic to people in custody. Later, in the detective division ... I continued my conversation with the female detective who ... said that she would like to see a return to the "dark ages", rather than having to put up with the liberal nonsense of today. Later, she clarified this.... She said that she would like a return to medieval forms of justice. She also expressed a prosecutorial mindset when it came to dealing with suspects; she believed that everyone who came into custody was a criminal, who was guilty and deserving of any negative consequences either in custody or later. For instance, at the time when I was speaking with her, she was dealing with a case in which a woman had beaten her pregnant sister, who then fell down the stairs. The injured party was in hospital and her baby was in foetal distress. She said that the injured party and a witness had identified the suspect, meaning that she was definitely guilty of the crime.
>
> (AMEPO3)

This prosecutorial and punitive mindset was part of a broader set of somewhat clichéd beliefs about the nature of "real" police work, which was seen as "catching criminals and throwing them in the bin," according to one custody manager in AUSPO3. As such, this prosecutorial mindset seemed to be a derivative of the "crime-fighter" mentality noted in other research (Reiner, 2010: 244; Loftus, 2009: 189; Waddington, 1999b: 117–8; Chan, 1997: 76; Reiner, 1992; Holdaway, 1983: 20; Ericson, 1982: 198).

Casual bigotry

One of the most unpleasant aspects of the informal rules of police detention in the research was the casual bigotry of a *minority* of staff. This must be seen against the backdrop of a lengthy history of police scholarship which has documented the racist and sexist attitudes of the police in Australia, the US and the UK since the 1970s (Reiner, 2010: 128–9; Blagg et al., 2005; see also Chapter 3). In the present research, this bigotry was most apparent in relation to the treatment of women, including myself, as well as in relation to minority ethnic and indigenous detainees. This bigotry was particularly apparent in the Australian city. In terms of the treatment of women, I had an early insight into the casual sexism of staff in the American city when I went to interview two detectives from AMEPO1.

When I left the custody area, the sergeant gave me a lift home. As we left, one of the other detectives we encountered in the parking lot wolf-whistled me. The sergeant ignored the wolf-whistle, as did I. It was humiliating and embarrassing.

Such casual sexism was also evident elsewhere. In AUSPO2, as discussed in more detail in Chapter 8, a distressed topless woman was left for a number of hours in the dock in full view of staff, and when asked why, one of the staff said to his more senior colleague that she was "just another topless Sheila." I later interviewed a custody manager who worked in the same detention facility where this woman had been detained. He explained how the incident had come about and then 'joked' that "unfortunately, it's not the good-looking ones that tend to do this." The casual sexism of this 'joke' left me flabbergasted.

Staff in England also made jokes that were sexist and in poor taste. In ENGPO1 a young woman arrested for being drunk and disorderly was taken directly to the cells, searched and her clothes removed in the presence of male officers. In the cells, her jewellery was removed by one of the male officers.

He held her down while female officers removed her top. While this was being done the detainee described herself as a 'fat slag'. The male officer commented to me later, 'she said it and she was!' He told me that she should have been accompanied by females in the cell but he was around at the time so he went.

Women were also, on occasion, accorded a particular kind of disrespect and mockery in the English cities. When a large number of women were brought in for drunk and disorderly offences, in ENGPO1, staff joked that it was "ladies' night." Women were also criticised, based on their looks, in ways that men were not; in ENGPO1, a male member of staff looked at pictures of a female detainee en route to the detention facility, saying "bloody hell. I was expecting a looker with that name." He then showed the picture to others and they all laughed. The casual and unselfconscious way in which male officers in all of these cities employed sexist language and engaged in sexist acts spoke volumes for the likely treatment of women in police detention. These matters are examined in more detail in Chapter 8.

Racist attitudes were also evident, though this time largely in the language staff used. In both the Australian and English cities, staff unselfconsciously used what I considered to be racist language in conversations with me, with limited attempts to moderate this language and with little discomfort evident amongst their colleagues within earshot, together suggesting that to some extent this language, if not commonplace, was considered acceptable. In ENGPO1, I noted that

two white custody officers were discussing what food they were going to eat later. One said he fancied a 'chinky' [meaning Chinese take
away food, but using language which is considered derogatory]. I nearly
choked. Thought about challenging him on this, but did not. Racist
language alive and well?

In the Australian city, a white duty officer spoke in disparaging and overtly
racist terms about the problems of alcohol in indigenous communities, hint-
ing at the fact that he thought that indigenous citizens were less evolved than
birds, whilst also calling them "niggers" and "black fellas":

> He noted how regulating the amount of alcohol had not worked in re-
> mote communities as "our little friends" simply drank their entire rations
> and then spent a few days hungover, before doing it all again when more
> "grog" arrived.... Consequently, he said that some communities were
> dry, but even in those communities, indigenous people had learned to
> dry out a certain type of frog ... with hallucinogenic properties and
> consume them instead. He described how birds and snakes had evolved
> to learn how to eat these kinds of frogs to avoid poisoning themselves.
> He seemed to be saying that indigenous groups were less evolved than
> these animals. He also noted fighting [in the city where the research took
> place] between different groups of Aboriginal people, those who were
> seen as "allowing" colonisation to take place and those who opposed it.
> This, he said, resulted in the "niggers" killing each other. He later mod-
> erated his language (perhaps when he saw the look of horror on my face)
> to talk about "the black fellas".
>
> (AUSPO2)

Such was my disgust at this conversation that I subsequently discussed its con-
tent with a key research informant and my initial chaperone. He fully agreed
that it was not acceptable for anyone to use such language, especially not a
senior officer, remarking also that "nigger" was not a usual part of the Australian vernacular, though "black fella" was and was considered derogatory
when used by the police, but less so when used by Aboriginal people. This
reveals the importance of placing these racist attitudes in their wider context.
As Reiner says,

> the crucial source of police prejudice is societal racism which places eth-
> nic minorities disproportionately in the least privileged and powerful
> social strata.... So they disproportionately become police 'property'. This
> structural feature of police-ethnic minority relations bolsters any prior
> prejudice police officers have.
>
> (2010: 131)

Conclusion

This chapter has provided an insight into what it is like inside police detention in terms of the terminology used, the physical conditions, routines and rituals in police custody and staff perceptions of the formal and less formal rules surrounding their discretionary decision-making. These are all necessary contextual prerequisites for understanding the extent to which staff abided by police policies and procedures, i.e. the legal fairness that is the subject of Chapter 6, but also for understanding how staff used their authority, which is examined in Chapter 7. It has been argued in the present chapter that, to an extent, all the detention facilities in the research exercised some degree of coercive control over detainees. This was evident in the routine use of the term 'prisoner' to refer to those who were merely suspected of having committed an offence, in the routinely poor-quality and physically oppressive conditions in which suspects were detained, as well as in how these physical spaces were used. Cramming detainees into a single cell to the point where staff "could feel the heat coming off of them," for example, and then expecting them to share an unscreened in-cell toilet, as was the case in the American city, was a particularly stark example of inhuman, degrading and coercive practices. This implied a disregard for police directives,[11] as well as for the importance of decency. To some extent, this was only possible because of the distant nature of the law from everyday police detention work in the American city, which contrasted markedly with the profound sense of importance that staff in the other cities attached to the legal rules framing their work.

What was also found to be coercive was the routinised and ritualised nature of the processes and procedures that detainees faced on arrival into police detention facilities. The booking-in process, for example, was strikingly similar in the way it was described by research participants in all four cities, suggesting that it was commonly routinised in all. During this process and often at the 'frontstage' of the 'backstage' of police work in the main part of the detention facility, detainees had to provide their name and date of birth, surrender their possessions and be searched. These similarities suggest that in all of the cities, police detention was the point at which detainees joined the endlessly churning criminal justice conveyor belt over which they had limited control as to when and at what point they could get off.

Together, these findings suggest that the police detention facilities in the American city, and, to a lesser extent, the Irish city, stood out from those in the Australian and English cities, in terms of the extent of coercive control exercised over detainees. However, at least in the Irish, Australian and English cities, this was to some extent tempered by the more profound regard that the police had for the legal rules surrounding their work. Next, we examine the extent to which this physically coercive environment was to some extent mitigated by adherence to legal rules about detainees' rights and entitlements, in police detention, and, furthermore, the role that police discretion played in decisions about these rights. This chapter further addresses the question of how police officers regarded the law and its impact on their day-to-day work in police detention. Answering this question is revealing as to the permissiveness or otherwise of the legal climate in which these police officers operated.

Notes

1 This is because in the context of globalised worlds in which there is an assumption of cultural convergence, "one can remain sure that as long as cultures, languages, public opinions and social discourses differ, so will criminal justice systems and the way they operate" (Pakes, 2004: 178, cited in Nelken, 2010: 86).
2 In spite of asking, these police directives were not available at the time of the research, though some of them have since become available online, including directives on adult, child, and intoxicated detainees, but not interviews and interrogations and rights of detainees.
3 This term was used largely in England and without any sense of irony.
4 The other terms in common parlance in the English cities were 'DP' which was short for detained person and sometimes detainee or suspect. In the Australian city, it was also commonplace for the police to refer to detainees as offenders.
5 Those in police custody might occasionally have been remanded or sentenced prisoners, in the English cities in the research. Operation Safeguard, which was ongoing at the time of the research, meant that prisoners were being temporarily held in police cells if the prisons were too full to take them. Similar usage of police detention has also been seen in some parts of Australia, such as in Victoria and New South Wales (Bibby, 2015; Bucci and Willingham, 2013), though this was not the case at the time of the research. Nonetheless, the term 'prisoner' was not reserved solely to refer to this group of detainees, who were being held awaiting transfer to prison.
6 Ink continued to be used up until at least 2007 when automated fingerprint machines were introduced in some police stations. However, ink was still in use in some police stations in 2009, when the present research was conducted, and even up until 2014, in part because the automated fingerprint machines had not been fully rolled out (Garda Inspectorate, 2014: 29).
7 I say most detainees here because some were not eligible for receiving information about their rights and entitlements in police detention. For example, in the Australian city, only those arrested for the investigation of an alleged criminal offence were eligible to receive information about their rights, meaning that those arrested for breach of bail or for a bench warrant were not.
8 Moskos (2008: 125–6) described the booking of an adult and a child arrested for drug dealing, which took 21 forms and labels, which had to be completed in three different places. The lengthy and bureaucratic nature of these procedures meant that officers would often complete them in quiet spells such as between 3am and 7am, so that they were not "out of service" during crucial periods of their shift, which would have earned them a bad reputation.
9 Following Holdaway, police culture is defined here as "the core of beliefs and values, of associated strategies and tactics relevant to policing, which remain a principle guide for the day-to-day work of the rank-and-file officer" (1983: 2).
10 By gallows humour, I mean when staff tried to make light of the difficulties of their job, in order to ease the strain upon them.
11 These directives stated that cells should contain a minimum of two people and four in exceptional circumstances such as if there were mass arrests, but that this should only be temporary and should also be approved by a senior officer.

Abiding by the rules? Legality in police custody

Introduction

In one detention facility in the American city where the research was conducted, I had an opportunity to talk to detainees who had been charged with an offence as they waited for their virtual court hearing to determine whether they would be bailed. This involved a lengthy line of mostly African American men waiting, without complaint, for a routinised decision-making process, which took no more than a few minutes for each individual. They talked about the dirty and freezing conditions and the difficulties of sharing cells, but also about access to their rights and entitlements. I asked one of them specifically about whether they accessed their rights and entitlements. He scoffed, "Rights? We ain't got no rights in here, you should know that by now" (AMEPO6). Similarly, a senior officer in AMEPO1 said to me whilst giving me a tour of the facilities that "suspects do not have any rights and entitlements" in here. Legally speaking, this was not true, as detainees did have some rights and entitlements in police detention in this American city – to silence, to legal counsel and to be informed of their rights – which collectively are known as Miranda rights. However, only those who were to be formally interviewed by the police would have known what those rights were, with suspects usually being informed of them immediately prior to interview, rather than on arrival, as was the case in the cities in England and Ireland. The exception to this was if they had been arrested before or had become of aware of their Miranda rights, given their centrality in American popular and legal culture (Weisselberg, 2017; Thomas and Leo, 2002).

The purpose of this chapter therefore is to examine the extent to which the police abided by legal rules, police policies and procedures with regard to detainees' rights in police detention and, furthermore, to examine the role of discretion in putting these rights into practice.[1] A further purpose of this chapter is to examine the extent to which the coercive custody environment outlined in Chapter 5 was moderated by the bestowing of rights and entitlements on detainees. Drawing on the data collected in the present research, as well as relevant existing research, this chapter thus examines the legality of police custody in the cities in the research. As noted in Chapter 2, for the purposes of this book, legality is defined as whether the police uphold the law as per established legal rules, which accord with the values and beliefs of the society in which these rules exist. Legality is also defined as one element of police legitimacy (Tankebe et al., 2016; Jackson et al., 2013: Chapter 11; Bottoms and Tankebe, 2012; Reiner, 2010: Chapter 3), though it is also recognised as having rhetorical potential, being used by the police to provide post hoc rationalisations of their discretionary decisions (McBarnet, 1981: 31–32). It thereby also helps to prop up notions of justice and equality before the law in democratic societies.

As will be explored in the rest of this chapter, the nature of and extent of suspects' rights varied tremendously between the cities in the research. Across the cities in the research, these rights encompassed four broad themes:

1   Key rights relating to police custody, including the right to know about the reasons for arrest, the role of the custody manager or equivalent, the maximum length of detention, the right to silence, the conduct of the police interview and about the information collected and recorded about a suspect.
2   Communication, including the right to have someone notified of the arrest and the right to telephone a family member/friend or to have visits.
3   Services for all suspects, including the right to legal advice (which may be publicly-funded) and to a certain level of treatment and welfare, including food, drink and access to medical assistance.
4   Specialist services for certain suspects, including the right to consular assistance for foreign nationals and the right to support from helping agencies for suspects with learning disabilities or mental health conditions, for children and for other vulnerable suspects, such as Aboriginal and Torres Strait Islander suspects.

It would be impossible within the confines of this chapter to look in-depth at all of these rights. Consequently, here the focus is on those custodial rights which were, in theory, available to suspects in all the cities in the research, namely, the right to silence, the right to legal advice and the right not to be detained indefinitely by the police. It is argued that the coercive custody environment was to some extent mitigated by the possibility of detainees making use of a range of custodial rights. However, this was to a lesser extent in the American city where, as shown in Chapter 5, the custody environment was more oppressive and where suspects had fewer rights on paper, which they were informed of, only if they were to be formally interrogated by the police. It is also argued that some legal rules – in particular, the rules about how long someone may be detained by the police in the American city – appeared especially distant from the day-to-day decision-making of police officers. This seemed to be rooted in police officer discretion, which has historically been seen as the "hallmark" of American policing (Brodeur, 2010:

71; Scott, 2010; Walker, 2008; Haller, 1976), and which has been accentuated under conditions of neoliberalism (see Chapter 3). It was also a consequence of the complexities and ambiguities of the law, as noted in Chapter 4. It is also concluded that such uncertainties and ambiguities have the potential to undermine the legality and, potentially, the legitimacy of police detention.

Right to silence

"Deciding whether or not to answer police questions is one of the most important decisions for the suspect," affecting how long they will spend in police custody and, ultimately, the outcome of their case (Blackstock et al., 2014: 322). Speaking to the police increases the likelihood of suspects providing incriminating evidence or a confession,[2] whether true or false, which then triggers a chain of events including charge, prosecution and sentence, which, once set in motion, are hard to challenge, even when exculpatory evidence comes to light (Kassin et al., 2010; Leo, 1996a). As Quirk (2017: 51) also notes, in the closely controlled environment of police detention in which the police decide nearly everything for the suspect, the decision about whether to speak to the police and about how they answer police questions is one of the few things over which suspects do have some control. Hence, the right to silence is enshrined in many legal systems around the world (Quirk, 2017: 24). However, this right is not always absolute. In the present research, suspects in the English and Irish cities had a qualified right to silence, with the possibility of negative inferences being drawn from their silence, whilst at the time of the research, suspects in the American and Australian cities had an absolute right to silence.[3] It is important to consider the right to silence first, in this chapter, as it is hard to disentangle it from the other custodial rights and entitlements which are the focus of this chapter, particularly the right to legal advice. As argued below, the right to legal advice and to have a lawyer present during police interrogations becomes all the more important in places where the right to silence is qualified and thus more difficult to understand and apply in practice (Blackstock et al., 2014: 323; Daly, 2014; Bucke and Brown, 1997: 31–39; Hodgson, 1992). This is because in such settings it shifts the focus of the criminal case from the courtroom to the police station, in particular to the police interrogation (Quirk, 2017: 121; Daly, 2014; Jackson, 2009; Dixon, 1997: Chapter 6).

In the European context, though the right to silence is not explicitly mentioned in the European Convention on Human Rights (ECHR), it is at the heart of Article 6, the right to a fair trial (Weisselberg, 2017; Ashworth and Redmayne, 2014: 34; Blackstock et al., 2014: 20). In England and Wales, a qualified right to silence was introduced in the Criminal Justice and Public Order Act 1994 (CJPOA), after a lengthy campaign by the police, which was rooted in prevailing concerns about the need 'to do something' about crime (Quirk, 2017: 24, 48; Dixon, 1997: 228).[4] The CJPOA enabled inferences to be drawn if a suspect failed to reveal something in an interview that they later relied on in court.[5] In Ireland, the right to silence is partially expressed through the Irish Constitution's right to a fair trial (Article 38.1).[6] However, this right subsequently became a qualified right to silence, initially, as a result of the Criminal Justice Act 1984. It permitted adverse inferences to be drawn at trial where someone failed or refused to account for certain matters on their person or clothing, or their presence at a certain place at a certain time, if this could reasonably amount to evidence of involvement in an offence (Daly, 2014; Walsh, 2009: Chapter 7).[7] The European Court of Human Rights (ECtHR) has accepted the lawfulness of these provisions with regard to the qualified right to silence, although it has sought to reduce their potential impact by declaring that silence cannot be the sole or main basis for conviction and requiring the provision of legal advice (Sanders and Young, 2008).

One interviewee, IREI5, said that the Irish approach to silence "echoed" what happened in England, which chimes with what Quirk says about the curtailment of the right to silence in England sending "shockwaves" around the world (2017: 160). Other scholars argue, however, that incursions into the right to silence in Ireland were also linked to 'The Troubles' in Northern Ireland, in which "extraordinary powers relating to paramilitary activity have become normalized" (Daly, 2014: 62). One area where England and Ireland differ, though, was that in England, the police caution was adjusted to reflect these changes to the right to silence, with officers having to inform people that, "You do not have to say anything. However, it may harm your defence if you do not mention when questioned something which you later rely on in court. Anything you do say may be given in evidence." Whilst in Ireland, the police continued to say, "You are not obliged to say anything unless you wish to do so but anything you say may be taken down in writing and may be used in evidence," with warnings about adverse inferences only being given to suspects through the course of the police interview (Walsh, 2009: 131). IREI5 said that the failure to change the police caution to reflect these incursions into the right to silence had "increasingly become an issue." He said that it made it harder for legal advisers to know how they should advise their clients about whether to remain silent in the police interview, particularly in Ireland, where legal advisers are not entitled to be present during police interrogations.[8] However, such practices are within the bounds of legality given that case law from the ECtHR is scant on whether and when suspects should be informed of the (qualified) right to silence.

In the past, similar kinds of adverse inferences were probably drawn in practice at court, even when suspects did have an absolute right to silence, so long as their case went to court (Sanders, Young and Burton, 2010: 267). Nonetheless, the qualified right to silence remains controversial partly because of the difficulties police, legal advisers and suspects, as well as juries, have in understanding what negative inferences mean in practice. In England, for example, police officers are duty bound to explain the caution in their own words to suspects who do not understand it (PACE Notes of Guidance 10.D), but some cannot do this as they do not understand it themselves (Quirk, 2017: 62–67; Blackstock et al., 2014: 378–80; Clare et al., 1998). Similarly, some legal advisers do not understand the caution and cannot explain it in their own words (Quirk, 2017: 62–67). Even when the caution is properly explained, some (vulnerable) suspects – including children, those with learning disabilities, and first-timers – still do not understand it (Quirk, 2017: 62–67; Blackstock et al., 2014: 378–80; Clare et al., 1998). Moreover, vulnerable suspects in particular may regard the very fact that the caution has to be explained to them as adding further pressure on them to speak to the police. At court, difficulties that juries have in understanding the qualified right to silence has also resulted in "more legal argument, more complex summings-up and directions and otherwise unmeritorious appeals" (Quirk, 2017: 155). As one judge in Quirk's study commented, the provisions have "made life more complicated (Judge/B1)" (Quirk, 2017: 155). Overall, this has shifted the status of what can be read into a suspect's silence to an increasingly central a role in the criminal trial. As such, the provisions have contributed more "to the complexity and cost of the criminal process than to justice" (Leng, 2001c: 125, cited in Quirk, 2017: 155). Furthermore, there may be a variety of reasons (fear, distrust, embarrassment, vulnerability etc.) why suspects do not answer questions put to them by the police and which may mean that they do not know or are unable to answer the question asked, rather than that they are exercising their right to silence (Daly, 2014; Dixon, 1997: 262).

By contrast, at the time of the research, in the Australian and American cities, there was an absolute right to silence. The police caution in the Australian city was, "You're not obliged to say or do anything unless you wish to do so, but whatever you say or do may be used in evidence. Do you understand?" Similarly, in the American jurisdiction, the police caution was: "You have a right to remain silent. Anything you do say can be used against you at court." The right to silence in the American city arose from the *Miranda* ruling requiring the police to inform suspects of their constitutional rights to silence and to legal counsel, which was the US' most significant attempt to rein in police discretion and to protect suspects from giving involuntary and unreliable confessions (Kassin et al., 2010; Leo, 2008: 4).

These different procedural contexts – with regard to the qualified right to silence in the English and Irish cities and the absolute right to silence, at the time of the research in the Australian and American cities – are key factors which can be used to understand the different proportions of suspects making using of the right to silence. As shown in Table 6.1, the uptake of the right to silence was mostly in the expected direction, in that the proportion of suspects answering no questions was higher in the US, where there is an absolute right to silence, and lower in England, where this right is qualified. Australia, in particular New South Wales (NSW), was anomalous, though: it had an even lower proportion of suspects answering no questions than England, in spite of the existence of an absolute right to silence at the time of Dixon and Travis' (2007) research. This finding is partially explained by the lack of legal advice in police detention in Australia (see later in this chapter). Regardless, what Table 6.1 does show is that even when the right to silence is absolute,[9] suspects are still more willing than not to speak to the police. This begs the question of why.

Part of the reason why such a high proportion of suspects speak to the police, in spite of an absolute right to silence, is because the police have been found to employ a variety of strategies to erode this right, in practice, with some of these strategies even being permitted by law. One such strategy is the use of non-custodial interrogations. In the present research, as noted in Chapter 5, it was not unusual to see detainees in custody in the American city who were detained but not formally arrested or booked-in. Leo (1996a) also notes that

Table 6.1 Estimates of the proportion of suspects exercising their right to silence[10]

Country	Proportion, year, study and jurisdiction (if relevant)			Estimate of suspects answering no questions (across all studies)
Australia	33% answered no questions or refused some in NSW, of which 3% answered no questions (Dixon and Travis, 2007: 96)			3%
England	11%–13% answered no questions and 9%–17% refused some pre-CJPOA (Zander and Henderson, 1993)	5%–9% answered no questions and 5%–7% refused some in 1992 pre-CJPOA (Brown, 1994)	13% answered no questions in 1995, post CJPOA (Bucke and Brown, 1997)	5%–13%
Ireland	No figures available			No figures available
US	16% answered no questions in 1994 (Cassell and Hayman, 1996)	22% answered no questions (Leo, 1996a)		16%–22%

a small percentage (4%) of suspects in his study were not deemed as being technically 'in custody.' Scholars have also noted that what is legally defined as 'custody' and thus entitling suspects to their Miranda rights, has changed over time. Weisselberg argues that originally in Miranda, 'custody' referred to someone being "deprived of his freedom of action in any significant way" (2008: 1547). Subsequently, questioning during roadside stops was no longer formally defined as custody (Weisselberg, 2008). Later still, following *California v. Beheler* (where a suspect was voluntarily held and questioned at the police station for 30 minutes and arrested five days later) and *Stansbury v. California* (where a suspect was voluntarily questioned at the police station initially as a witness, whereupon he revealed incriminating information, which led to him being read his Miranda rights and arrested whilst already at the police station), informal interviews in the police station without Miranda warnings were also no longer defined as 'custody.' In these two cases, all that mattered was whether a suspect was there 'voluntarily' and thus felt free to leave, regardless of whether the police brought them to the police station to eventually arrest them or whether the suspect believed they were in custody (Weisselberg, 2008).

Hence, in the present research in the American city, detainees appeared to be held at the police station and would speak to the police, all the while being told that they were not arrested and were free to leave whenever they wanted. For example, the following was observed:

> A number of 'volunteers' were observed waiting in the detective division to be interviewed about a recent escape from a correctional facility, in which prison guards were alleged to have colluded with the escapee. A detective told me that these volunteers had not been arrested and that they were simply being interviewed to clarify information they had already given to the internal affairs department at the prison. He said that these volunteers would only be read their rights if they incriminated themselves.
>
> Later, he said that he was probably the only detective to "Mirandarise" people if they had been detained but not arrested. He said this was preventative strategy because if he did not "Mirandarise" people when they were detained voluntarily then there was a risk that any incriminating information they provided would be simply thrown out at court.
>
> Furthermore, he said that at the end of these informal interviews, he would often know that the detainee had incriminated themselves and that they were likely to be later arrested and charged, but he would not say that to the detainee, at the time. Rather, he would let them walk out of the police station, as he had promised. That way, he could later call them and ask them to attend the police station, often making an appointment that was convenient to them, for instance, to fit around work and then he would arrest them.
>
> AMEPO7

This practice of detaining but not arresting those whom the police wanted to talk to in connection with an allegation of wrongdoing meant that the police could sidestep the reading of their Miranda rights. The staff said as much in the present research. Leo (1996a) also notes that the 4% in his sample who were not technically 'in custody' were not given any Miranda warnings. As a result, those participating in non-custodial interrogations would have been none the wiser that they had a right to silence, let alone that they had the right to exercise it, unless they had been arrested before perhaps. Of course, depending on what they said during their non-custodial interrogation, they might have been read their Miranda rights, but by this point it may have been too late as they may already have incriminated themselves, or at least said enough to the police to justify them being formally arrested. As such, this practice of detaining but not formally arresting someone can be seen as one of the strategies used by the police to 'soften suspects up,' such that they are more likely to confess (Leo, 2008: 121–2, 124). This contrasts markedly with what is legally permitted in England; for example, at the time of the research, those who voluntarily attended the police station to talk to the police continued to have a number of rights, such as to legal advice (Cape, 2006: 2.137).[11]

Second, suspects may waive their absolute right to silence because of *how* they assert this right or not. Such a high proportion of suspects end up waiving their right to silence in the US, for example, because, on the one hand, they have to *unambiguously and unequivocally assert their Miranda rights* both before and during police interrogations if they are to effectively exercise their right to silence. On the other hand, they only need to *imply that they wish to waive* their Miranda rights for the police to act on this and commence a full interrogation. With regard to asserting their rights, if during questioning suspects make an equivocal request for counsel, saying for example, "maybe I should talk to a lawyer", after initially waiving their Miranda rights, then the police can continue to question them. However, if they unequivocally request counsel mid-questioning, then questioning should cease. Clearly, not all suspects will be able to unambiguously and unequivocally assert their rights, seeing as they are on 'police territory' and in a position of relative powerlessness (Skinns, 2011a: 101; Weisselberg, 2008). With regard to waiving their rights, at least 43 states (including the one in which the American city in the present study was located) allow suspects only to *imply* that they wish to waive their rights in order for the police to interrogate them. For instance, if someone responds to questions put to them by the police, having heard their rights in a language they understand, this is taken as *implying* that they wish to waive their right to silence and there is no longer a requirement for them to formally waive their rights, verbally or in writing (Weisselberg, 2008). For these, as well as other reasons, Miranda has been seen as having been gutted, both in terms of how it operates 'on the books' and 'in practice,' thereby diminishing, if not killing off altogether, its protective safeguards for suspects (Rossman, 2017; Weisselberg, 2017; Weisselberg, 2008).

Third, the police have been found in the past to employ a variety of strategies during interrogations, which also have the effect of undermining the right to silence. Leo (1996a) found, in the US, that the police employed, on average, five to six tactics during interrogation, the two most common of which were to appeal to the suspect's self-interest or to confront the suspect with existing evidence of guilt. They also often used the tactics of offering a moral justification or psychological excuse for the suspect's alleged actions, as well as confronting them with false evidence of guilt. According to Leo (1996a), a typical interrogation involves a twin-prong approach in which the police use negative incentives (e.g. saying that the suspect should confess because there was no other plausible course of action, given the level of evidence they had against them) and positive incentives (e.g. saying that the suspect would feel better if they came clean and confessed). Unlike in England, some of these tactics are permitted by law and the police are trained to use them. For example, trickery and deception are permissible.[12] Leo (1996b) likens these techniques to a confidence game and one that has been enabled by Miranda, which gives their actions a veneer of legitimacy. He says

> [l]ike confidence men, police interrogators attempt to induce compliance from their suspects by offering them hope of a better situation in exchange for incriminating information. The interrogator exercises power through his ability to frame the suspect's definition of the situation, exploiting the suspect's ignorance to create the illusion of a relationship that is symbiotic rather than adversarial.
>
> (Leo, 1996b: 285)

In the present research, the police in the American city talked about employing some of these interrogation tactics as a way of securing a confession. For example, a group of detectives relayed the following to me:

> Later, I was introduced to one of the other white male detectives. He said to me, "So, what do you wanna know?" I hesitated. I said "what kind of practices do you use when you interview suspects", he replied "what, when we make them confess?" I said, "well, you can tell me about that if you like". He then said that "sometimes we remove their clothes for evidentiary purposes, if you know what I mean, and leave them sitting there in their underwear. We also try to show them who's boss because every time they want something they have to ask me. For example, if they want a drink of water they have to ask me or if they want to go to the bathroom they have to ask me."
>
> I then asked whether they varied their practices between suspects and how they knew which practices to use with which suspects. The detective said to me, "well, with you, for example, I would shout at you until you cried," then, turning to his female colleague, he said, "with her,

I would feed her, as she's a tough cookie and I would try to persuade her by giving her food."

Later, I relayed this conversation to one of the young police officers in the custody area and he said that this team of detectives were known as "badasses."

AMEPO3

Similarly, in the Australian city, the police were also observed to pressure suspects into talking. In one case (AUSPO3), a woman, who was arrested late at night for an assault on her boyfriend, was wavering about whether to talk to the police and eventually ended up incriminating herself after the police ignored her half-hearted attempts to exercise her right to silence. She repeatedly stated that it was late and that she was too tired and upset to recall things accurately, but the police still interviewed her at 4am. Two more experienced officers who observed this interview with me via video-link remarked that a lawyer would "go to town" on the interview, saying that the investigating officers put her under pressure to be interviewed. Eventually, she was given an apprehended violence order, which is a form of injunction prohibiting certain behaviours. Without her admission, there was no other evidence of assault, other than her boyfriend's injuries, his witness statement and broken items at the address where the alleged assault occurred. The research could not determine how routine it was for police officers in this jurisdiction to put pressure on suspects to waive their right to silence. However, others have similarly documented a tendency amongst the police, in some parts of Australia, to ignore suspects' attempts to exercise their right to silence (Dixon and Travis, 2007: 184–6).

In the Irish city, pressure was also applied to a legally unrepresented female suspect to encourage her to confess to a robbery. In this case, the arresting officer overstated the evidence against the suspect and also told her that if she cooperated with the police by confessing, she would be less likely to have her children taken away from her by social services. These proved to be effective techniques, at least for the police. The arresting officer reported that he interviewed her for three hours and that at the start of the interview she was saying nothing, but eventually she confessed. He was pleased as "they had nothing on her" (IREPO4). It is notable that these practices took place against the backdrop of repeated questions being asked about the ill-treatment of suspects in Garda custody, for example, by the European Commission on the Prevention of Torture in 1995, 1996, 2003 and 2007. More recently, the Morris Tribunal 2002–2008 found further evidence of malpractice in police interviews,[13] including evidence that some suspects were arrested/detained unlawfully, as well as being subject to verbal, psychological and physical abuse (e.g. being shown graphic autopsy photographs), denied access to due process rights and lied to in order to secure confessions (Conway, 2010: 66–79).

By contrast, no such interrogation tactics were spoken about or observed in the present research in England, though this is not to say that they were not used. Historically, the police in England have been found to use oppressive methods to obtain confessions. The 1991 Royal Commission on Criminal Justice (RCCJ), for example, took place because of a series of miscarriages of justice which arose prior to the introduction of the Police and Criminal Evidence Act 1984 (PACE), but only came to light between 1989 and 1991. These miscarriages of justice included the 'Guildford Four' and the 'Maguire Seven' and they shared in common the police suppressing evidence for the defence and obtaining incriminating evidence through oppressive means (Sanders and Young, 2007: 16). That said, since then, police interrogation practices have been improved by the widespread adoption of the PEACE model, (which stands for Planning and preparation, Engage and explain, Account, clarify and challenge, Closure, and Evaluation). This is an accredited approach to investigative interviewing which, in essence

> represents a pre-planned and orderly approach to the questioning of the suspect, which relies heavily on encouraging the suspect to give his account of the matter or matters of interest to the police, and probing his account to iron out conflict, ambiguity or evasiveness....
>
> (Walsh, 2009: 71)

This may be why Blackstock et al. (2014: 383–4) found little evidence of the police trying to persuade 'silent' suspects to speak in their research in England, unlike in some of the other countries in their research.[14] That said, this may not be routinely so, given that Quirk (2017: 69) found that police officers conducting interviews were not always trained to use PEACE and also tended to structure the investigation and the interview process in ways that constructed a case against the suspect, rather than seeking to uncover objective, factual evidence.

Right to legal advice in the police station

In England, following the introduction of PACE, access to publicly-funded legal advice is universal for all suspects who request it.[15] This right was given even greater legal weight in England and Wales, and other countries in the EU, including Ireland, as a result of the 2008 *Salduz v. Turkey* ECtHR ruling, which required suspects arrested by the police to be given access to a lawyer prior to their first interrogation, unless there are compelling reasons to restrict this.[16] This doctrine applies even if a suspect exercises their right to silence. The introduction of the right to publicly-funded legal advice in England may partly explain the increase in the number of suspects who request and receive legal advice in the police station. In 1985, immediately prior to PACE becoming operational, up to 27% of suspects requested legal advice and up to

23% consulted with a legal adviser (Bridges, 1985, cited in Maguire, 1988).[17] More recently, Skinns (2009a) found that 60% of suspects requested legal advice and 48% consulted with a legal adviser, whilst Pleasence et al. (2011) found that 45% of suspects requested legal advice and 35% consulted with a legal adviser. However, this increase may also be for other reasons such as the introduction of the qualified right to silence (Bucke and Brown, 1997).

Of course, in practice, not all suspects request legal advice and not all requests for legal advice are met. For example, Pleasence et al. (2011) found that 55% of suspects did not request legal advice, but of the 45% that did request legal advice, 22% of their requests for legal advice went unmet. The reasons for this are complex and wide-ranging. In sum, whether suspects request and receive legal advice is affected by: suspect-related factors, including ethnicity, haste to leave police custody, offence seriousness, self-defined guilt/innocence, prior experience of custody and of legal advisers; the police, including ploys and informal conversations which are used to suggest, for example, that a legal adviser will prolong detention; legal advisers, including their availability, experience, and competence; and prosecutors, including being slow to make decisions about case disposal (Blackstock et al., 2014: 247; Pleasence et al., 2011; Skinns, 2009a; Skinns, 2009b). What is unique about the provision of legal advice in the police station in England is that it is free at the point of contact for *all* suspects who request it; it is provided around the clock, for example, through the duty solicitor scheme; and suspects are mostly entitled to consult with a legal adviser in person at the police station, rather than just over the telephone.[18] This was not the case in any of the other jurisdictions in the research.

The practices in the Irish and Australian cities were more similar to each other than to those in England, in that publicly-funded legal advice was available to some suspects some of the time, albeit not all staff or suspects knew or understood this to be the case. This was of particular concern in the Irish city in the research, given the qualified right to silence, which necessitates a greater need for legal advice (Daly, 2014). In the Australian city, even if a suspect did request to see a legal adviser, this did not guarantee that they would consult with one. Since there was nothing equivalent to the duty solicitor scheme, suspects in the Australian city had to find and pay for a legal adviser themselves, reportedly being handed the phone book by the police to help them do this. In one facility, a custody manager said that he also relied on a list of legal advisers that had been faxed to him two or three years ago, suggesting that this list may have been out of date. In the Australian city, there was also confusion about who was entitled to publicly-funded legal advice: each interviewee told me something slightly different about this. AUSI5 said that there was a Legal Aid Commission legal information hotline which provided information about the giving of legal advice (not advice itself) for all suspects, albeit this was only available during office hours, whilst AUSI4 did not appear to know about this hotline. However, there was more of a consensus amongst research participants about the availability of support and advice for vulnerable suspects. For example, research participants told me that it was mandatory for the Aboriginal Legal Services to be informed of the presence of any Aboriginal/Torres Strait Island detainees. Children were also to be informed of their right to legal advice over the telephone. Staff also noted that information about the response of Aboriginal and Torres Strait Islander detainees and children, when provided with this information, was to be noted down in their custody record.

Altogether, this uncertainty amongst police officers in the Australian city about who was entitled to request legal advice and how they should access it suggests that legal advice was rarely requested or received. Therefore, as Dixon and Travis argue, the right to legal advice is little more than of "presentational value if no substance is provided in the form of legal aid and duty solicitor schemes ... Even if a suspect could afford a lawyer, the profession is not organised to provide in-station advice at all hours" (2007: 126–7). In practice, what the right to legal advice meant was that most could have legal advice, if they could pay for it, and the police should not unreasonably deny this, but few took up this right. Having to pay for legal advice seemed to be crucial in dissuading suspects from requesting it. In the case of the female suspect arrested for assault (in AUSPO3), described earlier in this chapter, for example, officers thought that she declined legal advice because of concerns about having to pay for it.

Consequently, compared to England, legal advisers did not have the same presence in the police detention facilities in the Australian city, a finding also noted by Dixon and Travis (2007: 126–7). They describe them as "marginal figures in the crucial early stages of the criminal justice process ..." and also found that a lawyer – a privately appointed one – was only present in 2 of the 262 interviews in their sample (2007: 126–7). If lawyers could be paid for by the suspect and persuaded to attend the police station, paradoxically, this may have further deterred detainees from continuing with the request to consult with them. AUSI6 said, for example, that if suspects wanted to have a face-to-face consultation, the police would call a "time out" on the investigation clock whilst they awaited the arrival of the legal adviser, thereby prolonging suspects' detention. Given the "let's get it over with" attitude of suspects (Skinns, 2009a: 58; Skinns, 2009b), this may have made some detainees change their mind.

In Ireland, legal advice in Garda stations and at court was publicly-funded, but this was means-tested. At the time of the research, it was only available to suspects who earned less than €22,000 per year. Suspects had to sign a form to this effect whilst they were in Garda custody. However, this legal aid scheme for legal advisers attending Garda stations was not provided on a statutory basis, meaning that there was no duty solicitor scheme, even though this placed the provisions in this city in Ireland at odds with European jurisprudence, such as *Salduz vs. Turkey*. This ruling emphasised the importance of legal advice as a precondition to police interrogation, particularly in situations where adverse inferences may be drawn (Walsh, 2009: 143; Daly, 2014). In light of this mixed set of provisions, the status of publicly-funded legal advice in Garda custody provoked some confusion amongst staff. For example, IREI3 believed that there was no duty solicitor scheme, which contrasted with what IREI8 said, that there was a publicly-funded scheme providing legal advice to persons detained in Garda custody, which had been introduced in 2001.

In terms of access, there is extremely limited information available about this in Ireland (Conway, 2017a), not least because custody records were and continue to be paper-based (Garda Inspectorate, 2014: 28). Based on figures from a 2013 working group and from the Irish Legal Aid Board, Conway (2017a) estimates that approximately 20% of detainees in police custody consult with a legal adviser (of which 7% have a legal adviser present during their police interrogation). Similarly, during 41 hours of participant observation in six Garda stations, I observed only one legal adviser in the police station and never observed anyone request legal advice, suggesting that access may have been limited. By contrast, IREI4 thought that around 60% of suspects requested legal advice, though this would seem to be an overestimation. He said that he did not know why people declined it, but made it clear that it was not because they were not told about it, even though there is no requirement for the police to do so (Daly, 2014). Rather he said suspects "get very complacent. They've been in a Garda station so often they know the way things go."

Other interviewees were more sceptical about the reasons why detainees in this Irish city did not request legal advice. IRE6 said that suspects declined legal advice (a) because Gardaí told them that they did not need a legal adviser "because all they [the police] wanted to do was ask them a few questions," which he felt was a "distortion of the interview process;" (b) because of an innate sense of trust in the police (see also Chapter 4), especially in the more rural parts of Ireland; and (c) because the suspect did not want anyone to know that they had been arrested. He spoke in particular length about the second of these, demonstrating the importance of understanding police custody with reference to wider police–citizen relations. Irish scholars have also pointed to the absence of a duty solicitor scheme as deterring suspects from requesting legal advice. Daly (2014) notes that there may be difficulties selecting a legal adviser, with some stations having informal lists of legal advisers, whilst in others, suspects are provided with a telephone book and asked to find one themselves, as was the case in the Australian city. The present research suggested that suspects may also have been deterred from seeking legal advice because of concerns about the potential cost. The information given to suspects in the present research indicated that they may consult with a solicitor, but in a separate paragraph on a different page, suspects were informed that eligibility for legal aid was determined at court. Therefore, suspects were required to connect these two paragraphs together, appearing as they did on different pages of the information sheet provided to them. If/when they did connect the paragraphs, they may have been deterred from requesting legal advice by ambiguities about whether they would receive legal aid at all, since means-testing was done prior to going to court, not in the police station.

In contrast to the cities in Ireland and Australia, access to legal advice in the city in the US was limited both in theory and in practice. However, this may be seen as less of a concern, given the absolute right to silence and the possibility therefore that suspects could, in theory, simply refuse to answer any questions put to them. According to case law, the right to counsel needs only to be available in practice at court. The right to advice from legal counsel during police interrogations was introduced into local, not just federal, police departments as a result of *Escobedo vs. Illinois 1964*, with the right to be informed of this being introduced as a result of *Miranda vs. Arizona 1966* (Walker, 2008). This right to counsel established in *Escobedo vs. Illinois* was initially only protected in court, as it was regarded as part of the right to a fair trial, though this was subsequently extended to initial judicial proceedings in *Massiah v. US* in 1964 (Leo, 2008: 277). It was "held that a suspect has a right to legal representation as soon as judicial proceedings have been initiated against him, whether by formal charge, preliminary hearing, indictment, information, or arraignment [first court hearing]" (Leo, 2008: 277–8). This means that if a suspect clearly and unambiguously asserts their right to legal counsel, the police must stop interrogating them, unless the suspect initiates further communication (Rossman, 2017; Weisselberg, 2017), with the requested legal advice becoming available to the suspect at their first court hearing, i.e. as a defendant in court, not as a suspect in the police station (Mulroy, 2013).[19] In fact, "[f]rom [the] inception [of Miranda], no lawyers were ever actually made available to suspects subject to police questioning" (Rossman, 2017: 1133).

Consequently, in the American jurisdiction, questions about whether public defenders attended police stations to consult with their clients were met with baffled looks. There was widespread agreement amongst research participants that, as one detective in AMEPO1 said, "there's no lawyers here [in the police station]." AMEI3 said that public defenders never came to the police station and even those who were privately appointed, rarely attended (see also AMEI5, AMEI6 and AMEI4).[20] In addition, detectives in AMEPO3 said that lawyers never came to the police station and the detectives preferred this, since lawyers would simply tell suspects to remain silent, whilst a detective in AMEPO2 said that even if a public defender were willing to visit a suspect in the police station that "the captain would not allow it." These baffled looks and the absence of public defenders in the police station stemmed from the fact that requesting a lawyer was tantamount to exercising the right to silence. If anyone requested legal advice, this would simply lead to them not being interrogated (AMEI2), as long as they made their request assertively.[21] Furthermore, others said that there was nothing much a lawyer could do at the police station because the police would simply charge the suspect anyway:

Truthfully, there really isn't much that a lawyer can gain from coming here because the process is the process and they're not going to come in here and change what goes on in here. Really the only use for a lawyer would be when they go to court because the detectives are going to charge them … I don't think a lawyer showing up is going to push things one way or the other.

AMEI4

As in the cities in the other three jurisdictions, decisions about the provision of publicly-funded legal advice at court (on preliminary arraignment) were based on defendants' ability to pay (AMEI5). Pretrial interviews, which took place over the telephone in specially designated cells in the custody area, were used to collect information that could be used by the judge during bail hearings to decide about a suspect's eligibility for legal aid. In these interviews, suspects were asked, for example, about their employment and family status. At the end of the bail hearing – which took place via video-link from the custody area – the judge would pronounce whether or not someone was entitled to bail and to a public defender on arraignment. In nearly all cases observed in the research, suspects were informed that they were entitled to a public defender on arraignment.

Length of detention

In England, under PACE and following amendments implemented as a result of the Criminal Justice Act 2003, suspects arrested for indictable offences can be detained without charge for a maximum of 24 hours, although the period of detention can be extended to 36 hours by a superintendent or above and up to 96 hours by a magistrate.[22] For non-indictable offences, the limit is 24 hours. The PACE clock puts pressure on officers to expedite cases so that suspects do not spend unnecessary time in police custody, and though the maximum permitted time is up to 96 hours, the average time spent in police custody is nine to ten hours.[23] Expedited police detention is in the interests of suspects, who experience a range of reactions to police custody as a result of the deprivation of liberty, autonomy, and importantly, their sense of certainty, as often times they do not know when they will be dealt with nor what the likely outcome of their case will be (Skinns and Wooff, forthcoming; Wooff and Skinns, 2017). Hence, ENG2D11 talked about how "happy" he was that, on this occasion, the police had done what they said they would do and had dealt with his case promptly.

It is also in the interests of the police to minimise the time detainees spend in police custody, given the resources required, particularly given the disproportionately vulnerable nature of the detainee population (see Chapter 8). In theory, detention reviews, which take place before six hours and every nine hours thereafter, are used to check on whether progress is being made with the investigation and therefore to exert additional pressure to expedite the case (PACE Code C, 2017: 15.1; Skinns, 2011a: 124–7). However, in practice, these have been shown to be routinised in the way they are performed. They ostensibly adhere to the legal requirements of PACE, but with few meaningful checks being undertaken to minimise the time spent in police custody, the result of which is the "rubber-stamping" of the decision to further prolong someone's detention (Skinns, 2011a: 226; Dixon et al., 1990). PACE S41(6) also allows the detention clock to be stopped, but only when the suspect is taken to hospital because they are in need of medical treatment.

A variety of factors have been found to impact on how long a suspect is detained without charge in England (Kemp et al., 2012; Skinns, 2010; Phillips and Brown, 1998; Bottomley, 1991; Brown, 1989; Irving and McKenzie, 1989; Maguire, 1988). First, there are factors that are connected to the suspect, including age, sex, offence seriousness and case disposal, with older male detainees arrested for more serious offences being significantly more likely to be detained for longer (Kemp et al., 2012). Second, there are police-related factors, such as the time of arrest, the time taken to investigate an offence, the police station someone is detained in, and the strength of the evidence (Kemp et al., 2012; Skinns, 2010). For example, Kemp et al. (2012) found that the length of detention was significantly longer for those detained between 8pm and 8am. Third, there are factors related to other practitioners, such as legal advisers, appropriate adults and interpreters. The research shows that, generally speaking, the involvement of such criminal justice practitioners can prolong detention (Kemp et al., 2012), albeit they are not always to blame for this (Skinns, 2010).[24] It is also important to note that being charged with an offence does not always mean that a suspect is then released from police custody. The police may decide that the suspect is unsuitable for bail, in which case, according to s46 of PACE, they may be held in police custody until the first available court sitting after charge. In practice, if someone is arrested on a Friday evening, this may not be until Monday morning.

Ireland was fairly similar to England in that it had a detention clock, albeit the length of time that a suspect could spend detained without charge was different. In Ireland there were three main sets of acts regulating the length of detention without charge: the Criminal Justice Act 1984, which permitted detention for up to 24 hours; the Offences Against the State Act 1939–1998, which permitted detention for up to three days; and the Drug Trafficking Act 1996, which permitted detention for up to seven days. The observational research in the custody areas in Ireland suggested that most suspects were detained under the Criminal Justice Act 1984. At various points, the grounds for someone's detention were also periodically reviewed by officers of increasing rank and then by the courts,[25] as also happened in England.

For suspects detained for up to three and seven days, the detention clock kept running, regardless of whether someone was taken to hospital. This was not so for detention under the Criminal Justice Act 1984, where the clock was stopped for trips to hospital, if their lawyer "has issues about their detention" (e.g. believing it to be unlawful) and if a suspect agrees to a rest period between 12am and 8am (IREI2 and IRE4). These rest periods, in which the detention clock stopped, could only begin if a suspect was arrested *before* midnight. If someone was arrested after midnight, the Gardaí had only six hours before the first detention review to show that they had begun their investigation and that someone's detention should continue, even though this meant their investigation had to be undertaken overnight. Another way of looking at this, however, is that if someone was arrested before midnight and agreed to 'rest' for eight hours, it effectively gave the police an extra eight hours on top of the 24 hours permitted under the Criminal Justice Act 1984, whilst the suspect 'rested.' In IREIPO4, a male who had been arrested for robbery was interviewed on and off from 5pm until 11.45pm. The suspect refused to admit to the offence, even though a large sum of money was found in his possession. The station house officer was keen for the arresting officers to quickly request the suspects' consent to a rest period. This was because the arresting officers wanted to go home and rest themselves. The suspect consented to the rest period and the station house officer made arrangements with the arresting officers about their arrival time for the following morning, once the rest period had elapsed. Similarly, in IREPO5, a taxi driver of Nigerian origin found to be in possession of a large amount of cocaine and cash had his detention extended and was told that "he *will* have a rest period," rather than being asked whether he would like one. However, rest periods for suspects were not just about giving the police time to rest and/or to conduct their investigation, it was also about "covering their backs" so that interviews were not seen to be oppressive because they took place overnight and whilst someone was "falling asleep" (IREI4).

In the Australian city, the length of detention without charge was managed in a different way. The police did not measure the time a suspect spent detained in police custody; rather, they measured the time spent under police investigation. Under the relevant legislation, the police had up to four hours (which could be extended to eight hours) to investigate an offence, but they also had 13 time outs that could be used to stop the investigative clock from running. AUSI5 and AUSI6 noted that time outs were mainly used to wait for responsible adults to arrive at the police station (e.g. parents of children); to take ill suspects to the hospital; to wait for intoxicated suspects to sober up; to wait for specialist investigators (e.g. homicide detectives) to arrive; and to conduct forensic procedures. In spite of the different approach to determining how long someone spends in police detention, similar to England, the mean average length of time spent in police custody was 11–12 hours (Taylor and Bareja, 2005: 43).[26]

The custody manager was responsible for keeping an eye on the investigative clock with the help of a computer system which added up the time a suspect spent under investigation and indicated whether someone was in a "time in" or "time out." There was no formal review process, as was the case the English and Irish cities, but part of the custody manager's role was to monitor the investigative process so that a suspect's overall length of detention met the requirement that it be "reasonable," a matter which could be challenged at court. AUSI1 said that the decision about the use of "time outs" was down to the custody manager. This meant that some staff like AUSI6 used their discretion to determine when they started the investigative clock. For example, he said that he would only start the clock once a suspect had been formally introduced to him and brought into the custody area, even if this meant the suspect spending lengthy periods in a police vehicle in the van dock waiting to be booked-in.

In spite of the numerous "time outs" available to custody managers, some felt that the four-hour investigation time was still not long enough to interview suspects and any witnesses, to carry out forensic procedures or execute search warrants, particularly when the police had to investigate multiple suspects at once or when they were investigating complex crimes, such as armed robbery or murder (e.g. AUSI5). Concerns about not having enough time to investigate an alleged offence also arose because the process was believed to have been slowed down by the growing regulation of police custody practices over the last 15 years, meaning that suspects were no longer simply arrested, detained, indicted and bailed within a short space of time (AUSI6).

In the US, the laws relating to the length of police detention were considerably more complex, reflecting the "byzantine" nature of criminal procedure in the US (Mulroy, 2013: 867). For those arrested without a warrant and then *charged* with an offence, the conventional process would be for the suspect to be afforded a preliminary arraignment hearing "without unnecessary delay,"[27] as required by federal laws and state codes in the jurisdiction of interest.[28] Depending on the jurisdiction, "unnecessary delay" has been interpreted as from a few hours up to 72 hours, though in the selected jurisdiction there were no rules per se about how long the arrest to preliminary arraignment period should be.[29] On top of this conventional route through police detention, there were also legal provisions which had, in effect, enabled the police to detain some suspects for 48 hours, *without charge* (and also without probable cause),[30] even though some argue that this is unconstitutional (Mulroy, 2013).[31] Following *County of Riverside, California. v. McLaughlin 1991*, a person arrested without a warrant must be promptly taken before a judge to enable them to check the evidence for probable cause and whether or not someone should indeed be charged with an offence.[32] In *County of Riverside, California v. McLaughlin*, "promptly" was interpreted as 48 hours.[33] Therefore, broadly speaking, this case enabled a harsher set of police procedures and practices with regard to the permitted period that someone may be detained without charge by the police, than had hitherto been the case. Hence, Olano concludes that the ruling de-emphasised the importance of "individual rights," such as the right to liberty, relative to other considerations, such as limited criminal justice resources (1992: 1315). At the time, the 48-hour rule that emerged from the case was also seen as resulting in a more rigid procedural framework which, in theory, impacted on police practices nationwide, replacing what had previously been a more flexible set of rules, which were left to individual states to interpret (Chavey, 1992).[34] However, since then, it has become clear that it has not had the intended effect. In fact, the *County of Riverside v. McLaughlin* ruling has been applied in a variety of ways across the US, including in ways that subvert the need for probable cause and for a determination of charge prior to arrest (Mulroy, 2013).[35]

Given this complex and ambiguous legal context, no wonder the police interviewees in the US city in the research were uncertain about the upper time limits for detaining suspects in police custody. As noted in Chapter 1, responses varied, with officers stating that there was no time limit to 72, 24, 12 and 6 hours. In practice, though, officers said that they did not detain people for unnecessarily long periods and that police detention usually lasted for a couple of hours, for the mostly mundane matters that they dealt with, though this could be up to one or two days for more serious matters such as repeat robbers (AMEI1, 2, 3, 4, 6). AMEI5 also pointed out that the facilities were not appropriate for suspects to be held for lengthy periods, saying that

> conditions here are not built for you to stay here for 24 hours, let alone for 72 hours. You're sitting on steel, it's either the steel or the concrete, and we don't have pillows, and cushions and things of that nature because it wasn't set up for any prisoners to be here no more than 24 hours, technically.

Though it was highly likely that these uncertainties stemmed partly from police officers misunderstanding the legal rules about the length of time that they may detain a suspect, it was also likely that there was some more cynical and deliberate rule-bending at work. After all, the complexities and ambiguities of the rules provided scope for decisions about the length of detention to be left to the discretion of individual officers, which meant that the rules could easily be shaped to suit their own ends. For example, it seemed that one of the primary influences on decisions about how long someone was to be detained was the progress of the police investigation, including the taking of fingerprints, the examination and photographing of the crime scene and talking to potential witnesses (AMEI3). A further influence on decisions about the length of detention was the conscientiousness of staff, as this cell block attendant explained:

> If you get an officer that is just going to sit there and do absolutely nothing, you get a drone,[36] but if you have an officer that's in there making sure that everything is going the way it's supposed to step by step, and is conscientious, and looks and says, hey, look this person got locked up at 6 o'clock, now it is, almost 10 o'clock at night, four and a half, almost five hours later, this person doesn't have any charges, well, you don't need to run out and see the corporal, you need to pick the phone up and call up to the detectives and find out what's going on, and then once the

detective gives you an answer, then you go out and you say to the corporal, hey corp, I've had this person sitting here for five and a half hours, he hasn't been charged yet, I called up, I talked to the detective, they're still investigating, oh OK, fine, the corporal knows, I know.

AMEI3

Altogether, this suggests that police practices in relation to the length of detention, in the US city, were relatively unregulated, particularly if "drones" were involved, unless perhaps it could be established in court that a suspect's detention was unlawful because it involved unnecessary delay or because it breached the 48-hour rule, whereupon evidence might be excluded in court. This seems unlikely, though, given the growing use of plea bargaining and declining numbers of contested cases, including in the jurisdiction of interest (Frampton, 2012), meaning that there were likely to be few opportunities for defendants to challenge the lawfulness of the length their detention.

In the American city, as noted above, there was also an important distinction to be drawn between the time spent 'voluntary' detention and the time spent *formally* arrested and detained, awaiting interrogation and possible release after a bail hearing. As a result, as noted in Chapter 5, some suspects were detained 'voluntarily' in cells in the detective division, before being formally charged and sent down to the cells in CCTV/booking, where they would await a bail hearing. Apart from eroding suspects' access to their Miranda rights, this practice of detaining but not arresting someone, in effect, extended the time that someone might be detained in the police station. This period of 'voluntary' detention was also unlikely to count towards the legally permitted maximum period of detention by the police, as much as the police paid attention to this in this American city.

Conclusion

In sum, drawing on the data collected in the present research, as well as the existing research, I have examined the way in which three key rights – the right to silence, the right to legal advice and the right to be detained by the police for lawful periods of time – operated in theory and in practice. With regard to the right to silence, in the English and Irish cities, the possibility of adverse inferences being drawn from a suspect's silence made for a complex and contentious set of arrangements, not least because of the difficulties that police and suspects have in grasping what this qualified right to silence means. In the American city and, at the time of the research, in the Australian city, there was an absolute right to silence, meaning that once suspects exercised their right to silence, it was, in theory, no longer possible for the police to continue with an interrogation. Irrespective of whether this right was qualified or absolute, it is likely that large numbers of suspects agree to be interviewed by the police, including potentially in the cities in the present research. This may be because suspects fail to assert their right to silence in an appropriate manner (e.g. they do so tentatively) or because of police practices, such as preliminary non-custodial interrogations, which then lead to a formal interrogation.

The right to silence is closely linked to the right to legal advice, particularly in England and Ireland, given the qualified right to silence. The complexity of the rules about when and how adverse inferences may be drawn requires interpretation by legal counsel and ideally their presence during a police interrogation. In this regard, Ireland offers less protection to suspects, compared to England, largely because, though means-tested publicly-funded legal advice is available to suspects in police custody, there is no statutory duty solicitor scheme. Moreover, there is no requirement for the police to inform suspects of their right to legal advice and for legal advisers to be present during police interrogations. It was hard to robustly compare how the two approaches to custodial legal advice operated in practice, in part because of a lack of data in Ireland about the extent of uptake of legal advice. However, participants in the research suggested the uptake to be low in the Irish city in the research. Even when publicly-funded legal advice is available free of charge at the point of contact and suspects are informed of this, as was the case in the English cities, this is not to say that suspects avail themselves of this right. Indeed, there are multiple reasons why they do not, including because they see a legal adviser as likely to prolong their detention or because of police ploys. Access to legal advice was even more limited in the Australian and American cities, though not because this right did not exist. In the Australian city, the lack of a duty solicitor scheme for all suspects was seen as largely to blame for this, whilst in the American city, there was a sense that public defenders did not belong in police stations, as they were seen as irrelevant until arraignment, that is, until someone's first judicial proceeding.

Knowing their likely length of detention is of major concern to detainees, for example, influencing decisions about whether they exercised their due process rights, such as to legal advice. Yet, across all the cities in the research, there was a sense of uncertainty about the likely length of police detention, but to different extents and in different ways. In the English and Irish cities, there were clear and well-known rules about the maximum period someone could be detained without charge, but uncertainties arose about whether the police would use up all of this permitted time or encourage detainees to 'rest' in the Irish city. In the Australian city, uncertainties about the likely length of detention were largely due to the discretionary decisions that custody managers were able to make about whether to call a time out. Though these decisions operated within clearly defined legal rules, such as about what constituted a time out, it was up to the police how they put these rules into practice, with suspects thus having to wait for indefinite periods. By contrast, in the American city, uncertainties about the length of detention were due to the complexities and ambiguities of the law, but also due to a sense of the permissiveness of the law, with police officers regarding the law as somewhat elastic, for example, when subjecting suspects to non-custodial detention. In practice, this suggests that police discretion was widest of all in this American city, compared to the other cities in the research. Therefore, with regard to the length of police detention, the legal rules appeared particularly distant from the day-to-day decision-making of police officers in this American city.

The purpose of this chapter was two-fold. The first purpose was to examine the legality of police detention, focusing on the extent to which the police abided by legal rules with regard to detainees' custodial rights, whilst also examining the role that discretion played in any departures from these rules. Second, the purpose of this chapter was to examine the extent to which the effects of the coercive custody environment, the features of which were outlined in Chapter 5, were mitigated by the bestowing of rights and entitlements on detainees.

In terms of whether custodial rights mitigated the coercive effects of the custody environment, this seemed likely to be only partial and none more so in the American city in the research.[37] As noted in Chapter 5, in the American city, the physical conditions of nearly all detention facilities were particularly poor and accompanied by routinised and ritualised processes, all of which likely added to the coercive pressure on detainees to comply with the police, irrespective of whether they regarded it as right to do so. These conditions, routines and rituals then combined with a fairly limited set of rights and entitlements, in theory and in practice. At best, on paper, suspects in the American city had the right to absolute silence, to legal counsel and to be informed of these rights, but only if they were to be formally interrogated by the police. This contrasted markedly with the wide range of rights available to suspects in the other cities in the research – including that they only be detained for pre-specified lengths of time – most of which suspects would be informed of on arrival into police detention, at least in the Irish and English cities. Of course, these legal rules were not always put into practice in a straightforward manner. As a result, in practice, suspects in the American city only really had access to the right to silence and, even then, they had to be assertive in how they used this right.

In terms of the legality of police detention, to some extent, departures from the legal rules were evident across all of the cities. They were evident, for example, when suspects were persuaded to talk to the police when they would have preferred to rest; when they were detained but not formally arrested; or when they were put off from requesting legal advice due to a lack of a duty solicitor scheme or due to police ploys used to suggest that legal advisers prolong detention. This was for a variety of reasons connected to suspects, as well as the procedural, legal and wider socio-cultural context of the rules. These departures from the legal rules were also, however, rooted in the discretionary power of the police, particularly in the US (Brodeur, 2010: 71; Scott, 2010; Walker, 2008; Haller, 1976). This discretionary power was evident, for example, in determining whether and when to call a time out or when to act on someone's request for legal advice or when to release them from police detention. However, also important was the perception and the reality that the legal rules were complex, ambiguous and were thus in need of interpretation. Such complexities and ambiguities were evident with regard to the qualified right to silence in Ireland and England, for example, but particularly with regard to the length of police detention in the American city.

The foregoing discussion has a further important implication for the legality of police custody. Where rules are especially complex, ambiguous and thus hard to understand or to interpret, this suggests that police custody is likely to be lacking in legality and also potentially in legitimacy, given the intertwined nature of legality and legitimacy (Tankebe et al., 2016; Bottoms and Tankebe, 2012; Jackson et al., 2013: Chapter 11; Reiner, 2010: Chapter 3). This was especially evident with regard to the length of police detention, in the American city, as well as the qualified right to silence in the English and Irish cities. This was in contrast to other aspects of police detention, such as suspects' rights to legal advice and to be informed of their rights, where in most of the cities in the research, there were a clearer set of rules and more of an attempt to thus abide by them, at least some of the time.

Notes

1 An earlier version of this chapter, "Police custody in common-law jurisdictions: early findings from a comparative study," was presented at the American Society of Criminology conference in San Francisco in 2010.
2 For example, Bucke and Brown (1997: 31–39) found that 58% of suspects confess in their interview with the police.
3 In the Australian city, a qualified right to silence was introduced in 2013, with adverse inferences being drawn if a defendant failed or refused to mention a fact that they could reasonably have been expected to mention in the circumstances existing at the time, which is also then relied on in a court proceeding. These restrictions to the right to silence were implemented in spite of the Australian Constitution implying the right to a fair trial and thus a need to restrict any incursions into the right to silence (Dixon and Cowdery, 2013).
4 Quirk (2017: 25, 48) traces the campaign to erode the right to silence back to the 1970s and to growing concerns about terrorism connected to "The Troubles," with this campaign gaining particular momentum in the 1990s (Quirk, 2017: 25, 48). Dixon (1997: 228), however, traces this campaign back even further to the early 1960s before "The Troubles" began.
5 This act enabled four kinds of adverse inferences to be drawn: (i) if a defendant uses a defence in court which they failed to mention earlier when questioned by the police (s34) (ii) when a defendant aged 14 years or over refuses to give evidence at trial (s35) (iii) when a suspect when issued with a special warning fails to account for incriminating objects, marks, or substances (s36) (iv) when given a special warning, a suspect refuses to account for their presence at a particular place (s37). The provisions in this Act were subsequently tested in the ECtHR in Murray (John) v. UK (1996) 22 EHRR.
6 Daly (2014) notes that Irish courts have expressed different views in terms of the constitutional locus of the right to silence.
7 Further adverse inferences have subsequently been added to these original provisions. For example, the Offences Against the State Act (1939–1998) and the Criminal Justice (Drug Trafficking) Act 1996 permitted adverse inferences to be

drawn from a suspect's failure to mention any fact during questioning, about an offence under these two Acts, which they could reasonably be expected to mention when questioned (Daly, 2014).

8 This has proven to be a controversial part of the criminal process in Ireland. Since 2014, the DPP has instructed the Gardaí to allow legal advisers into interviews with their clients, albeit this has not yet been legislated for (Conway, 2017b). This was in part because in *DPP v. Doyle*, the Supreme Court refused to recognise this right as a constitutional right in Ireland. In this case, the Irish Supreme Court rejected an appeal from a defendant who received advice from a solicitor but did not have his counsel present during interrogation. Those justices in favour of rejecting the appeal acknowledged that ECtHR jurisprudence meant that legal counsel is required from the time of arrest, but that there is no requirement that a solicitor be present *during* questioning by the police (Weisselberg, 2017).

9 Bearing in mind the different ways in which the data from these various studies were collected and given the varying sizes and compositions of the populations in each country, the figures in this table should not be seen as representative of the countries from which they derive. Therefore, caution should be exercised when trying to compare between the countries shown here, in terms of the extent of access to the right to silence.

10 In this table CJPOA refers to the Criminal Justice and Public Order Act 1995 and NSW refers to New South Wales.

11 Since the research on which this book is based was conducted, voluntary attendance has been explicitly encouraged as a way of diverting suspects from police custody, though data is not routinely collected on this. What has been given less thought, however, is how to provide access to these voluntary attendees' rights and entitlements and how to protect their welfare, as risk assessments may not be conducted, for example.

12 *Miranda* was critical of deceptive practices but did not outlaw them, and such practices were subsequently given the "green light" in *Frazier v. Cupp* (1969) (Kassin et al., 2010). In this case, it was ruled that police deception – in which the police told the suspect that their co-defendant had confessed when he had not – is insufficient to render a confession involuntary.

13 The Morris Tribunal investigated allegations of police corruption arising out of the investigation of the death of Richie Barron in Donegal in 1996.

14 In the Netherlands, for example, Blackstock et al. (2014: 364) observed and heard from police officers that they used a variety of tactics to persuade silent suspects to speak. These included asking a suspect why they were silent, telling them that they had an opportunity to tell their side of the story, asking seemingly innocuous questions, provoking them, telling them that a co-suspect had confessed and implicated them, undermining the advice from their lawyer who would not be present, and saying that silence would either prolong detention or lead to a higher sentence.

15 There are two separate but connected rights: the right to consult a solicitor (s58(1) PACE), and the duty of the police to inform suspects of this right (PACE Code C, 2017: e.g. 3.1).

16 This ruling placed renewed pressure on European countries to improve the practices of defence lawyers and the police. Some countries, such as England, were better prepared for this than others, such as France, the Netherlands, and Scotland. For example, in France, the Netherlands and Scotland there was no centrally organised training for lawyers and no requirement that they have expertise in criminal defence work (Hodgson, 2013).

17 This may have been an overestimation given that legal advice had to be paid for by suspects and also given that earlier estimates were much lower than this.

Softley et al. (1980), for example, estimated that, in 1978, 11% of suspects requested legal advice and 7% received it.

18 Telephone legal advice is provided by the Criminal Defence Service Direct, which was piloted in 2005 and then hurriedly rolled out nationally in 2008 (Bridges and Cape, 2008: 22). Legal advice is only provided over the telephone in cases where the suspect has been arrested for driving with excess of alcohol, driving whilst unfit through drink or drugs, drunk in charge, failing to provide a specimen; non-imprisonable offences; cases of warrants for failing to appear in court or failing to pay court fines; and cases of breaches of police or court bail conditions (Legal Services Commission, 2007; Pattenden and Skinns, 2010).

19 This legal framework and the interpretation of it are at odds with what suspects were told in the research about their rights in police detention. Immediately prior to their formal police interview, suspects would be informed of their Miranda rights to silence and to legal advice from a public defender if they could not afford to pay for a lawyer themselves. They were not told, however, that they would have to wait until arraignment before they would be able to speak to a lawyer.

20 In some states, such as New York State and Washington State, it is possible for suspects to telephone a lawyer from police custody (Tong, 2018), but this was not observed to happen in the present research.

21 However, if someone requested legal advice as opposed to exercising their right to silence, this does not prevent the police from trying to interview them again later.

22 For terrorist suspects, the maximum length of detention without charge is dramatically higher at 14 days.

23 In a study of 24,992 custody records in 44 police stations, Kemp et al. (2012) found the average length of detention to be 9 hours and 18 minutes, whilst in a smaller study of 871 custody records in 2 police stations, Skinns (2010) found the average length of detention to be 9 hours and 55 minutes. This seems to suggest an increase in the length of detention without charge. In 1987, Bottomley et al (1991) found that 73% of suspects were released within 6 hours.

24 For example, the time of arrival of an appropriate adults or legal advisers at the police detention facility may be because the police arrange for them to arrive at this time so as to suit the demands of the police investigation.

25 These review periods vary depending on which power of detention is being exercised (Walsh, 2009: 56–57).

26 For non-indigenous suspects, the average was 11 hours, whilst for indigenous suspects, the average was 12 hours (Taylor and Bareja, 2005: 43).

27 At this preliminary arraignment, a suspect would be informed of their right to counsel, be provided with details of the charges and of probable course, and have the date for a preliminary hearing set and their bail determined. In the city in the research, this preliminary arraignment hearing was held in police detention via a video-link with the courts.

28 See Fed. R. Crim. P. 5(a).

29 "Without unnecessary delay" has been interpreted as a few to 72 hours in Tennessee, for example (Mulroy, 2013). In the selected jurisdiction, in the 1970s, a six-hour arrest to arraignment rule was established but then eroded by numerous exceptions to it, such that by the 2000s, there were no rules per se about how long someone may be detained prior to preliminary arraignment so long as any delay did not amount to coercive pressure to confess.

30 This case was a class action brought against Riverside County where, at the time of the case, determination of probable cause by a magistrate only needed to be assessed within two days of arrest, excluding public holidays and weekends, meaning those arrested during public holidays could be held sometimes for up to seven days (Olano, 1992). These practices were challenged, as they were seen as undermining detainees' right to liberty.

31 This reflects a fundamental difference between the US city and all the others. Detention *without charge* is lawful and commonplace in England, Ireland, and the Australian jurisdiction so that the police may investigate a case, but this is not the case in the US. Mulroy (2013) argues that in the US, arrests are unconstitutional without probable cause, except in certain circumstances (e.g. brief in situ Terry stops on the street based on reasonable suspicion), and without probable cause it is impossible to charge someone on arrival into police detention, which therefore makes their detention unlawful. Nonetheless, some police departments have continued to detain suspects under 48-hour holds without charge, such as in parts of Tennessee, although not without controversy (Mulroy, 2013).

32 With hindsight, this legal context suggests that asking how long a suspect could be detained without charge may have involved unfamiliar language for the police in this US city. It might have been more accurate to phrase the question as "how long can a suspect be detained after a warrantless arrest, before their preliminary arraignment via CCTV?" or "how long can a suspect be detained after a warrantless arrest, before probable cause must be checked by a magistrate?" This underscores the importance of language, especially when conducting comparative research, in which the same terms do not necessarily have the same meaning (Nelken, 2010: 86; see also Chapter 5).

33 This was in spite of dissenters in the 5:4 ruling suggesting that 36 hours or 24 hours would be more appropriate time limits, given that several states require/d determinations of probable cause to be made by magistrates within 24 hours, including Arizona, Delaware, Iowa, Utah, and Idaho (Cedrone, 2016; Chavey, 1992; Olano, 1992). Justice O'Connor nonetheless concluded in *County of Riverside, California. v. McLaughlin* that 48 hours were necessary in the interests of minimising administrative costs, as the police and courts would require extra resources to process suspects any quicker than this (Cedrone, 2016; Olano, 1992). Not only does such a conclusion neglect suspects' right to liberty, but recent technological advances, such as computerised booking-in and fingerprint procedures, have reduced the time required before a case may be passed to a magistrate for their consideration, such that 36, not 48, hours would be sufficient time for this to happen (Cedrone, 2016).

34 *County of Riverside v. McLaughlin* sought to clarify and reinterpret *Gerstein vs. Pugh 1975*, which stated that probable cause determinations had to be made "either before or promptly after arrest" (Olano, 1992: 1312) but did not specify a time frame. Rooted in "broad federalism concerns" *Gerstein vs. Pugh* also advocated flexibility with regard to local control over these decisions, so that "the constitution does not impose on states a rigid procedural framework" about the period of time, before which probable cause determinations must be checked by a magistrate (Chavey, 1992: 405).

35 For example, in Shelby County, Tennessee, the police claimed to have ascertained that probable cause existed prior to filling in the forms requesting a 48-hour police hold without charge. In fact, all that was often included on these forms was a re-statement of the allegations made, rather than proof that the case passed the threshold for probable cause (Mulroy, 2013). In the US jurisdiction, where the research took place, *County of Riverside, California v. McLaughlin* was mentioned in the relevant state code, but it was unclear the extent to which it informed police practices. It was not mentioned by the police officers in the research and no relevant state-level case law could be found.

36 By "a drone" this officer seemed to mean someone that did little and cared little for the job (e.g. the expediency of the investigation or someone's detention) or for the welfare of detainees in custody.

37 To some extent, Irish suspects were also less likely to have had the effects of the coercive custody environment mitigated by their custodial rights, in light of qualified right to silence but also the absence of a statutory duty solicitor scheme.

Styles of authority

Whilst it was important that staff did (or were at least seen to) abide by legal rules, such as about detainees' rights in police detention (as discussed in Chapter 5), what was also important was *how* they treated detainees, including whilst bestowing these rights and entitlements. The focus of this chapter is thus on how the authority of staff was used and understood in the cities in the research. It draws on the theoretical framework set out in Chapter 1. There, the use of police authority and detainee compliance was conceptualised as, first, coerced – that is, based on sanctions and rewards used to deter unwanted behaviour, which sometimes involve the use of force, for example. Second, it was conceived as legitimate, based on softer forms of power, connected to the fairness and respectfulness of police-citizen encounters. Third, it was conceptualised as symbolic, such that detainees complied out of a sense of 'dull compulsion' and because they felt they had to, rather than because they saw themselves as in moral alignment with the police. Fourth, it was conceptualised as involving inducement by staff, in which extra drinks or cigarette breaks were used to secure suspect compliance. Since this last form of authority rests on the giving of sanctions and rewards, albeit ones that are less obviously coercive, inducement can thus be seen as a form of coerced compliance. Therefore, for the purposes of this chapter, compliance based on the use of force and on the use of inducement will be considered together.

This chapter next explores the empirical evidence about the way staff used their authority across the police detention facilities in the cities in the research. What was clear was that staff craved for a socially ordered detention facility in which detainees were compliant with police orders, as this research participant explained:

> [Y]ou can have good shifts down there, you can have bad shifts, and it's not necessarily a good shift because nobody came through, you might have heaps of people through, but as long as they're all sort of doing as you ask them to do, and they're not kicking the doors and carrying on and all that sort of stuff, it's okay.
>
> AUSI5

In this chapter, I examine how this social order was created and maintained through strategies which mapped on to the four different styles of authority. In particular, I examine the politeness and respect afforded to some detainees (legitimate authority); the use of force or delays in detention as well as rewards, such as cigarettes (coerced authority including inducement); and the total and all-encompassing power of the police, which rendered detainees relatively powerless (symbolic authority). These strategies have been separated in this way to ease the interpretation of the data, but it is important to recognise the fluidity of them. Within a single interaction and over the course of someone's detention, staff could switch between different strategies, selecting the approach that best suited how they subjectively viewed the demeanour of a detainee in any given moment (See also Skinns et al., 2017a).

Coercive forms of authority – based on the use of force and inducement – existed across all detention facilities and cities in varying degrees and forms, as did more legitimate styles of authority. However, in the American city and, to a lesser extent, the Irish city, there was a greater sense of the symbolic authority of the police. Therefore, in the American city, detainees were particularly meek and compliant with the police, rarely complaining or resisting their authority. This meant there was also less recourse to physical force. At the same time, given the also poor physical conditions of custody, the coercive nature of the routines and rituals of custody and, further, given the limited access to rights and entitlements, this made for a particularly oppressive police detention environment for American detainees in this city. At least in the English city, for example, coercive conditions, routines and rituals were to an extent counterbalanced by the more legitimate forms of authority that the police used to encourage compliance.

It is also argued that discretion featured heavily in these varied manifestations of authority. Staff had some degree of choice as to whether they used force or talked politely to detainees, for instance. These discretionary decisions seemed to be moulded primarily by what the police regarded as acceptable behaviour, as determined by them and their fellow officers. That is, how staff used their authority was shaped largely by the informal rules of police detention work that made up the occupational culture of the detention facility, such as notions of solidarity between staff (see Chapter 5). This contrasted with the granting of access to detainees' rights and entitlements (discussed in Chapter 6), with such decisions resting to a greater extent on the formal legal rules of police detention work, except perhaps in the American city.

More legitimate forms of authority

Respect

To some extent, there was evidence of staff employing more legitimate styles of authority in the police detention facilities in the research. This partially revolved around staff being respectful or at least showing respect to detainees, irrespective of the allegations made against the detainee or their demeanour and behaviour towards staff. This was because staff saw the payoffs in terms of improved detainee compliance and thus less work for them. There were a few staff that stood out across the research in terms of the level of respect that they showed or described themselves as showing towards detainees. AUSI1 said that "treating people properly in custody has its rewards" for all parties. To illustrate this, he gave an example of when a detainee was in custody – someone who was not a "troublemaker," a 45-year-old businessman who had never been arrested before – after experimenting with drugs. In spite of the detainee being abusive towards him, he was supportive of him and his girlfriend, who visited the detainee whilst he was held in police custody. This interviewee described how when he later saw them both at court, they both smiled and waved at him, which was to the surprise of the judge. This interviewee seemed to be saying that showing respect to this detainee meant he received respect and gratitude in return, which in this case had long-term pay-offs. The respect shown by this cell-block attendant also stood out in the American city, in part, because it was a rarity. He talked about the importance of respect, albeit he would also assert his authority if necessary:

> I asked the cell-block attendant about what enabled him to keep people calm in here. He said that what was important was that suspects were talked to with respect, that they were processed quickly and that he had a thick skin and did not react to the abuse that some of them shouted at him…. He said that the small things really mattered in here, such as being given a drink of water. He also said that it was important to forget about the offence that suspects were alleged to have committed and just treat them all the same.
>
> AMEPO3

However, there were also numerous examples across all cities of staff displaying disrespectful attitudes and behaviour towards detainees, as well as a general lack of kindness. Staff, at times, spoke in a disrespectful way about detainees. Sometimes this was directed at detainees or happened whilst they were in earshot, whilst on other occasions, it involved private conversations between staff:

> Male suspect of Turkish origin arrested on suspicion of theft. He was known for dipping [pickpocketing] people. The female jailor intensely disliked this man, who she had encountered before, calling him a "creepy fucker" within earshot and "a fucking idiot" to his face, albeit he did not seem to register this. He was intoxicated but claimed not

to have taken any drugs or alcohol. She kept shouting at him to "stand up! Don't lie down" and when he looked at me she said, "don't look at her."

IREIPO5

Male of Fijian origin in his 40s – Arrested for allegedly punching his 13-year-old daughter and telling her to hang herself. He is drunk, rude, belligerent and shouting. When he is brought to the custody desk to be booked in, he asks for a glass of water. The staff say that he can have one, once the booking-in process is complete. He becomes annoyed at this. He is asked to surrender his property as part of the booking–in process. When he is asked for his belt by the custody manager, he also removes his T-shirt and throws it in the direction of the custody manager. This lands on the custody manager's shoulder and falls to the counter. The custody manager and the custody assistant then forcibly remove the suspect to the dock, where he continues to shout that he wants a glass of water and that he is diabetic.... Eventually, one of the patrol officers (a sergeant) passing through the custody area gave him a drink of water.... This suspect regularly asked to go to the toilet and the custody assistant complained about this, saying "far out" in response to one of the suspect's later requests. She also asked him "why have you farted in my custody area?" and then told the suspect he was "stupid". She also muttered that he was a "fucking cunt" under her breath whilst sitting at the booking-in desk. [It was probably not loud enough for him to hear, but I heard]. Later the suspect urinated in a cup, whilst the staff were not watching.... The suspect denied that he had done it, saying it was the person who had used the dock before him.

AUSPO4

Staff were also disrespectful towards detainees in that they laughed at them in front of them, which the detainees did not appreciate. In AMEPO6, as a large group of detainees were leaving police detention, having been bailed, staff laughed at them for not being able to "follow a simple instruction to go straight on." As the staff laughed at them, one of the male suspects who I had spoken to said, "I hope that you're writing this down." Staff also proceeded to laugh at photos of detainees who had been multiply arrested:

[Two cell-block attendants] and a Corporal from the Operations room proceeded to look at photos on their computer, whilst laughing loudly and visibly in front of the detainee. They said things like, "oh, he's a man of a 1000 faces" and "oh look, there's his rock face". I deliberately did not go and look at the photos, as I did not want to be complicit with them. I looked, instead, at the suspect and he rolled his eyes at me. He did not react to them at all, although it was pretty clear from his expression and his eye rolls that he felt humiliated by what the police were doing.

AMEPO7

These incidents showed a lack of respect towards these detainees and, though not necessarily representative of how all detainees were treated, they still raised questions about the likelihood that the police would have been re-garded as a legitimate authority by the suspects who were treated like this. The incident described in AUSPO4 was particularly revealing about the relationship between respect and detainee compliance. Being unkind and disrespectful, as well as failing to respond to a straightforward request for a drink of water served only to further antagonise this detainee, who was prob-ably already reacting poorly to being detained by the police, causing further non-compliance and upset for him, as well as more work for the police. There were, however, a few staff who could, at times, put to one side their feelings about detainees and accord them respect, regardless of what they did or said to staff.

Humanity

More legitimate forms of power were also manifest in the extent to which staff recognised and treated detainees as fellow human beings, rather than seeing them as a criminal 'other,' undeserving of their respect. Some staff explicitly acknowledged the importance of seeing detainees as human beings and detainees similarly acknowledged the importance of such sentiments to them:

> At the end of the day they're human beings really, even though they have committed a crime, or they're alleged to have committed a crime, they're still, it could be my brother or sister, it could be anybody, so they have to be looked after.

IREI2

> These people [detainees], they're people for God's sake, albeit damaged stock, may not be the type of person you want to take home and have dinner with, or introduce to the wife and kids, or husband, or boyfriend, or whatever, but they're people.

AUSI1

A lack of humanity with regard to how staff treated detainees could have harmful consequences. It could result in detainees becoming upset, agitated and non-compliant, as was the case of a woman in AUSPO2 who was left topless and audibly crying in full view of a nearly all-male team in the docks (see Chapter 8). As suggested by ENG1S2, police detention which lacks humanity could also leave detainees at risk of self-harm or possibly even su-icide. By contrast, acting with humanity towards detainees, particularly for detainees who were upset, was a way of keeping them safe, as well as securing compliance. This custody manager, for example, acted with humanity by keeping the dock door open for a detainee who was in distress:

> The other day, there was a young lady particularly upset who had been brought in for a relatively minor offence and she was despondent and crying and all of the above, and it would have just exacerbated the issue by closing the door in a fairly small space…. You could look at it from a humanitarian aspect, or you could look at it, that if the custody manager puts the detained person offside immediately, then the arresting officers aren't necessarily going to get anything out of them when they decide to talk to them about the offence that they may have committed. If we can keep the detained person onside, it just makes the process go a lot quicker, and probably more beneficial to police having a happy detained person than an obstructive one or a non-compliant one.
>
> AUSI6

As he explains, this had the effect of keeping her safe and "on side" with po-lice procedures, such as police interviews. This suggests that sometimes police actions were, in fact, *displays* of humanity, which were performed for utilitar-ian reasons, such as the benefits that the police could accrue to the criminal investigation. Indeed, this illustrates one of the criticisms raised about the procedural justice literature, in which there is a concern that procedurally just treatment may be used to hoodwink citizens into accepting unfavoura-ble outcomes, in this case subservience to police investigations (MacCoun, 2005). Moreover, it also implies that the police may only treat citizens with dignity and respect because of the compliance that it encourages, rather than because it is morally the right course of action.

The use of sanctions and rewards

Staff across all the police detention facilities also displayed a more obviously coercive style of authority in their relationships with detainees; this involved staff, on occasion, using a variety of sanctions and rewards to encourage but also reward compliance. One of the main rewards on offer, at the time of the research, were opportunities to smoke. Smoking was used as a bargaining tool. It was used as a way of encouraging detainees to comply with police procedures, such as fingerprinting, photographing and police interviews:

> Male 3 – Drunk and disorderly. Found staggering on a busy main road. Because he had been given an adult caution on a previous occasion he was to be charged … [the jailor] was asked to go down to the cells and

take a picture of him. However, to do this, she had to get him to sign a consent form first. She openly admitted that she was going to use a cigarette to bribe him and she took this cigarette from the property of Male 2. She gave this detainee the cigarette first, lighting it through the cell wicket and then asked him to sign the form.[1]

IREPO4

Smoking and, in one facility in the Australian city, access to television and a choice about what was watched were also used to reward compliance with the police. They were used to reward things like not complaining, 'kicking off' or demanding too much of staff, which resulted in a more peaceful and socially ordered detention facility, which was more pleasant for staff. Rather than it being a case of "if you do x police procedure, I will give you a smoke break," it was more a case of "if you behave well, you can watch TV or I will let you have a smoke in your cell." For example, the following was observed in the Australian city:

In the charge room, I notice that the television is pointing out into the custody area. It has a notice on it, which says that it is there to keep suspects quiet so that they don't yell at staff, along with some quip about it being wobbly, heavy and best not moved. I say to the sergeant that it seems like a good idea to have the television positioned so that the suspects can see it. He says that it is used as a "bargaining tool" in that if suspects "behave", they let them choose, within reason, what they watch.

AUSPO1

The sanctions for non-compliance were more wide-ranging in scope across all the cities in the research, with the exception of the American one, where there was seemingly no need for such sanctions given the meekness of most detainees (which is discussed later in this chapter). There seemed to be three main kinds of sanctions. The first and most obvious sanction employed by staff for non-compliance was the use of force, of which there were many examples. By and large, the use of force involved handcuffs and/or the taking of detainees directly and forcibly to the cells if they were non-compliant in the charge room, where they may be forcibly searched and then left until they were calmer, at least in the eyes of the police.

One young man was brought in for criminal damage. From the beginning, he was belligerent, talking over the arresting officers and the custody officer. The custody officer was patient and explained to him why he had been arrested and what was going to happen to him, but he did not listen. He became increasingly agitated, angry and visibly upset. He then began flailing around and had to be gently restrained by the arresting officers. He became increasingly violent and was talking about self-harming. It was quickly decided he needed further restraining. All male staff … disappeared into the cell area and he was restrained by three officers, one lying across his legs, two holding his arms.

ENG1PO1

What was notable about many of the incidents observed, where force was used to take someone directly to the cells, was that it tended to involve detainees who were intoxicated and/or were mentally disordered, with the intoxicated often becoming more compliant and respectful towards the police, once they were sober again. This association between use of force, drugs, alcohol and mental health conditions raises questions about whether the use of force was appropriate, given the vulnerabilities of some of these detainees (see also Chapter 8).

Second, the police would adjust the way they communicated with detainees, as well as making threats of different kinds when they wanted detainees to comply with them. Sometimes they would shout at them or threaten them with the use of force and sometimes they would remind detainees about who was "in charge." More often than not, these forms of coercive authority had the desired effect of securing detainee compliance, perhaps because detainees feared the repercussions of doing otherwise. For example, in AMEPO4, staff shouted at a detainee who started to protest about not having been released, even though his bail bond had been paid. He was then taken (non-forcibly) to the cells and threatened with further time in the cells if he did not stop complaining. Similarly, this custody manager talked about having to intervene when he came back to "his" detention facility to find arresting officers and a detainee in a "pissing competition" over who could threaten whom the most:

> I had to leave temporarily, and when I returned, I missed the part where the offender gave the police some death threats, and the police started with, 'so you want to threaten me' …. And I walked in and, hang on a moment, there's about to be bloodshed here, so I got the arresting police to leave, and I put the offenders on notice. It may not be totally appropriate but I told the offender that they know they're there for a serious crime, they were there for aggravated breaking and entering, and armed robberies, and … I told them bluntly, you're in a world of shit … and I actually tapped him on the chest and side of the head when I said it, and he listened, and I did not have a problem with him …

AUSI1

In contrast to the arresting officers, this custody manager felt that threatening this detainee with the seriousness of his offence, rather than with physical force was the more effective way to secure detainee compliance. This was in spite of the fact that it resulted in a conflict between him and the arresting officers, who questioned whose side he was on after he sent them out of the facility.

More serious threats about the use of force were evident in the American city, all of which contributed to the view that police authority in police detention was all-encompassing, meaning that detainees seemed to comply out of a sense of fear, rather than because they felt it was the right thing to do (see also later in this chapter). As this interviewee noted, most detainees did cooperate and, if they did not, supervisors would be brought in who were allowed to use Tasers in police detention, and this would be "explained" to detainees in order to secure their compliance:

> [T]he reality is that the people that are intent on being a problem usually that's known from the time they walk in the door, and that person is going to be treated differently ... They'll be brought out by themselves and we'll have three or four people escort them, and the supervisor will often be standing by with a Taser ... Now I often, myself, will walk back there with the Taser, talk to a person, before we open it up explain to them what's going to occur, explain to them the situation, and explain to them that one way or another you're going to be fingerprinted, now you can be an adult and walk out on your own, or we can do it the hard way. And 99% of the time you will eventually make sense with them, and they'll come and out and they'll comply. They'll run around while it's happening, maybe try and insult you, but 99% of the time you're going to do fine, just treating them professionally, overwhelming them with force, as you're there with four or five other people, and it's a no-win situation, and when they realise that they usually comply.
>
> AMEI6

Third, in the Australian city, where the police were involved in bailing detainees and then setting bail conditions, the police could use these bail conditions as a way of sanctioning non-compliant behaviour. AUSI6 noted that the police used bail in "a punitive manner," giving bail conditions that would "stuff up someone's life," such as having to report for bail seven days a week in one city, knowing that they had a holiday booked in another state. Using bail punitively and to sanction detainees was also observed in the research:

> Male − white, British, 27, drunk and verbose. He was deliberately winding up the police by calling the arresting officer "tubs", commenting on the cricket, loudly saying that his dad was a lawyer and that

they would all lose their jobs. The arresting officers took a particular dislike to him. Admittedly, he was behaving like an idiot, but was the bravado a front for the fact that he was scared? Noone explained to him what was happening, what his rights were, where he was going etc.... He gave a false name and the police could not verify his identity. He was asked to consent to having his fingerprints and a photo taken, but refused, although no-one told him it was an offence to do so. He was eventually charged with hindering the police, failing to follow a direction to move on, assaulting a police officer (chest to chest, kicking door of van into the police) and failing to provide fingerprints. He became angry on reading the charge sheet, querying each of the charges on it.... He was given police bail, but the requirements were deliberately set so that it was impossible for him to meet them, which seemed like punishment for being rude and non-compliant. For instance, the sergeant made the arresting officer ask the suspect, whilst the sergeant was filling in the bail details, whether he had someone that could bring his passport to the police station to verify his identity and who was willing to pay $500, if he failed to show up in court at the specified date. He said he did not and so he put these as requirements of his bail conditions.

AUSPO2

As he could not meet these requirements his bail was refused and he was held until the next available court session the next day. This had the effect of significantly prolonging this detainee's detention.

Symbolic authority

Within police detention, there was also a sense of the total and all-encompassing power of the police, meaning that detainees felt they had no choice other than to follow police directions. Evidence for this could be found in the subtle and not so subtle ways that the police reminded detainees of who was in charge. In AMEPO5 below, a police officer made it abundantly clear that he was not at the beck and call of detainees, no matter how often and how loudly they sought his attention. AUSI3 was a bit subtler in his attempts to convey to detainees who was in charge.

It was quiet in the custody area, so I spent time talking to one of the (Puerto Rican) police officers down there.... Whilst we were talking, people began banging and shouting in the cells and asking for his attention. He shouted down the corridor 'I can't hear you' in a sarcastic tone of voice and remained sitting down.

AMEPO5

[I]t's like, here's the carrot, you're never going to get the carrot, I know you're never going to get the carrot but I'm still dangling the carrot out here … 'I want the doctor', and you'll say, 'why?' and he'll go, 'I don't have to tell you, you're not a doctor, get me a fucking doctor, I want a doctor, and I want him here now, you get me a doctor, I know my rights, get me a fucking doctor', and you go, 'I actually need to know why because if you work with me I can maybe help you, this is not helping, you're not helping me to be able to help you at all' …

AUSI3

In the face of this symbolic authority of the police, this 'total police detention,' it is not surprising that detainees tended to meekly and unthinkingly comply with the police, doing as was asked of them because they felt there was no other choice.

This symbolic authority of the police was particularly evident in the American city, where detainees were notably meek and compliant during their time in police detention. In my research diary, I noted the following:

Detainees here are remarkably compliant. I have not yet seen one fight or anyone being aggressive, which surprises me…. I wonder if it is because people are more scared of the police here or because they are less informed about what their rights are in custody? For instance, people were waiting in AMEPO4 for 6-hours or more in a cramped, overheated cell, without a toilet, water or food, which was inhumane. Yet, no-one complained.

As noted here, detainees seemed to accept their lot when it came to things like their limited rights and entitlements, the grim conditions and outcomes that were patently unfavourable to them, such as the prohibitively high cost of bail bonds, with failures to pay resulting in the prolonging of their detention. For example, in this case, a detainee simply accepted that he was not going to be able to pay his bail bond:

Only two suspects were brought before the judge [deciding on bail] … [one] of them was accused of three things, including stalking and breaching a protection order and was given a bail of $5000 for each of the three charges. The suspect sat there extremely nervously whilst he waited for the magistrate to inform him of the amount of his bail. He said that when he had been arrested, only two weeks previously, for the same offence that his brother had paid his bail bond, but that this would not happen again. I thought he was going to get upset and aggressive when he was informed that bail was to be set this time at $15,000, but he did not. He simply signed electronically and went meekly back to

his cell, even having a laugh and a joke with the turnkey who took
him back.

AMEPO7

This tendency amongst detainees to simply accept their treatment in police
detention in this American city, without question, was seemingly rooted
in their fear of the police. As noted above, non-compliance would be dealt
with through threats of the use of force by the police, sometimes including
being Tasered. How could this not be seen as threatening and intimidat-
ing? One officer in AMEPO5 also said of detainees, "in here, they cry
like babies, but outside they play the big man." This sense of 'total police
detention' and concomitant dull compulsion to accept police treatment in
police detention was also rooted in the conditions, routines and rituals of
police detention in this American city, which were seen and experienced
in the main as coercive (see also Chapter 5). However, this tendency to
accept their lot may also have been connected to repeated contact with
criminal justice institutions. Lerman and Weaver (2014: 10, 200) show that
"custodial citizens" – often young, African American men from deprived
communities who become excluded from political and social forms of citizenship through contact with the criminal justice system – become socialised into accepting their lot, not making demands, staying quiet and below
the radar, so that they do not attract further unwanted attention from the
police. They also come not to trust criminal justice institutions, such as
the police, which are seen as exerting "near total control" over them, a
view which they extend to all political institutions, which are consequently
seen as "authoritarian, hierarchical and all-powerful" (Lerman and Weaver,
2014: 141). The 'total police detention' found in the research, largely of
African American men, must also be understood as historically situated and
part of the lengthy history of racism, discrimination and exclusion (see also
Chapter 4), in which African Americans were pathologised and thus readily
seen as deserving of authoritarian policing practices (Muhammad, 2010:
225; Bass, 2001).

Conclusion

Drawing on the theoretical framework set out in Chapter 1, this chapter
has examined the empirical evidence from the research with regard to the
different styles of authority that staff employed and how these styles of authority impacted on detainee compliance. Staff used their authority in three
main ways. First, they exhibited a more legitimate style of authority, which
encompassed elements of procedural justice, including showing respect and
acknowledging detainees as human beings. Whilst staff could be deliberately respectful and humane with regard to how they treated detainees,

recognising the benefits in terms of detainee compliance, this was not routinely the case. There were clear instances across all cities of disrespectful treatment, which was also lacking in humanity. The predominant tendency across all detention facilities, however, was for staff to employ their authority in a coercive way, employing rewards and sanctions in order to secure detainee compliance. This second style of police authority in police detention thereby encompasses both authority based on coercion and authority based on inducement, as set out in Chapter 2. Third, particularly in the American city, there was a strong sense of the symbolic authority of the police in police detention, that is, of 'total police detention,' leaving detainees with the impression that they had little choice other than to do as they were asked by staff. This was rooted not only in the fear induced in detainees by threats of the use of serious forms of force, including Tasers, but also in the manifestly coercive police custody environment as a result of its physical conditions, routines and rituals as described in Chapter 5. It can also be understood as a product of the political socialisation of "custodial citizens" through multiple contacts with criminal justice institutions, with this particularly impacting on young black men from deprived communities, both in the past and present (Lerman and Weaver, 2014: 10, 200; Muhammad, 2010: 225; Bass, 2001).

Given the focus of this book on the impact of discretion, the law and other rule structures on police powers and citizens' rights in police custody, it is important to examine the impact of these features of police work on the styles of authority examined in this chapter. None of the research participants explicitly connected their sense of discretion to how they employed their authority in police detention. Nonetheless, it is clear that the styles of authority seen in the research, that is, *how* the police used their authority, were a discretionary matter and one in which there was limited influence on it by formal legal rules and procedures, in part, because there were fewer legal rules to influence such matters. By contrast, as documented in Chapter 6, *whether* someone should be given access to rights and entitlements was more patently influenced by relevant laws and associated codes of practice, at least in the English, Irish and Australian cities.

This raises the possibility that discretionary decisions about *how* the police employed their authority in police detention were to a greater extent determined by the informal rules of police work, namely, the attitudes, values and beliefs of staff. The incident that the custody manager AUSI1 recounted above, in which he had to step in to prevent arresting officers and a detainee engaging in a "pissing competition" about who could threaten whom the most, was revealing in this regard. This incident led these arresting officers to question this custody manager about whose side he was on, eventually also putting together a complaint against him, which was eventually dismissed. In trying to prevent the use of such heavy-handed and coercive practices in police detention, it would seem that this custody manager violated what the arresting officers considered to be the informal rules of the detention facility, one of which seemed to revolve around the importance of solidarity between colleagues (see also Chapter 5).

Note

1 There was an interesting paradox here in that he was believed to be too intoxicated to be out in public and, hence, he was arrested, and yet he was sober enough to consent to having his photo taken and to sign a form to this effect.

Meeting individual needs

Vulnerable detainees in police custody

Introduction

In Chapters 5–7, I examined the ways in which the largely coercive custody environment and its routines and rituals were to some extent mitigated by detainees' access to their due process rights, as well as by the styles of authority that the police employed, albeit at varying degrees across the different cities. The purpose of this chapter is to further examine these issues, looking at the ways in which police custody was adjusted for detainees deemed vulnerable. I explore how vulnerability was defined, identified and responded to in police custody in the cities in the research, as well as examining the implications of this for police–citizen relations.[1] Here the focus is on children, detainees who had medical conditions, mental health conditions or learning disabilities, women and those from linguistically diverse backgrounds. My argument is that the effects of the coercive custody environment and coercive styles of authority were only partially mitigated for vulnerable detainees: adaptations of police custody tended only to occur when detainees visibly demonstrated their vulnerability (see also Dehaghani, forthcoming: Chapters 5 and 6). This was also largely only in the Australian, English and Irish cities. When detainees' vulnerability was less obvious in its manifestation and detainees were unwilling or unable to divulge such details, specialist safeguards for vulnerable detainees could be sidestepped, suggesting that the law was also being sidelined, as a consequence of the discretionary powers of the police. Before exploring these findings from the research, it is important to examine understandings of vulnerability as they relate to police custody.

Rules and police policies on vulnerable detainees

The police interact often with vulnerable citizens, whether as suspects, witnesses, victims and during calls for service (Adebowale, 2013: 11). Indeed, this may be a growing tendency in England, in light of neoliberalism and austerity politics, in which cuts across the public sector have resulted in the police becoming even more of an 'agency of last resort' (Cribb et al., 2014).[2] After all, the police are part of an interconnected set of governmental institutions who respond to problems of vulnerability, meaning that shortcomings in one set of institutions, such as those dealing with mental ill-health, affect the functioning of the rest, including the police. Hence, Grabosky says, "much police work arises from the malfunctioning of the other social institutions" (2012: v). It is against this backdrop that there has been growing academic interest in the policing of vulnerability, which is more broadly about the policing of increasingly diverse and complex societies in the 21st century (Asquith and Bartkowiak-Théron, 2012).

Since the 1980s, concerns about vulnerability in police custody have resulted in sustained attempts to ameliorate the treatment of vulnerable detainees in England. For example, the Royal Commission on Criminal Procedure 1981 (RCCP) was, in part, prompted by the Maxwell Confait murder case in which there were grave concerns about the way that children with learning disabilities were treated by the police, resulting in false confessions and a miscarriage of justice (Skinns, 2011a: 8; Hodgson, 1994; Dixon et al., 1990). The Court of Appeal quashed the convictions of the three children arrested in this murder case and the RCCP recommended extending the use of appropriate adults (AAs) in police custody from children and those with learning disabilities to those with a mental illness too,[3] a measure that was eventually implemented in the Police and Criminal Evidence Act 1984 (PACE).[4] Since the RCCP and the introduction of PACE, there have been subsequent attempts to examine but also improve the treatment of vulnerable detainees in police custody. Various reports have looked at how to improve the treatment of children (Skinns, 2011b; HMIC, 2011), those with mental health conditions and learning disabilities (Adebowale, 2013; Bradley, 2009), as well as vulnerability, generally, in police custody (HMIC, 2015). There has also been growing emphasis in police policies, codes of practice and laws about the need to divert and refer vulnerable detainees to appropriate services. This has been evident in attempts to reduce the number of children detained overnight in police cells (Skinns, 2011b); changes to the law about whether and the circumstances in which children and adults experiencing a mental health crisis may be held in police detention;[5] and the growth of Street Triage schemes and mental health liaison and diversion teams in police detention over the last decade.[6]

Similar trends to improve the treatment of vulnerable detainees have been observed in Australia. Concern arose in the 1980s about the treatment of Aboriginal and Torres Strait Islanders by the criminal justice system. The Royal Commission into Aboriginal Deaths in Custody (RCIADIC) was established in 1987, following 99 deaths of Aboriginal and Torres Strait Islander citizens in police and prison custody nationwide between 1980 and 1989, with particular concern being raised about the standard of care in police cells. It is "widely acknowledged as the most thorough legal inquiry ever conducted into the lives of Indigenous Australians" (Marchetti, 2005: 104, cited in Bartels, 2012), and resulted in 339 recommendations to improve the treatment of Aboriginal and Torres Strait Islander in state custody, including through independent investigations of deaths in custody; improved data collection on detainees in police custody; greater use of alternatives to police detention for the intoxicated; and the development of policies and programmes relating to indigenous suspects, including the opportunity to have a support person and access to legal advice. As a result, in most states in Australia – including the one in which the present research was located – children, people who have impaired intellectual or physical functioning, those with mental health conditions and from non-English speaking backgrounds, and people who are Aboriginal and Torres Strait Islander – have the right to have a support person present, and in most cases, the interview should not proceed without them (Bartkowiak-Théron and Asquith, 2012; Moston, 2009).

In Ireland, various cases have come to light of inappropriate treatment of (vulnerable) detainees (The Morris Tribunal 2005–2008, cited in Conway, 2010: 66–79; European Committee on the Prevention of Torture, 1995, 1999, 2003, 2007), though there has not been the same sustained programme of reform to tackle the issues they raised. For example, the Grangegorman murder investigation in 1997 resulted in a false confession and the wrongful conviction of Dean Lyons. This was not due to oppressive or coercive conduct by the police, so an inquiry into the circumstances of his wrongful conviction found. Rather, it was because the police failed to fully take into account the effects his learning disabilities had on the information he provided, even though some of the investigating officers raised misgivings about the reliability of his evidence, "referring to him as a Walter Mitty" character (Birmingham, 2006: 7). However, given its limited terms of reference, it was not within the remit of this commission of inquiry to make recommendations for police reform. That said, there have been more recent attempts to improve the treatment of vulnerable detainees during police interrogations. There are plans to focus on the kind of interaction that an interviewee is already having with the police – that is, whether the person is being cooperative, uncooperative, resistant, or, importantly, whether they are vulnerable – rather than whether they are a suspect, victim or witness (Noone, 2015: 295–6).

Though there has not been a sustained programme of reform of police custody in Ireland with respect to vulnerable detainees, this is not to say that there are no protections for vulnerable detainees in Garda custody. As Walsh notes, Garda ethical codes state that "police investigation must be sensitive and adaptable to the special needs of persons such as children, juveniles, women, minorities including ethnic minorities and vulnerable persons" (2009: 44). This can be interpreted as meaning, so Walsh (2009) argues, that care should be taken, for example, with children and single mothers not to detain them any longer than absolutely necessary. The guidance notes for the Criminal Justice Act 1984 also state that a "responsible person" – who plays a similar role to the AA in England – should be found for those under 18, the "mentally handicapped" and the mentally disordered.

In the US, though research has pointed to the susceptibility of vulnerable detainees to false confession and thus to miscarriages of justice (Kassin et al., 2010),[7] there is little by way of additional rights or safeguarding measures. For example, police practices with regard to how they relay suspects' Miranda rights to them are assessed by the courts with respect to whether they cover the requisite information, rather than whether this information is given simply, accessibly and in a way that pays attention to the vulnerabilities of suspects (Weisselberg, 2017; Weisselberg, 2008). As argued later in this chapter, in the American city in the research, there was also a presumption that suspects' vulnerabilities were something that would be dealt with by the courts, not by the police.

Even in countries where safeguards for vulnerable detainees do exist, they do not always have the intended effects. For example, with regard to the provision of AAs in England, there have been difficulties identifying who needs one, as well problems of under-identification (Dehaghani, 2016; NAAN, 2015; Skinns, 2011a: 63–64; Newburn and Hayman, 2002: 48, 131; Hodgson, 1994); there have been difficulties finding and contacting suitable people to act as AAs, particularly for vulnerable adults, given the non-statutory funding of AA schemes (Kemp and Hodgson, 2016; NAAN, 2015; Blackstock et al., 2014: 243–6; Skinns, 2011a: 60–61; Quinn and Jackson, 2003: 66; Hodgson, 1994; Dixon et al., 1990); there have been misunderstandings over the role of the AA (Kemp and Hodgson, 2016; NAAN, 2015; Blackstock et al., 2014: 243–6; Skinns, 2011a: 62; Jacobson, 2008: 31; Quinn and Jackson, 2007; Pierpoint, 2006; Brookman and Pierpoint, 2003; Quinn and Jackson, 2003: 66; Bucke and Brown, 1997: 11; Hodgson, 1994; Dixon et al., 1990); and, there has been an increasingly less robust interpretation of the AA provisions, in which the absence of an AA alone was not seen as sufficient to merit the exclusion of evidence (Hodgson, 1994). Similarly, with regard to indigenous suspects in Australia, whilst the overall number of Aboriginal and Torres Strait Islanders dying in police custody decreased in the eight years after the RCIADIC (Dalton, 1999), they continue to be over-represented amongst those proceeded against by the police (Australian Bureau of Statistics, 2017), thereby placing them at greater risk of dying in police cells.[8] In addition, high-profile deaths in police custody have a particularly damaging effect on relationships between Aboriginal and Torres Strait Islanders, criminal justice institutions and the state, contributing to the feeling that nothing has changed in the 25 years or so since the RCIADIC (Wahlquist, 2016). In part, this may be due to the inconsistent way in which recommendations from the RCIADIC have been implemented, with some Australian states (such as Victoria, New South Wales and Australian Capital Territory) making more progress than others (South Australia and Northern Territory) (Bartels, 2012).

Nonetheless, attempts to improve the safeguarding of vulnerable detainees illustrate why a focus on vulnerability is important. Vulnerability affects the fairness and integrity of the criminal justice process. If vulnerability is not taken into account, vulnerable detainees are likely to experience police custody as unfair and may be more willing to provide false confessions, and this may result in a miscarriage of justice. Moreover, this potentially has consequences for them and their families, especially in parts of the US where the death penalty may be used (Roberts and Herrington, 2012; Kassin et al., 2010; Sanders and Young, 2008; Weisselberg, 2008). Such miscarriages of justice also potentially impact on victims and society as a whole, if the person responsible for an offence is not discovered and they go on to reoffend. As the RCIADIC and other research show, vulnerable detainees are over-represented amongst those who die in or following police custody; for example, a large proportion of those who die are intoxicated due to drugs and/or alcohol or have a mental health condition (Angiolini, 2017: 87; Hannan et al., 2010; Sanders and Young, 2008; Best, 2004). This suggests that failures to adapt police custody to vulnerable detainees' needs affects its survivability. There is a real possibility that such vulnerable detainees may self-harm and/or die prematurely whilst being detained by the police (Cummins, 2008). Furthermore, as Grabosky notes "the quality of a society will be evident in the way it treats its most vulnerable citizens" (2012: viii). By the same reasoning, the quality of police detention and policing, more generally, can also be judged by the way police organisations treat the most vulnerable.

Conceptualising vulnerability

The foregoing discussion hints at some of the ways in which vulnerability is understood in police custody.[9] It has tended to be understood in terms of a range of characteristics which afford the detainee extra protections. In Australia, for example, vulnerable populations are thought to include children and young people, elderly people, people with culturally and linguistically diverse backgrounds, the mentally ill, the disabled, victims of crime, Indigenous Australians, people with addictive behaviours, and sexually and gender-diverse communities, as well as the homeless in some jurisdictions (Bartkowiak-Théron and Asquith, 2012). As discussed later in this chapter, with the exception of indigenous groups, to varying degrees, a similar list of protected groups was identified across the Australian, English and Irish cities in which the research took place. What this means is that if detainees possess these characteristics, they are deemed to be vulnerable and thus at a disadvantage when compared with others. In particular, they are seen "as more susceptible to abuse, discrimination, misunderstanding or miscommunication. They therefore need additional support to navigate the intricacies of the system" (Bartkowiak-Théron and Crehan, 2012: 6).

However, such conceptualisations of vulnerability are also problematic. These lists of protected characteristics are far from exhaustive (Bartkowiak-Théron and Asquith, 2012; Bartkowiak-Théron and Crehan, 2012). Moreover, though pragmatic, the very act of listing protected characteristics encourages the police to see them as separate and individual rather than over-lapping and multiple in the way they impact on detainees. Furthermore, the laws and policies which offer protection to detainees have similarly developed in a silo-like fashion, meaning that the police have to interpret a variety of relevant police policies and legislation at once when dealing with vulnerable people. This has "created an organisational maze (complete with obligatory paperwork or data entry) which requires a radical re-think ..." (Bartkowiak-Théron and Asquith, 2012: 47). This rethink entails a need to work from an assumption that everyone is potentially vulnerable and in a variety of ways, until proven otherwise. This notion of universal vulnerability draws on the work of Martha Fineman, an American socio-legal scholar. Because of the centrality of her vulnerability thesis to the present chapter, it is set out in some detail here.[10]

The starting point for Fineman's vulnerability thesis is that all human beings' bodies are susceptible to harm or injury from external forces – whether accidentally, intentionally or otherwise – as well as to internal disintegration. Indeed, this creates a continual degree of uncertainty throughout the life course, given the "ever present possibility that our needs and circumstances will change" (2008: 12). What she also notes is that many of the harms that lead to vulnerability, such as illness, ageing or death, are beyond individual or human control (Fineman, 2010). As such, vulnerability is a universal feature of the human condition. This idea of the universalism of vulnerability challenges negative connotations of the term, in which vulnerability is connected to stigmatised groups, such as those with HIV-AIDS or those confined in prisons or other state institutions (Fineman, 2008). She also notes the complex and multiple forms of vulnerability, which can be cumulative in their effects; for example, harm to the body can result in harm to employment prospects and to family re-lationships (Fineman, 2010).

She also describes vulnerability as particular and individualised, but also situated, saying, "[u]ndeniably universal human vulnerability is also particular: it is experienced uniquely by each of us and this experience is greatly influenced by the quality and quantity of resources we possess or can command" (2008: 10). Her thesis thus emphasises the embedded nature of human beings in social relations and within social institutions. After all, were we to succumb to harm or injury, then we would depend on others, including the state, for survival. Hence, for example, she describes vulnerability as a "universal, inevitable, enduring aspect of the human condition that must be at the heart of our concept of social and state responsibility" (2008: 8). This positioning of the vulnerable subject within society and its institutions encourages the view that societal institutions are collectively and independently involved in "lessening, ameliorating and compensating for vulnerability" (2008: 13). These institutions provide us with "assets," i.e. advantages and resources, which together provide individuals with "resilience" in the face of vulnerability, which Fineman (2010: 268) also sees as the counterpoint to vulnerability. Her point, therefore, is that when examining vulnerability, there is a need to consider both "individual position and institutional relationships" (Fineman, 2010: 269).

This socially situated understanding of vulnerability, therefore, offers a way of tackling inequalities and disadvantage, which does not focus on anti-discrimination measures and identity politics, in which protected groups become pitted against each other and in which the quest for equality becomes narrowly focused on individual responsibility and autonomy, with limited recognition of governmental responsibility (Fineman, 2010; Fineman, 2008). Rather, she focuses on "shared vulnerabilities and building a political movement around unequal institutional arrangements attendant to those vulnerabilities," which she sees as "a far more promising and powerful approach in addressing and correcting the disadvantage that persists in society" (2008: 17). Hence, her vulnerability thesis can be seen as an explicit attempt to move beyond the identity politics paradigm, as well as an attempt to create an alternative, which places the actions of institutions, not just individuals, under scrutiny. This is important, for example, because privilege and disadvantage "migrate across identity categories" (2008: 21), but also because confronting discrimination against certain social groups has eclipsed the elimination of inequalities for *all* social groups. As noted later in this chapter, this reimagining of vulnerability offers an important challenge to the tick-box approach to identifying and responding to vulnerability in police custody; across all the cities in the research, if detainees did not obviously fit into these criteria, then few adaptations were made, thereby excluding them from the possibility of fair and equal treatment.

Fineman's thesis therefore turns a number of understandings on their head: the liberal, rational, responsible subject becomes the vulnerable subject, who is characterised by an inevitable and shared sense of vulnerability with others; vulnerability becomes disconnected from any negative connotations; identity politics and anti-discrimination measures become replaced by the seeking of assistance from societal institutions. All of this takes place against the backdrop of an active and responsive state, which acts to ensure a more equitable distribution of assets and privilege across society. However, Fineman also acknowledges that such a conceptualisation of citizens and the state would be particularly difficult to implement in the US, as it requires moving beyond American ideological attachments to notions of individual autonomy and a limited state. Next, I examine findings from the research about who was considered vulnerable and how they were identified.

Identifying vulnerability

Across the cities in the research, when asked who was vulnerable, most in-terviewees mentioned children, those who did not speak English as a first language and detainees who were physically unwell. Some would also mention suspects with learning disabilities and mental health conditions, though there seemed to be confusion about the difference between them and thus about how best to safeguard detainees with either set of conditions. Interviewees also pointed out that a key vulnerable group in the Australian city were suspects who were Aboriginal and Torres Strait Islanders, with staff taking at face value anyone who said that they were a member of an indige-nous group, even if staff felt that they were not. The varying ways that these groups were treated by staff will be explored in more detail later in this chap-ter, but for now, I explore the process by which vulnerability was identified in the first place.

In all of the cities in the research, there were a mixture of formal and informal methods for identifying vulnerable suspects, involving risk assess-ments and medical checklists, with differing degrees of formality, as well as reliance on the instincts and intuition of police officers and on suspects to provide accurate information (see also Chapter 5). In the Irish city, staff seemed to rely on a more informal hunch-driven process to assess vulnera-bility. IREI1 said, "a lot of it's down to what people notice, common sense prevails, I mean, a lot of these people [his colleagues] have had a lot of experience and they'll pick up fairly quickly if something's not right." He also said that they would contact a doctor to assess someone if they were concerned that they may be vulnerable. In the other cities in the research, however, the process of identification tended to be more formal, involving risk assessments and medical checklists. For example, in the American ju-risdiction, AMEI4 said that one of the first things completed with a suspect when they arrived into police detention was a medical checklist, and the main thing they looked for was whether or not someone was diabetic or had any other kind of "extreme medical condition." This checklist contained seven visual checks that staff were supposed to carry out concerning, for example, whether they appear intoxicated, withdrawing from drugs, de-spondent/suicidal or irrational. There were also eight questions asked of detainees concerning, for example, whether they had any serious medical problems (including diabetes), mental health conditions or were receiving any type of treatment.

In spite of these mechanisms for identifying vulnerability, there were a number of potential difficulties. First, vulnerability was hard to spot, par-ticularly if staff were unfamiliar with the signs of vulnerability or they were inconspicuous, as well as if staff were untrained and unsure about identifying them. Staff also implemented formal risk assessment and medical checklists with varying degrees of stringency. Some staff took this medical checklist seriously, though this was not observed to be the case in all custody areas in the American city. In field notes from AMEPO1, I noted that

> [w]hen suspects arrived in the cell area, they were asked to sign a form about their welfare. I never saw staff ask detainees to answer the questions on this checklist. Rather staff ticked no for all the boxes and then handed the form over to detainees and asked them to sign it.

As such, staff here seemed to focus on filling out the paperwork, rather than meaningfully engaging with whether or not the detainee in front of them had vulnerabilities that required their attention. This was also a violation of the police directive relating to this checklist. As argued later in this chapter, what this seemed to mean, therefore, was that only the most obvious forms of vulnerability were identified and addressed (see also Dehaghani, forthcoming: Chapters 5 and 6).

Second, in all of the cities, staff relied on detainees to provide them with accurate information about their vulnerabilities. Without this information, it was difficult to assess someone's vulnerability. Yet they would sometimes try to elicit this information in blunt and insensitive ways. In ENGPO2, one of the research team observed a woman being booked-in for a drunk and disorderly offence, in which the custody officer as usual went through a risk assessment, saying "'we are going to go through your problems now,' to which the detainee replied 'what problems?' and the custody officer replied 'I dunno, schizophrenic, for starters aren't you?'" What was also notable was that, more so than in the other cities, staff in the American city saw this provision of accurate information as the responsibility of detainees, rather than seeing it as incumbent on staff to ask appropriate questions. For example, AMEI5 felt that it was suspects' responsibility to be honest with staff and to provide information that would ensure that they received an appropriate level of care. He said that when detainees were not forthcoming in relation to the medical checklist, for example, then police officers ended up having to deal with the consequences, such as medical emergencies, which he felt was unfair.

Third, what was also problematic was the timing and the purpose of the requests for information, which could be used to assess whether a detainee was vulnerable. In the American city, AMEI2 said that the questions asked on booking-in were fairly rudimentary, with more detailed questions only being asked if and when a detainee was to be interviewed by the police (see also Chapter 5). This suggests that these questions were concerned to a greater extent with ensuring the admissibility of the evidence in court than with assessing someone's vulnerability so that they could be appropriately dealt with throughout the duration of their detention. In one of the English cities, staff also talked about taking extra-special care when assessing and dealing with potentially vulnerable detainees to prevent complaints being made. ENG2S7, for example, said, "it's just, covering your back, you've got to cover your back, and to make sure you do the job professionally, and not leave yourself open to complaints." What this suggests is that questions asked of detainees about their vulnerability served a variety of purposes; they were partly used to assess the level of their vulnerability, so that appropriate measures could be put in place to ensure their safe custody, though they were also used to prevent complaints being made or evidence being rendered inadmissible in court. Next, I consider the way that police responded to detainees, once their vulnerability had been identified.

Responding to vulnerability

Physical health conditions

Suspects in all the cities in the research were observed to experience a wide range of physical health conditions – from diabetes to concussion, from drug-related abscesses and sores to HIV, and from heart conditions to cuts and bruises[11] – most of which were easier to identify and address than other kinds of vulnerabilities, such as learning disabilities or mental health conditions (which are considered in the two sections that follow). Either these physical health conditions were more visible to staff or staff were more willing to ask and detainees were more willing to volunteer information about them. In addition, staff spoke with greater certainty and confidence about what they should do with detainees with physical health conditions, which largely entailed facilitating access to medical staff. In particular, custody staff had to determine whether to summon a medical practitioner (in the English and Irish cities), whether to take the detainee to hospital themselves or, in an emergency, whether to summon an ambulance. In addition, in the American city, where there were concerns about a specific range of physical health conditions, detainees could also be taken to a specialist police custody area in the centre of the city, which held women, diabetics and detainees with other serious illnesses.

Learning disabilities

Staff in the Australian city said that they rarely came across detainees with learning disabilities. For example, AUSI4 said that he had encountered few suspects in custody who had learning disabilities, despite his many years of service as a police officer: "intellectually disabled, I could probably count on my hand the number of people who have been intellectually disabled that have come into a police station. You very rarely get ones like that." However, this contrasts with what the research shows about the higher prevalence of learning disabilities amongst the suspect population, which is particularly problematic because of its comorbidity with mental health conditions. For example, in a US prison survey cited in Weisselberg (2008), it was found that

12.3% of inmates had, at most, an eighth-grade education. English research suggests that 9% of suspects had an IQ score which was in the learning disability range (Gudjonsson et al., 1993), which compares to a prevalence of 1%–2% in the general population (Roberts and Herrington, 2012). Similarly, at 6.7%, Young et al. (2013) also found the prevalence of learning disabilities to be much higher amongst detainees in a South London police station than in the general population. Learning disabilities have also been found to overlap with mental health conditions, such as depression and anxiety, with research showing that 52% of the prison population has a learning disability *and* depression compared with 19% of the general population (Talbot, 2008: 27). Similarly, McKinnon and Grubin (2012) found that 8%, 5%, 3%, 11% and 19% of the detainees in their sample, respectively, had psychosis, depression, learning disabilities, current suicidal ideation or previous suicide attempts and that the proportion of detainees with learning disabilities (and also psychosis) were higher than in the general population. McCausland and Baldry (2017) also note the over-representation of people with mental and cognitive disability in the criminal justice system, both in Australia and internationally.

The fact that AUSI4 noted the rarity of learning-disabled detainees suggests that under-identification may have been a problem in this city and almost certainly in the other cities in the research too.[12] The consequences of this are grave given that safeguards – such as the provision of a support person or AA – would not have been activated. It might also have resulted in staff failing to regard such detainees as suggestible and/or they may have misconstrued their behaviour as purposefully uncooperative or as deliberately failing to recognise the authority of the police (Bartels, 2012). Together, this may increase the likelihood of detainees providing unreliable information and thus being particularly vulnerable to miscarriages of justice (Roberts and Herrington, 2012). Aside from staff failing to spot learning disabilities, under-identification of such detainees may also have arisen because of the public nature of the circumstances in which they were expected to declare personal details about their disabilities at the charge desk, which may have had an inhibitory effect on some.

If they were recognised by participants in the research, learning disabilities seemed to create confusion for officers in the Australian and Irish cities, in terms of what they should do about them. For example, in the Irish city, whilst there were safeguards in the Criminal Justice Act 1984 guidance notes for the "mentally handicapped" in police custody, for example, that they be allowed a responsible adult with them during the police interview, all barring one staff interviewee did not seem to put this into practice. They noted, instead, that they would treat those with learning disabilities the same as everyone else. In the Australian city, AUSI4 believed that seeking a support person for someone with a learning disability was discretionary, when in fact it was statutorily required. This may help to explain why Dixon and Travis (2007: 104–5) found evidence of suspects with clear signs of learning disability being interviewed without a support person present.[13] Similarly, in the

English cities in the research, though AAs were supposed to be sought for vulnerable adults (i.e. those with learning disabilities and/or mental health conditions), there was evidence to suggest that this did not always happen. For example, in ENG2PO2, a man of Moroccan origin suspected of shoplifting, who was observed rocking in his cell and who staff described "as not the full ticket," was not provided with an AA (nor a lawyer or an interpreter).[14] In this case, race, nationality, language barriers, mental health and possibly learning disabilities interacted, thereby compounding this suspect's vulnerability. Yet, he was still not regarded as vulnerable enough for the additional safeguards that he almost certainly deserved.

It was only in the American city that treating learning-disabled detainees the same as everyone else was permitted by law. Weisselberg (2008) notes that there is an assumption in case law that all suspects will be able to understand their Miranda rights and make a reasoned choice about whether to exercise these rights. Furthermore, the Supreme Court has made it clear that the police are not required to provide additional information that might enable suspects to make a more informed choice (Weisselberg, 2017; Weisselberg, 2008). Officers are also trained to believe that most suspects, whether they are children, or those with learning disabilities or mental health conditions, are able to understand their Miranda rights and are capable of waiving them. Training manuals emphasise that the same legal standards apply to all suspects. For example, one notes that

> [b]eing mentally slow, uneducated, drunk, injured and/or criminally unsophisticated does not mean we cannot get a valid waiver out of a person if the problem is recognized and extra precautions are made to insure the suspect understands what it is he is giving up.
>
> (Weisselberg, 2008: 1574–5)

Indeed, police officers may interpret this as meaning that they can pressure suspects to talk to them, irrespective of what the police may believe about the suspect's possible learning disabilities and level of comprehension.

Part of the reason why the police were reluctant to recognise the importance of learning disabilities to police detention was that they saw courts, not the police, as the main player in determining someone's capacity. This was the case in the Irish, Australian and American cities. IR EI3 said that it was up to the courts to determine whether a detainee's mental capacity had a bearing on what they did and whether they knew right from wrong. Indeed, this interviewee said that he did not see the identification of learning disabilities as part of his job, which was to investigate the facts of the case. IR EI8 (who was one of two non-police interviewees) confirmed the reluctance of the police to acknowledge learning disabilities:

> Very often you simply find yourself arguing the appropriateness of interviewing your client with a police officer who does not want to listen.

The attitude is we're going to interview your client and if you object to what we're doing or you believe that anything we obtain has been obtained unfairly, you should make that application in court and seek to have the evidence excluded … it's not even seen as a problem, the idea that you can interview a vulnerable suspect and get admissions from them, it's sort of seen as a perfectly legitimate of a police investigation, and that, if it's found to be unfair, then a court will rule that way, and the admissions, whatever they are, however they were obtained, will be ruled out, and the person will not suffer for it.

AUSI4 and AMEI4 expressed remarkably similar views to those of IREI3 and IREI8 about the limited role of the police in determining capacity and responding to vulnerabilities arising from learning disabilities. AUSI4, for example, said that "'mental problems' were not something considered in the police station, though they would be considered during court hearings, affecting the admissibility of evidence." In theory, whether a defendant has learning disabilities may be considered in court, and, if so, this could be a mitigating factor used to divert them to specialist services and treatment, but this is not happening systematically, in practice (McCausland and Baldry, 2017). Indeed, McCausland and Baldry conclude in relation to Australia that "[p]olice management of highly disadvantaged young people and adults with mental and cognitive disability has served to criminalise them, and courts, criminal justice diversion and therapeutic approaches have failed to stem their flow into and return to prisons" (2017: 303). Therefore, the presumption made by the police that picking up on "mental problems" is not their responsibility is problematic, likely resulting in the criminalisation of vulnerable suspects.

Mental health conditions

By contrast, participants in the research seemed more likely to respond to the more obvious signs of mental illness. If someone's behaviour was evidently disturbed in police custody, then this would prompt the police to seek help from medical staff in police custody or by taking someone to hospital for an assessment. In the American city, the police detention directive for adults contained a section on suicidal detainees, including information about the profile and characteristics of people who were most likely to be suicidal and how to deal with them. This was the only information it contained on mental health conditions. Nonetheless, staff also responded where other mental health conditions were clearly in evidence. AMEI4, for example, recounted taking a suspect for a mental health assessment, after he smeared himself with excrement. However, this suspect was released back into police custody as he was seen as "crazy," rather than as "endangering anybody else," which was not the response the police were hoping for. In spite of this, staff still made this detainee clean up the mess he made of his cell on his return to the detention facility.

These decisions about whether or not someone was vulnerable and how best to deal with this became more difficult where detainees exhibited multiple signs of vulnerability, including mental health conditions. For example, in AUSPO1, the custody manager was initially unsure whether to seek a mental health assessment for an intoxicated detainee who was also exhibiting behaviour, which the custody manager felt was odd. After consulting with a more experienced colleague, he decided to contact the mental health crisis team, and it transpired that this detainee had been released earlier in the day from hospital for a drug overdose. The mental health worker agreed with the hospital that this detainee was intoxicated and eccentric, but not mentally ill. There were also other similar cases in the English cities. In ENGPO2, staff could not deduce whether a woman arrested following an allegation of shoplifting, and, with a crack pipe in her possession, was acting oddly due to drug use or due to a mental health condition. The forensic medical examiners contacted to assess her in the detention facility also struggled to decide, though they eventually decided that drug use was to blame. In ENGPO1, the arrest of a woman for shoplifting, who was distressed, but also physically aggressive towards staff, resulted in a similar conundrum for staff about how best to respond to her. In her case, though, staff connected her behaviour to her mental health conditions and learning difficulties, rather than her drug use, in part, because she was known to the team of drug workers in the detention facility.

Aside from seeking medical advice and assessment of obviously disturbed detainees, in the English, Australian and Irish cities, the police would also alter their observation of detainees, increasing their frequency the more concerned they were, even putting someone under constant observation either in the cells or in secure waiting areas in the main charge room. ENG2S10, for example, noted the high levels of mental illness amongst detainees, which could make people vulnerable and at risk of self-harm (see also Cummins, 2012; McKinnon and Grubin, 2012; Payne-James et al., 2010; Cummins, 2008). This police officer, therefore, felt duty bound to eliminate the risk of this happening, as far as this was possible, including by altering the frequency of observation. However, others in this English city were more sceptical about the ability of staff to identify those with genuine mental health conditions, given the tendency of some detainees to "play the system" such as by "superficially self-harming" so that they would be dealt with more quickly. In addition, acknowledging the mental health conditions of detainees necessitated a more caring role for staff, such as whilst they sat outside someone's cell door when they were on constant watch, which was seen as far from a "plum posting" by one custody officer.

Particularly, in the Australian and American cities, as was the case for detainees with learning disabilities, research participants tended to view the courts and not the police as the primary decision-maker about the impact of a detainee's mental health on their legal capacity, particularly with regard to serious offences. AUSI2 said that for serious offences, even where a mental health condition was suspected, the police should interview and charge someone and then let the courts decide whether they were fit to plea. Similar beliefs about the limited role of the police in determining capacity led the police in the American city to simply treat mentally ill suspects the same as other suspects, except that they may be put in a "suicide cell" if they were threatening to self-harm. Unlike for suspects who were physically unwell, they would not be transported to hospital or to the central detention facility (for women, diabetics and those suffering other forms of serious physical ill-health). AMEI4 said, for example, that

> I would say a good 70% of the people that are arrested, it's very, very high the people that have mental problems, like schizophrenia, bipolar disorder, that kind of thing. Honestly, there is no special facility for them … we house them here [in the district police stations].

Similarly, AMEI6 said that for those with mental health conditions things were "a little trickier" than for those with physical ailments, saying that these kinds of conditions would only be addressed, once someone arrived at prison and if ordered by a magistrate during arraignment proceedings. This lack of consideration given by the police to the capacity of suspects, with regard to their mental health condition or learning disability (as discussed in the section above), seems to amount to a fait accompli. In the Australian and American cities, if a suspect did speak to the police, it is likely that, in court, the suspect would have few options other than to go along with any evidence they had provided in the interview, unless they had a legal adviser to stringently argue that their mental disorder should, in fact, be taken into consideration in court.

Overall, it seemed that detainees with mental health conditions had minimal safeguards available to them relative to other vulnerable suspects, unless their symptoms were obvious and they were in imminent danger of harming themselves or others. Otherwise, staff would simply contain them — sometimes humanely and sometimes not — believing that it was not the police's role to determine their capacity and assuming that they would receive the care they needed elsewhere in the criminal justice process. As was the case for those with learning disabilities, particularly in the Australian and American cities, in all but the most obvious of cases, research participants overlooked the fact that mental illness impairs detainees' ability to cope with police custody and with police investigative procedures, such as the police interview. This suggests that there would be a greater chance of such detainees providing unreliable information and thus of miscarriages of justice (Roberts and Herrington, 2012; Kassin et al., 2010).

Children

Across all of the cities in the research, the picture was even clearer still as to the treatment of child detainees,[15] as there could be far less confusion than for adults with learning disabilities or adults with mental health conditions about their need for additional support. After all, a detainee's age was harder to dispute.[16] Across the cities, there was a requirement for a parent, guardian or a responsible/appropriate adult or support person to be contacted about their child's detention; for them to be contacted and their permission sought about the need to interrogate their child; for them to be present at the police station for police procedures (e.g. the reading of rights and entitlement, the interview, charging and signing of the bail paperwork).

There were a number of similarities across the Australian, English and Irish cities in the research in terms of police responses to child detainees and the challenges involved. First, as documented in the extant research (Blackstock et al., 2014: 243–6; Skinns, 2011a: 60–61; Quinn and Jackson, 2003: 66; Hodgson, 1994; Dixon et al., 1990), police officers in the cities in Australia, England and Ireland noted difficulties contacting parents, guardians or other responsible adults, particularly in the evenings and on weekends. In the Irish city, for example, IREI4 said that there were issues contacting parents/guardians because of difficulties in his particular police division with unsupervised children. Participant observation in IREPO1 confirmed this picture. In one case, for example, a 15-year-old boy suspected of criminal damage was in Garda custody for nearly six hours after difficulties contacting a responsible adult. His father was uncontactable and apparently in the pub, and staff then telephoned four Peace Commissioners,[17] before finding one that was willing to attend the station and act as a responsible adult. Gardaí also had to collect this elderly Peace Commissioner from her home and bring her to the police station. Her presence meant that the detainee could be interviewed and released, with Gardaí driving him home around midnight and releasing him into the care of his older brother. Similarly, in the English cities, there was a perception that seeking an AA for children (and for vulnerable adults) prolonged their detention, making staff reluctant to call one for some vulnerable adults, for whom the decision about an AA was considered to be more discretionary.

Second, unsurprisingly given the difficulties of finding a support person for children in police detention, in the English, Irish and Australian cities, these adults were sometimes inappropriate. Again, this is something documented in the existing research (Blackstock et al., 2014: 243–6; Skinns, 2011a: 60–61; Quinn and Jackson, 2003: 66; Hodgson, 1994; Dixon et al., 1990). Staff in the Irish city, for example, reported asking security guards at a nearby shopping centre, members of the public waiting for a bus, bar staff and traffic wardens, if they were struggling to find a responsible adult. It was also commonplace, as noted in the paragraph above, for Peace Commissioners to be used where parents could not be contacted. However, as IREI3 pointed out, in the more rural parts of Ireland, the Peace Commissioner might be the wife of the police officer in charge of custody. In parts of Australia, support persons could be similarly inappropriate; Dixon and Travis (2007: 114–26) found, for example, that in one case, the support person was a firefighter with no connection to the child detainee. In the English cities in the research, the research team were asked from time to time to be an AA, revealing a similarly misplaced view about who was suitable to be an AA.

Third, when parents, guardians and responsible adults were present in the Australian, English and Irish cities, they sometimes played a limited role. This was, in part, because of the ambiguities of the role and the concomitant uncertainties that parents/guardians/responsible adults felt about what they should be doing. It was also because they appeared to feel intimidated by being in 'police territory' (see also Blackstock et al., 2014: 243–6; Skinns, 2011a: 62; Jacobson, 2008: 31; Quinn and Jackson, 2007; Pierpoint, 2006; Brookman and Pierpoint, 2003; Quinn and Jackson, 2003: 66; Bucke and Brown, 1997: 11; Hodgson, 1994; Dixon et al., 1990). Interviewees in the Irish and English cities remarked that responsible/appropriate adults often did nothing and said nothing, except sometimes to admonish their child if they thought they were being cheeky to the police. This was also found by Dixon and Travis (2007: 115). They found that support persons in New South Wales played a limited role, in part, because they were seated behind the suspect in the interview, but also because the police failed to clarify their role from the outset. Most observed and listened but said nothing and, when they did speak, sometimes their comments were inappropriate (e.g. admonishing their child or encouraging them to tell the truth) and were rarely acknowledged. Parents were right to feel intimidated in 'police territory': police officers across the Australian, English and Irish cities noted that they would eject adults supporting children in custody if they saw them as "interfering," such as by telling their child to say nothing during their interview with the police, albeit it was rare for this to happen (IREI2, AUSI4).

However, this was still better than there being no role for appropriate/responsible/supporting adults for children detained by the police, as appeared to be the case in the American city. Without them being present, this seemed to give the police carte blanche with regard to the treatment of child detainees, including how/when they were interviewed. AMEI4 said that parents did not need to be present during police interrogation if the parents consented over the phone first:

> if they can get consent from the parent, 'can we interview your child?' Most of the time they'll say, 'yes', because when the juvenile is arrested, 9 times out of 10 the parent doesn't want to be bothered with the kid, anyway, so they'll say, 'yes, go ahead and interview them' … I haven't run across that, where the parent refuses … and you know what, if the

parents aren't going to allow the detective to interview the child, chances are the detectives are going to charge the child, no matter what.

However, whether or not a parent or guardian's permission was sought was seen as a flexible rule by some. In AMEPO3, whilst talking to the so-called "badass" detectives, these detectives suggested that permission *should* be sought to interrogate child suspects, but they did not always get it and they still went ahead and interrogated the child anyway.

Indigenous detainees

Unlike in any of the other cities in the research, membership of an indigenous group was used in the Australian city as an indicator of vulnerability, resulting in additional legal safeguards. This is because of the history of relations between the police and indigenous people and also because Aboriginal and Torres Strait Islanders are more likely to have undiagnosed hearing problems, for example (Bartels, 2012: 3–4). It is furthermore because speakers of indigenous languages are more likely to have limited English and a tendency to freely answer 'yes' to questions whether they understand them or not (Bartels, 2012: 3–4). Historically, this treatment of Aboriginal and Torres Strait Islanders as vulnerable suspects dates back to the 'Anunga Rules.' These nine rules, which were issued by the Supreme Court in the Northern Territory in 1976, included requirements that: Aboriginal and Torres Strait Islander suspects have an interpreter, if they were not fluent in English; care be taken in the giving of the police caution (e.g. it should be read back by the suspect) and in the formulation of questions put to detainees in police interviews (e.g. they should not be leading); the suspect has a "prisoner's friend" present; the custody manager contact Aboriginal Legal Services (Bartels, 2012: 4; Moston, 2009). Though somewhat paternalistic in nature, these rules, as well as the additional legal safeguards that they have spawned, reflect an awareness of the complications that can arise with indigenous suspects connected to miscommunication arising from the use of different languages and their wider sociocultural context (Moston, 2009). Additional support for Aboriginal and Torres Strait Islander suspects is also rooted in their over-representation in custodial populations,[18] as well as in their greater involvement in deaths in police custody.

In the city in the research, if a detainee indicated that they belonged to an indigenous group, this meant that custody managers were supposed to contact Aboriginal Legal Services for these detainees. Aboriginal and Torres Strait Islander detainees were also entitled to have a support person contacted and present during investigative procedures. It was also required that Aboriginal and Torres Strait Islander detainees be placed in a cell with each other and, wherever possible, that they not be placed in a cell alone. These additional legal safeguards applied, irrespective of the capacity of the detainee.

Bartkowiak-Théron and Crehan regard such blanket policies as ethically problematic because they override citizens' autonomy and right to self-determination, as well as resulting in "the 'unlevelling' of the playing field" (2012: 43–44). However, this argument seems to presume that the "playing field" was level in the first place, which is clearly not the case for Indigenous Australians. Research participants agreed that these additional safeguards for indigenous detainees were unnecessary, though for different reasons. For example, one implied that they were undeserved, by saying that indigenous people are given "a heck of a lot of, well, certainly a big free ride, and a big helping hand in regards to government handouts. They are given pretty much whatever they ask for as a group ..." (AUSI6). This failure to appreciate the colonial conditions which have contributed to the marginalisation of indigenous people, as well as the unforgiving attitude towards and stereotyping of Aboriginal people by the police, represent further aspects of the casual bigotry described in Chapter 5, all of which compounds the vulnerability of indigenous detainees. In some ways, this bigotry was unique to Australia, but in other ways it was not, given that someone's status as an Aboriginal and Torres Strait Islander can also be read as a marker for race and ethnicity. This suggests, therefore, that given the histories of racism, as well as over-policing and under-protection, especially in the US, Australia and England, all racialised groups who enter and are confined in police spaces, to some extent, are rendered vulnerable.[19]

Nonetheless, officers in the research were observed to understand and act on the safeguards for detainees who were Aboriginal and Torres Strait Islanders, ensuring for example that they contacted Aboriginal Legal Services and that they did not place indigenous detainees in cells on their own. However, it was also clear that relationships between police officers and Aboriginal and Torres Strait Islander detainees were tense. Moreover, on occasion, police officers sometimes inflamed these relationships. In this case, this female Aboriginal suspect's 'contempt of cop' had political overtones, whilst staff responses to her had racist undertones:

> Female, Aboriginal suspect, 23 years – She was arrested for malicious wounding, after allegedly attacking a male with a bottle. She lived on the street and staff suspected her to be a sex worker. She fluctuated between being extremely aggressive (banging on the dock, and shouting and swearing at the arresting officers) and calming down ... Part of what she was shouting was political. She was saying to the arresting officers that all their family were criminal because they were white and it was the white people who had stolen the land of the Aboriginal people ... At one point, the custody manager got annoyed with her, saying that she should be proud of her culture, rather than letting them down by being in police custody ... He then promised her a McDonald's and a cigarette if she calmed down. However, in order to deliver this promise, he had to

take a McDonald's meal (in a paper bag) from the garbage and microwave it. He gave this to her in the dock which she ate extremely hungrily. It transpired that she had not eaten for over 24 hours... She was asked if she would like to speak to Aboriginal Legal Services, and she said "nah." She then put her head down and slept. She was later charged and bail refused.

AUSPO2

On the surface, it seemed that this custody manager's actions were simply about treating her with kindness and calming this detainee down. An alternative interpretation, though, is that he did not see her as deserving of a fresh meal or perhaps he was secretly punishing her for shouting insults at him. Indeed, such attempts to distinguish the 'respectable' and 'deserving' from the 'rough' and thus 'undeserving' is seen as part of the mandate of the police in Australia, as well as elsewhere (Bronitt and Stenning, 2011; Reiner, 2010: 123–5). These judgements are sometimes based on race (Muhammad, 2010: 225), but also on whether people fulfil their obligations as citizens (Humpage, 2015: 234–5).[20] The actions of this custody manager may not have been directly racially motivated, but race formed a significant part of the context in which this interaction took place. They arose in the context of the casually racist language used in conversations between the researcher and other police officers, the stereotyping of indigenous suspects (see Chapter 5) and racism documented in other research on the police in Australia.[21]

Women

Across all the cities, there were limited attempts to provide additional safeguards for female detainees. Generally speaking, female detainees were not searched by male officers. However, this was not always the case, due to shortages of female staff. In one of the English cities, for example, the researcher observed an older teenage girl arrested for being drunk and disorderly – who was not complying with police directions on arrival into police detention – being indirectly searched by a man. In order to secure her in a cell and remove any potential risk, a male member of staff removed her jewellery and then helped to hold her down whilst two female officers removed her top, after which she was given a paper suit to wear (ENG1PO4). In the American, Irish and Australian cities, other safeguards included women being separated from men, either in different cells/wings or by being transported to a separate detention facility. For example, AMEI3 said that women were sent to the central police detention facility if they were arrested because of allegations that they had committed a misdemeanour or felony offence,[22] but that women with citations (who were required to appear at court) stayed in divisional custody areas, so they could attend court there.

Otherwise, staff in the cities appeared to operate with a degree of gender-blindness, in which they claimed to treat women equally to men. This was partly because women were not necessarily seen as vulnerable or in need of additional support. This stance towards female detainees was apparent, for example, in a recent thematic inspection of vulnerable detainees in police custody in England, which did not include women (HMIC, 2015). Yet, research suggests that women have a particular set of needs,[23] which shape how they respond to and cope with places of detention. When combined with a male-dominated custody environment and the sexist attitudes of some officers, as documented in Chapter 5, this is likely to create particular challenges for female detainees. Together these factors may render women situationally vulnerable, including to confession. For example, it has been found that women are likely to confess at a significantly higher rate than men, the result of which is that they may also be more likely to be found guilty (Cassell and Hayman, 1996).[24]

This gender-blindness and failure to recognise the particular needs of female detainees also seemed to feed into the disrespectful and insensitive treatment of women in some of the cities in the research. As noted in Chapter 5, in one of the English cities, women were accorded a particular kind of disrespect and mockery, as well as being criticised for the way they looked, unlike male detainees. The staff in the Australian city also acted with a particular level of insensitivity towards this vulnerable female detainee:

> Female – white, late 20s, arrested on warrant, no rights given as not required by law. When I arrive in the custody area, there is a female suspect in her late 20s being held in a small Perspex holding cell (the dock), which is directly opposite the custody desk. She was being detained because of an arrest warrant (relating to a previous alleged offence), meaning that she had to stay in police custody until her case could be heard at court the next day. This suspect was in full-view of all the staff at the custody desk. She was topless and noticeably angry; she was shouting and banging on the Perspex and glaring at the all-male team. I pointedly asked one male constable why she was so upset and, more importantly, why she was topless. He looked at me sheepishly and said that she took her vest off and that, earlier, before I got there, she was threatening (or attempting – it is not clear which) to hang herself with it and so it had been confiscated.
>
> It took 20 minutes before the sergeant, who had just come on duty, suggested that she be put in one of the regular cells and be given a blanket. However, I did not know how long she had already been like this. A female officer was found to escort her to a cell. When this officer arrived in the custody area, she looked surprised that the woman was semi-naked and asked (with slight irritation, glancing at me, as the only other woman in the custody area) why this was so. She gave the woman a blanket and then led her to a cell away from the gaze of the custody staff. As this happened, the suspect shouted something along the lines of "this is all I wanted all along." The all-male team of staff in the custody area

laughed at her, as she was led away. She then spent the next few hours audibly and continually crying. Because the woman was so distressed she was later taken to hospital to have her mental health assessed, still wrapped in a blanket and without her top and audibly crying. However, an hour later she returned from the hospital (still crying), with officers reporting that she had refused to answer any of the doctors questions, meaning that they could not assess her. She was still topless and wrapped in a blanket. When the Duty Officer asked the sergeant in charge of the custody area what had happened, he said of the female suspect "oh, just a topless Sheila."

AUSPO2

Overall, it seemed that this woman was treated insensitively by staff and possibly also punished for being non-compliant, and this had serious consequences for her, given that she was vulnerable and distressed. Subsequently, I discussed this incident with an experienced custody manager. He said that this detainee may have been placed in the dock because of the opportunities this afforded for her to be on constant watch. However, he also said that whether a suspect of this kind was in a cell or in the dock, staff should have provided an approved blanket or a paper suit.

Language barriers

Linguistically diverse detainees may have difficulties communicating with staff in police custody and with understanding what will happen to them and how they will be treated whilst they are there. Given that many of those in the research who were from non-English speaking backgrounds were also non-white and sometimes migrants, this illustrates how language barriers can often be a marker for racial/ethnic groups, nationalities, the citizenship status of detainees and their foreignness relative to the white Australian/American/English/Irish majority.[25] Whilst such suspects may be fluent in conversational English, this does not guarantee that they can cope with a police interview, for example, because of the specialist language involved; concepts such as 'free will' may be hard to grasp (Dixon and Travis, 2007: 112). In their study of police interview recordings, Dixon and Travis (2007: 112) found that around 2% of these interviews involved suspects who needed an interpreter, raising concerns about the reliability of what they said. Hence, steps were taken in some of the cities to alleviate obvious language barriers. For example, detainees in the Australian, English and Irish cities could be provided with their rights and entitlements written in their first language. Independent interpreters could also be sought in the Australian, English and Irish cities, with interpretation services being provided over the telephone or in person across all of the cities in the research, although it varied as to when and whether this happened.

In the English and Australian cities, interpreters were typically contacted to help with booking someone in and with the reading of detainees' rights, as well as with police interviews and when relaying charging decisions. For example, in the Australian city, AUSI5 said that if interpreters were called, then this counted as a time out and then "it takes however long it takes." He said that it generally took an hour and a half for an interpreter to arrive at the custody area. Though this interpreter would be used to read someone their rights, they were also required at other points in the process, including those unconnected to the police investigation. They were used, for example, when someone was being treated by ambulance crews (AUSPO4). Whether an interpreter was required was determined by the custody manager / custody officer in the Australian and English cities. Sometimes they would request one so as to 'cover their backs' and even if the detainees protested that they did not want one, as was the case in ENG2PO6 for a man of Algerian origin suspected of stealing a mobile phone. Whilst on other occasions opportunities would be missed to contact an interpreter, including in one case in ENG2PO2 (as described above), in which a man of Moroccan origin who was also a drug user and suspected to be mentally disordered had neither an AA or interpreter nor a legal adviser. This highlights the fluidity of officers' decision-making about linguistic difference (linked, in these cases, to race, ethnicity, nationality and possibly citizenship status), which was invoked or not to suit their purposes.

In the Irish city, interpreters were only seemingly sought when the police were ready to interview or charge someone, which meant that, in some cases, staff continued to read detainees their rights, even though they may not have understood them properly. For example, in IREPO5, three detainees arrived in the custody area having been arrested for working illegally. Two of these detainees were from Bangladesh and were eventually charged with working illegally with the help of an interpreter, though initially they were given their rights and entitlements in English. The third detainee was a Chinese woman in her early twenties. She was released almost immediately after she was booked-in, as she was able to supply the necessary paperwork to confirm her right to work in the country. It took around 20 minutes for her to be booked in and given her rights and entitlements. She said that she understood 80% of what was said to her, and staff were fairly patient in explaining things until she understood them. Interestingly, when she was asked to agree to be photographed and fingerprinted, she only agreed to have her photograph taken. She was worried that having her fingerprints taken would harm her right to stay in Ireland. The jailor told her that having a photo taken was "for her benefit," as it meant that if this ever happened to her again, then it would be easy to verify that she had a right to work in Ireland. She eventually had her picture taken. No interpreter was called for her and she was released without charge. These cases show that, in theory, detainees can have their rights read to them in a different language but, in practice, this may only have happened once the police deemed it worth having an interpreter present, that is, if they were ready to interview or to charge the detainee. Yet there is a range of complex questions asked of detainees and decisions to be taken *prior to* the police interview, such as about fingerprinting and photographing, for which a detainee may also need an interpreter.

The American city was different to the others in that interpreters were often police officers and also because interpreters were only requested for police interrogations, as was the case in Ireland. By and large, interpretation, including during police interrogations, was provided by (certified) police officers. This meant that interpreters were readily available over the telephone or in person, given the ethnically diverse and multilingual nature of the police force in which the research was undertaken. At the same time, their lack of independence and lack of specialised expertise was potentially problematic. Even for skilled and specialised interpreters, their role in the police interview is potentially laden with risks. For example, interpreters can contribute to a loss of accuracy in the information conveyed and a loss of non-verbal communication, as well as altering the dynamics of the interview, such that the investigating police officers experience a loss of control over the interview (Goodman-Delahunty and Marschuk, 2016). As for untrained bilingual interpreters, they pose even greater risks to the police interview. They may misconstrue their role as being about assisting the police, not the suspect, or may switch between roles of investigator and advocate for the suspect, all of which can compromise the interview and render evidence inadmissible at court (Bucke et al., 1997; Dixon et al., 1990). These ambiguities in the role of the interpreter are particularly likely where the interpreter is a police officer.

Conclusion

In sum, obvious forms of vulnerability prompted attempts to address inequalities in police custody through measures written into policies, codes of practice and legislation in the Australian, English and Irish cities, which were also incorporated to some extent into police practices. This was less obviously the case in the American city, thereby echoing Kassin et al.'s conclusion about police interrogation practices in which they suggest that "juveniles and individuals with cognitive impairments or psychological disorders are particularly susceptible to false confession under pressure. Yet little action has been taken to modulate the methods by which vulnerable groups are questioned" (2010: 30). However, even in the Australian, English and Irish cities, staff sometimes failed to address seemingly obvious needs, such as of female suspects, partly due to sexist attitudes and a perception that women were not vulnerable. Moreover, where suspects had a range of vulnerabilities, the police tended to respond to the more obvious of these, rather than to all of them. As for forms of vulnerability that were harder to spot, especially learning disabilities, particularly in the American and Irish cities, these went unidentified and unaddressed. This was partly as the police presumed that the needs of the learning-disabled would be addressed later in the criminal justice process, such as in court or in prison, suggesting also that they understood the law as retrospectively, not prospectively, filtering such cases out of the criminal justice process.

To conclude I seek to argue that decisions taken about vulnerable detainees were more *discretionary*, *individualised* and thus potentially more susceptible to *neoliberal* sentiments about the importance of personal responsibility, than for the rights and entitlements examined in Chapter 6. Here, I unpack each of the elements of this argument. First, this high level of discretion arose, in part, because of the greater level of ambiguity across all of the cities about the meaning of vulnerability and how the police should respond to it. For example, in England and Wales, even though definitions of vulnerability exist in the PACE codes of practice, they are so lacking in clarity and real-world relevance that they are rarely referred to by staff (Dehaghani, 2016). This vacuum is thus filled by police officers' hunches and intuitions, as well as by their values and beliefs, such as about deserving and undeserving detainees and about who was and who was not vulnerable. In addition, though indigenous detainees in the Australian city did receive mandatory additional support, this was sometimes provided grudgingly, in practice, in part because staff did not believe them to be deserving of this extra level of help. Similarly, in the Irish and American cities, for detainees with learning disabilities, the police presumed that it was the court's role, not theirs, to determine capacity, and thus they decided to focus on processing and charging them.

This high level of discretion places the police in a position of power to reinforce and possibly entrench the existing distribution of inequality in society, as part of a wider climate of neoliberalism. As the research showed, if detainees did not obviously fit into fixed vulnerability criteria, then few adaptations were made and detainees could be excluded from measures which might have mitigated the effects of police custody on them, and thus from the possibility of experiencing fair and equal treatment in police custody and in other parts of the criminal justice process. Yet, the police showed limited recognition and reflexivity about this position of power in which they found themselves by dint of their discretionary decision-making about vulnerable detainees.

Second, decisions about vulnerable detainees were also individualised in the sense that the police considered each vulnerability separately, rather than holistically, using non-exhaustive lists, as found in previous research (Bartkowiak-Théron and Asquith, 2012; Bartkowiak-Théron and Crehan, 2012). Across all of the cities, the police employed a tick-box approach to identifying and responding to vulnerability. They looked for detainees to manifest, in an obvious way, a narrow range of 'deficiencies' – connected to health and mental health conditions, their age, their status as indigenous and their first language – which could thus necessitate additional safeguarding and support. This meant that those who did not readily fall into police-defined categories of vulnerability could be excluded from receiving help. Women were one such group. So too were detainees who exhibited multiple vulnerabilities (e.g. mental health conditions, learning disabilities and drug use). When confronted with such detainees, staff were uncertain about which vulnerability to respond to first. When they did respond, it tended to be to one form of vulnerability, rather than all of them. To some extent, this individualised approach to vulnerable detainees is to be expected as, at an institutional level, holistic joined-up multi-agency responses to the varied needs of those engaged in the criminal justice process, including in police custody, have tended to be beset by difficulties (Loftus et al., 2014; Skinns, 2011a: 164–7; Turnbull and Skinns, 2010).

Decisions about vulnerable detainees were also more individualised, than decisions about other rights and entitlements, because suspects were expected to not only self-identify when they needed help, but also to perform their vulnerability (see also Dehaghani, forthcoming: Chapters 5 and 6). This was in order to make it obvious, so that their vulnerability could be readily noticed by staff, irrespective of suspects' ability or desire to do so. After all, some detainees may try to hide their vulnerability, for example, because they may feel too embarrassed to mention it to staff in a public setting (Kemp and Balmer, 2009: 13). To a lesser extent, responsibility was also placed on individual staff too – particularly custody officers / custody managers / members in charge – to identify and respond appropriately to vulnerability, irrespective of their skills, knowledge and training, with the possibility that they might also be blamed if things were to go wrong. Reliance on individual detainees to perform their vulnerability and staff to notice this suggests a lesser role for institutional processes and procedures in decisions about vulnerability in police custody. As such, the identification of vulnerability was a highly responsibilised matter, thereby showing it to be one of the ways in which the logic of neoliberalism has penetrated into the police custody domain. In particular, it illustrates how the "cultural trope of individual responsibility" noted by Wacquant (2009b: 306–7), is of relevance to police detention in the selected countries.

Taken together, this underscores the fact that current approaches to vulnerability in police detention, particularly in the American city, are a far cry from the universal notion of vulnerability articulated by Fineman (2008, 2010). As such, a pivotal societal institution, the police, is unlikely to be offering the kind of protection that it should be to vulnerable citizens. The tick-box approach employed by the police demonstrated that vulnerability was defined, identified and responded to in terms of individual detainees' 'deficiencies,' with vulnerable detainees being seen in terms of the problems they caused the police. Fineman's thesis suggests that the police should work from the position that everyone is vulnerable until proven otherwise. However, given that such understandings of vulnerability were not part of the beliefs and values of staff who worked in the police detention facilities in the research, neither were they part of police policies or the legal rules, this would require a fundamental reorientation of their formal and informal rule structure. It would also require a major shift to the institutional context in which staff worked, including the policies and practices of partner agencies engaged in supporting vulnerable detainees in police custody. Without such changes, though, what the research suggests is that, through their dealings with vulnerable detainees, the police are likely to reinforce and entrench existing inequalities experienced by vulnerable citizens.

The foregoing analysis makes an important contribution to the overall thesis of this book. It shows that, as noted in the previous chapters with regard to other aspects of police detention, the American city was exceptional relative to the rest in terms of its treatment of vulnerable detainees. It seemed to have the most discretionary and individualised approach to the decisions taken about them, rooted in the historical importance attached to discretionary decision-making by the police and amplified by the wider neoliberal climate. In a city/jurisdiction in which neoliberal values, such as of individualism, personal responsibility and a limited state, have a particularly prominent place, it is unsurprising to find such values embodied in the day-to-day practices of police officers in the American city in the research, namely, in the individualised, discretionary decisions taken about vulnerable citizens in police detention. Furthermore, it is likely that these discretionary and individualised decisions taken about vulnerable citizens in police detention, especially in the city in the US, enabled the perpetuation of neoliberal values, whilst also potentially adding to and compounding the inequalities neoliberalism encourages. Therefore, echoing Kaplan-Lyman (2012), the police can be seen as an important site of neoliberal governance.

Notes

1 An earlier version of this chapter, 'Diversity, difference and vulnerability in police custody: key issues from comparative research in common-law countries' was presented at the American Society of Criminology Conference in Washington DC in November 2011.

2 In 2013, at 5.7 million and representing 20% of the workforce, the public sector was at the lowest level it has been in 40 years (Cribb et al. 2014).

3 Appropriate adults are supposed to advise and support children and vulnerable adults, as well as ensuring that police interviews are fairly conducted and, furthermore, assisting detainees with communication.

4 In 2015, following an amendment to the PACE Codes of Practice, appropriate adult provision was extended again to include 17-year-olds who had previously been excluded from accessing their services.

5 The Policing and Crime Act 2017 has amended the Mental Health Act 1983 such that children experiencing a mental health crisis may no longer be taken to police custody as a place of safety. Furthermore, the new Act has clarified the "exceptional circumstances" in which adults in crisis may be taken to police detention as a place of safety and reduced the maximum time that they may be detained there from 72 hours to 36 hours.

6 Street Triage entails the police and mental health practitioners working together whilst attending to someone experiencing a mental health crisis in the community and who may be at risk of being sectioned under mental health legislation. This enables the person in crisis to be assessed and referred onwards, if necessary, to the most appropriate mental health care. Liaison and diversion teams are present in police detention in most police detention facilities nationwide for significant parts of the working day, enabling detainees to be assessed and more appropriate decisions to be taken about their care in police custody and, in other parts of the criminal justice process, if they subsequently go to court or to prison. See also Cummins and Edmondson (2016) and Horspool et al. (2016).

7 Kassin et al. (2010) note that certain groups are over-represented amongst those who are likely to falsely confess, including children, in part, because of their developmental immaturity, which means they have less comprehension of legal terms, and less understanding and appreciation of their Miranda rights; those with learning disabilities due to their diminished capacity for understanding Miranda and its implications for them; those with mental health conditions, such as anti-social personality disorder or depression, though the evidence on this is not as extensive.

8 For example, in 2017, Aboriginal and Torres Strait Islander adults made up 2% of the general population and 27% of the prison population. They also have an imprisonment rate of 2,434 per 100,000 of the Aboriginal and Torres Strait Islander population compared to 160 per 100,000 of the non-indigenous population (Australian Bureau of Statistics, 2017).

9 In terms of its etymology the word, 'vulnerability' can be traced back to wound or injury in Latin, *vulner-, vulnus,* thereby linking notions of vulnerability to harm (Bartkowiak-Théron and Crehan, 2012).

10 Fineman's vulnerability thesis stems from an attempt to develop a human rights discourse for an American audience, in which she became more focused on the 'human' than the 'rights' part of this discourse (Fineman, 2010). Her thesis is largely set out in Fineman (2008), though was subsequently expanded on in Fineman (2010), particularly the notion of the responsive state. Since then it has been further explored conceptually and empirically in a range of fields from housing to reproductive rights to animal rights in Fineman and Grear (2014) and in relation to privatisation in Fineman et al. (2016).

11 These findings correspond with what McKinnon and Grubin (2012) found during their screening of 237 detainees in two London police stations. They found that detainees had the following health conditions, as well as looking at the extent to which they were picked up in police screening processes: 16% had asthma which was picked up in 49% of cases; diabetes, 5% and 67%; epilepsy, 2% and 60%; cardiovascular complaints, 19% and 2%; communicable diseases, such as HIV, 3% and 38%; abdominal symptoms, 3% and 38%; serious injuries, 6% and 57%; head injury, 5% and 75%; heroin use, 11% and 84%; crack cocaine use, 22% and 64%; risk of alcohol withdrawal, 18% and 83%. They also found that the proportions of detainees with asthma and epilepsy were higher than for the general population. See also Payne-James et al. (2010) and Cummins (2012) for further data on the prevalence of physical and mental health conditions amongst detainees and Cummins (2008) for data on the prevalence, methods, and causes of self-harm in police custody.

12 Under-identification is likely given that learning disabilities are difficult to spot. Gudjonsson et al. (1992) found that even clinical psychologists struggled to identify learning disabilities over the short periods for which suspects were detained, and that the police only identified 4% of a possible 20% of suspects as in need

of an AA. Nearly 20 years later, Young et al. (2013) found similarly high levels of under-identification of "intellectual disabilities" and ADHD in police custody, both of which have been linked to high levels of suggestibility. Screening by the researchers found 6.7% of their sample to have an "intellectual disability" and 23.5% to have ADHD but only 4.2% were provided with an appropriate adult. McKinnon and Grubin (2012) also found that of the mental disorders that they examined in their research, learning disabilities were the least likely to be identified by the police during routine screening. They found that 8%, 5%, 3%, 11%, and 19% of the detainees in their sample, respectively, had psychosis, depression, learning disabilities, current suicidal ideation or previous suicide attempts and that these were picked up in police screening in 79%, 69%, 50%, 84% and 68% of cases.

13 For example, one suspect reported to the police that he had brain damage and had attended a "special school" and had difficulty answering the questions asked of him.

14 See Skinns (2011a: 64) for a fuller discussion.

15 Across the cities in the research, children were considered to be those aged 17 years or under, with the exception of the English cities where it was 16 years and under, at the time of the research, though since 2015, this has changed to 17 years and under.

16 Though harder, it is possible to dispute a detainee's age. For instance, if a detainee is unwilling to provide their date of birth, it may be difficult to ascertain their age and thus become the subject of dispute, particularly for those in their mid-to-late teens. Furthermore, for older teenagers, staff may also dispute whether they need additional support. For example, in AUSPO3, even though the law defines a child as 17 years and under, the custody manager decided, with regard to a 17-year-old arrested on a warrant, that after unsuccessfully trying to contact a support person at 4am, not to wait for a support person to arrive before processing this detainee.

17 Peace Commissioners replaced Justices of the Peace in the 1920s. This is an honorary title and Peace Commissioners are appointed by the Minister of Justice and Equality to perform a range of civic duties within the communities in which they live (Hennessey, 2014).

18 Taylor and Bareja (2005: 12) found that 26% of all custody incidents in October 2002 involved Aboriginal and Torres Strait Islander detainees, meaning that indigenous people were 17 times more likely to be involved in a custody incident (per relevant population) than non-indigenous people. They also note that this over-representation has declined since 1992 when the first National Custody Survey was conducted.

19 This point was recently recognised by HMIC (2015: 16) in a thematic inspection on vulnerable people in police custody in England, where it was noted that (Afro-Caribbean) black citizens should be considered vulnerable because of "pronounced concern" about their relationships with the police, for example.

20 In the 19th and 20th century "[t]aking action against intoxicated persons, pimps, prostitutes, Aboriginals, vagrants and other 'disorderly' subjects formed the focus of uniformed policing from its inception in Australia" (Bronitt and Stenning, 2011: 324). As a result, the police therefore play a role in reproducing existing inequalities in society.

21 There is a significant body of literature which has explored racist attitudes and behaviour, as well as individual level and institutional racism in the police and other parts of the criminal justice process, including the Royal Commission into Aboriginal Deaths in Custody (1991), Chan (1996), Blagg et al. (2005: 52–3).

22 Misdemeanour and felony is the distinction drawn in the American criminal process between less serious offences (such as minor thefts and drug offences) and more serious offences (such as rape and murder).

23 Women in the criminal justice system are more likely to be sole carers for children, as well as to have experienced sexual and physical abuse as children and domestic abuse as adults, and furthermore, they are more likely to have experienced precarious living circumstances connected to deprivation, homelessness, and unemployment (Wyld et al., 2018: 6). Hence, female prisoners exhibit higher rates of self-harm than men and generally do not cope as well in prison (Corston, 2007: 70, 23).

24 This high confession rate may partly arise because women's specific needs are more amenable to exploitation by the police to secure confessions. For example, in Ireland, the Morris Tribunal found that Roisin McConnell, who was unlawfully arrested as an accessory to Richie Barron's murder, was denied information on who was caring for her child and was told he would be taken into care, in order to encourage her to confess (Conway, 2010: 66–79).

25 These factors also intersect with gender and socioeconomic status in police custody (Parmar, 2018) which, when conflated, may contribute to stereotyping, discrimination, and criminalisation (Bosworth, 2018).

Conclusion

The book in short

The book began with a 'research puzzle.' Whilst collecting data in police detention in an American city in 2009, I was fascinated by why it was that police officers provided such varying responses to the question of how long they were legally entitled to detain someone in police custody. This was particularly so given that the same question in the other cities in the research in Australia, England and Ireland elicited a straightforward answer and possibly also a reference to the relevant piece of legislation. In order to explore this puzzle and in the spirit of engaging in comparative research which hopefully avoids the related pitfalls of ethnocentrism and relativism (Nelken, 2010: 22; Zedner, 1995), I have taken a somewhat circuitous route in trying to unravel it, by providing as much relevant theoretical and contextual material as possible in Chapters 2–4. This provided a platform on which to base subsequent empirical chapters. This contextual information is also vital given the underdeveloped nature of comparative research in police studies (de Maillard and Roché, 2016; Body-Gendrot and de-Wenden, 2014: 2, 9–10; Mawby, 1990: 4–5). As such, Chapters 2–4 are a mine for comparative researchers and students with an interest in police work in Australia, England, Ireland and the US.

Chapter 2 set out the conceptual framework for the book. I examined the significance of *whether* citizens are accorded their rights and entitlements in police detention, that is, their legality, which has traditionally been framed through notions of crime control and due process (Packer, 1968). Also noted was the importance of *how* the police used their authority. It was argued that legitimate styles of authority, resting on notions of procedural fairness (Donner et al., 2015; Tyler et al., 2015; Mazerolle et al., 2013), are accompanied by more coercive styles of authority, based on sanctions and rewards, including the use of force or the provision of hot drinks and cigarettes (Crewe, 2009: 8–86; Bittner, 1970: 26). They are also accompanied by symbolic styles of authority rooted in the tacit sentiments and beliefs that the public hold about the police, which inform the culture of policing (Loader and Mulcahy, 2006: 55). It was also argued that, for the most part, police officers exercise discretion about whether and how they use their authority, with a long history of scholarship pointing to the centrality of discretion to police officers of all ranks, though especially for more junior officers on the street. This chapter also explored the way that police authority is held to account through formal and informal rules, examining the evidence for Ericson's (2007) conceptual schema of "following the rules," "using the rules," "beyond the rules," "within the rules," and "without rules," paying particular attention to how this framework applies to police detention.

In Chapter 3, I examined the configuration of neoliberalism in the selected countries. For the purposes of the book, neoliberalism is understood as varying in its effects both within and between countries. It coalesces around a series of interlinked ideas, including free-market fundamentalism and the idea that the state should play a more limited role in the lives of citizens, for example, through the rolling back of the welfare state or the deregulation of markets. In addition, neoliberalism is understood as encouraging a growing emphasis on individualism and personal responsibility for supposedly free-willed, rational social actors, who can be held responsible for perceived failings. This includes those in the criminal justice system, who are also particularly susceptible to a growing grip on them by the state, particularly young black men from deprived communities (Lerman and Weaver, 2014: 181; O'Neill and Loftus, 2013). Drawing on Cavadino and Dignan (2006a), who regard the US as archetypal, in terms of its neoliberal climate and its effects on penality, I examined the evidence on how this neoliberal climate is manifest in Australia, England, Ireland and the US. I argued that the US is exceptional in terms of its embracing of neoliberal policies, as well as in terms of its high levels of economic inequality and low levels of human development, according to the UN Human Development Index (UN, 2015; Wilkinson and Pickett, 2010: 174), relative to the rest. The UK is also neoliberal but less so than the US, based on these measures, with its social democratic history partially moderating the effects of neoliberalism. Whether Ireland or Australia follows next is contentious. On the one hand, Australia has higher levels of income inequality than Ireland. On the other hand, Ireland is more avowedly neoliberal in terms of its economic and social policies, as indicated all too well by the rise and fall of the 'Celtic Tiger.'

In Chapter 4, I turned my attention to patterns of policing, briefly noting, first, the shared history of the police in Australia, England, Ireland and the US. It was argued that the concept of the 'police' originated in France, but was then borrowed and reinterpreted by the English, most notably by police reformers like Sir Robert Peel, who was central to the creation of the Metropolitan Police in 1829. However, the idea that a police force could be hierarchically organised and publicly-funded had, in fact, emerged 45 years earlier in Dublin in 1786. The model of the New Police in England was then exported and reinterpreted in the US and Australia to suit local conditions, such as large and hard-to-govern populations and indigenous opposition to colonial rule. It was also argued that elements of this police history have continued into the present, in particular, the localised and discretionary nature of American police work (Brodeur, 2010: 70; Scott, 2010; Walker, 2008; Haller, 1976), which contrasts with the more impersonal, but also slightly less localised, statewide and nationalised forms of policing in England, Australia and Ireland, respectively. With reference to legal accountability arrangements, it was furthermore argued that the highly discretionary nature of police work in the US is symbiotically linked to the limited codification of police powers in statutes in the US. This places the US further at odds with Australia, England and Ireland, contributing to ambiguities in what police officers understood about the legal rules and a looser approach to putting police powers into practice.

Chapter 5 was the first of the empirical chapters, in which I examined perceptions of the language, conditions, routines, rituals, and informal and formal rules inside police detention. It was argued that to an extent, all the detention facilities in the research exercised some degree of coercive control over detainees. This was evident in the routine use of the term 'prisoner' to refer to those who were merely suspected of having committed an offence, in the sometimes poor-quality and physically oppressive conditions in which suspects were detained, as well as in how these physical spaces were used (e.g. the cramming of multiple detainees into a single cell). Such coercive control was particularly evident in the American city in the research, which was to some extent enabled by the (perceived) distant nature of the law from everyday police detention work. This contrasted markedly with the profound sense of importance that staff in the other cities attached to the legal rules surrounding their work. The cities in the research were more similar, however, in terms of the routinised and ritualised nature of the processes and procedures that detainees faced on arrival into police detention facilities. This included when they were booked-in, risk-assessed and searched. They were also similar in terms of the informal rules that guided police practices, connected to suspiciousness, solidarity, a prosecutorial mindset and casual bigotry.

In Chapter 6, drawing on the empirical and existing research, I examined the legality of police custody. Specifically, I considered how the right to silence, the right to legal advice and the right not to be detained indefinitely by the police were put into practice in the cities in the research. It was argued that the coercive custody environment was to some extent mitigated by the possibility of detainees making use of a range of custodial rights, but this was to a lesser extent in the American city. This was because, as shown in Chapter 5, in the American city, the custody environment was more oppressive and suspects had fewer rights on paper, about which they were informed only if they were to be formally interrogated by the police. It was also argued in this chapter that some legal rules – in particular, the rules about how long someone may be detained by the police in the American city – appeared especially distant from the day-to-day decision-making of police officers. This seemed to be rooted not just in police officer discretion, which has historically been seen as the "hallmark" of American policing (Brodeur, 2010: 71; Scott, 2010; Walker, 2008; Haller, 1976) but also in the ambiguities and complexities of the law (see Chapter 4). This personalised and discretionary approach to police work has also been further accentuated under the more extreme conditions of neo-liberalism in the US (see Chapter 3), particularly as a result of the emphasis on individualism and the need for personal responsibility. It was also concluded that such uncertainties and ambiguities have the potential to undermine the legality and potentially the legitimacy of police detention.

In Chapter 7, I explored *how* the police used their authority, considering the different styles of authority that the police were found to employ in police detention. Staff were found to use their authority in three main ways. First, they sometimes exhibited a more legitimate style of authority, which included showing respect and acknowledging detainees as human beings, though there were also clear instances of disrespectful treatment too. The predominant tendency across all the police detention facilities, however, was for staff to employ their authority in a coercive way, employing rewards and sanctions in order to secure detainee compliance, which was the second style of authority. Third, particularly in the American city, there was a strong sense of the symbolic authority of the police in police detention, which seemed to leave detainees with the impression that they had little choice other than to follow police directions. This was rooted in threats of the use of force, including Tasers, and in the manifestly coercive police custody environment, as described in Chapter 5. It can also be understood as a product of the political socialisation of "custodial citizens." That is, through multiple contacts with criminal justice institutions, with this particularly impacting on young black men from deprived communities, both in the past and present (Lerman and Weaver, 2014: 10, 200;Muhammad, 2010: 225; Bass, 2001).

Finally, in Chapter 8, drawing again on the empirical evidence from the present research, as well as the existing research, including Fineman's (2008, 2010) vulnerability framework, I examined the ways in which police custody was adjusted for detainees deemed vulnerable. Specifically, I considered how vulnerability was defined, identified and responded to in police custody in the cities in the research, as well as examining the implications of this. For the purposes of the chapter, those considered vulnerable were children, detainees who had medical conditions, mental health conditions or learning disabilities, women and the linguistically diverse. It was argued that the effects of the coercive custody environment and coercive styles of authority, as documented in Chapters 5 and 7, were only partially mitigated for vulnerable detainees: adaptations of police custody tended only to occur when detainees visibly demonstrated their vulnerability. These adaptations largely occurred only in the Australian, English and Irish cities. When detainees' vulnerabilities were less conspicuous, specialist safeguards for vulnerable de-tainees could be sidestepped, as a consequence of the vagaries of the law, as well as the discretionary powers of the police. As a result, I concluded that decisions taken about vulnerable detainees were more discretionary (due to the vagaries of the law), but also more individualised (due to the dependence on individual detainees to demonstrate their vulnerabilities), than for the rights and entitlements examined in Chapter 6.

Together these chapters help to illuminate and explain the 'research puz-zle,' which prompted this book. My main thesis is that discretion played a role, both in *whether* and *how* the police used their authority across the police detention facilities, in all of the cities in the research. This was particularly the case in the US city, for example, in relation to decisions about the length of police detention. By contrast, in the other cities/jurisdictions of interest, the law seemed to feature more heavily in discretionary decision-making and appeared to have a more central place in the culture of police detention. The exceptionalism of the city in the US and the greater similarity between the cities in England, Ireland and Australia, with regard to the role of dis-cretionary decision-making and the law in police work, may be partially explained by the historical centrality of discretion to American police work (Brodeur, 2010: 71; Scott, 2010; Walker, 2008; Haller, 1976). Also important are the closer ties between Australia, England and Ireland, geographically speaking, in the case of Ireland, but also in terms of their values as indicated, for example, through Australia's current and Ireland's past membership of the Commonwealth. However, a further important explanation of the difference between the city in the US and the rest is its exceptionalism when it comes to neoliberalism. In a city/jurisdiction in which neoliberal values, such as of individualism, personal responsibility and a limited state have a particularly prominent place, it is unsurprising, therefore, to find such values embodied in the day-to-day practices of police officers in the American city in the research, namely, in the individualised discretionary decisions taken about citizens in police detention. That is, neoliberalism and its associated values seemed to accentuate historical tendencies towards highly discretionary police practices in the city in the US. The particularly wide discretion in the American city in the research, provided scope for disparities and unfairness in the way that the police treated citizens in police detention. This was particularly so for vulnerable detainees, where vague laws combined with discretionary police powers and a particularly individualised way of applying them to detainees. Therefore, discretionary decision-making in relation to (vulnerable) citizens in police detention, especially in the city in the US, perpetuated neoliberal values, whilst also potentially adding to and compounding the inequalities wrought by neoliberalism. Therefore, echoing Kaplan-Lyman (2012), the police can be seen as a site of neoliberal governance, albeit neoliberalism is not the only explanation provided in the present book for the highly discre-tionary nature of police decision-making in the US.[1]

The foregoing chapters also further elaborate on the relationship between police detention and citizenship set out in Chapter 1. With reference to the Marshallian tripartite conceptualisation of citizenship involving the right to civil, political and social rights, I considered why it was important to conceptualise those held in police detention not just as suspects, but as citizens. Regarding suspects as citizens has a humanising and valorising effect, whilst also acknowledging the political aspects of police work, including the potential for police detention to add to existing inequalities, under conditions of neoliberalism. What the book has shown is that there were indeed barriers to civil rights, particularly to justice, based on due process and that this was especially so in the US city, judging by the limited access that suspects had to rights, such as legal advice or silence, in theory or practice (see Chapter 6). There was also an apparent lack of access to the right to justice based on equality before the law, given the limited adaptation of police detention for vulnerable suspects (see Chapter 8), but also given the way that neoliberal values seemed to influence staff expectations of suspects. For example, the need for vulnerable suspects to perform their vulnerability seemed to mirror the need for citizens to actively, rationally and responsibly perform their duties to demonstrate themselves as active, not passive, citizens in neoliberal societies. Similarly, police detention also mirrored or perhaps enabled narratives about those considered deserving and undeserving, which are evident in the literature on neoliberal citizenship. For example, some police officers took the view that rights and entitlement should only be available to 'good' and thus deserving suspects, of which they did not encounter many. Together this adds nuance and texture to Lerman and Weaver's (2014: 28) concept of custodial citizenship, revealing additional layers linked to blame and personal responsibility, vulnerability and its individualising effects, and the police role in reinforcing these neoliberal values.

In the remainder of this conclusion, I now further elaborate and unpack the overarching thesis of this book. I also examine the implications of the work for how the relationship between neoliberalism and police authority might be conceptualised in future research, as well as for state-citizen relations in neoliberal countries. Finally, I end by offering some suggestions about what might be done about the entrenchment of inequalities, as a result of discretionary decision-making in police detention.

Discretion, and the formal and informal rules of police detention

This book began by exploring the uncertainties about the length of police detention expressed by participants in the American city, relative to participants in cities in Australia, England and Ireland. My initial hypothesis was that police officers in this American city lacked familiarity with the legal rules and, as a consequence, acted with a greater degree of discretionary power. Together this was suggestive of a larger gulf between the law in the books and the law in practice in this American city compared to the other cities in the research. This book has shown partial support for this initial hypothesis. When it came to decisions about *whether* to apply legal rules, such as about silence, legal advice and length of detention, police officers in the American city considered themselves to have a greater degree of leeway than in the other cities in the research (see Chapters 5 and 6). However, this was not just because of a lack of familiarity with the legal rules. Though the Miranda rules are fairly straight-forward, how they have since been adapted and amended by the courts is not (see Chapter 4). Crucially, this made for a complex set of legal rules which were harder to apply in practice than in the other cities in the research, where such case law relating to police powers has been, generally speaking, eventually codified in statutes. As such, the discretionary power of the police in the American city in the research was rooted not only in the sense of importance that police officers attached to discretionary decision-making, but also to the vagaries of the legal rules, arising from the complex ways in which they were incorporated into practice. Moreover, it was hard to disentangle the relative importance of each of these elements of the discretionary decision-making process in this American city. Regardless, taken together, they afforded the police in the American city a greater degree of power when it came to discretionary decisions about whether to put legal rules into practice.

In terms of Ericson's (2007) typology (set out in Chapter 2), this suggests that, broadly speaking, police officers in the Australian, English and Irish cities tended to operate according to the "within the rules" type, whilst in the American city, particularly with regard to the length of detention, police officers seemed to operate according to the "beyond the rules" type. In the Australian, English and Irish cities, legal rules about the right to silence, to legal advice and to not be detained for unspecified periods were embedded in various forms of communication within the police organisations in these cities, some of which were shared with detainees. For example, they existed in the statutes and their accompanying guidance, with such guidance being available for detainees to read (in Australia, England and Ireland); booking-in processes, such as when detainees were read their rights on arrival into police detention and prior to interrogation (in Australia, England and Ireland); the police caution (in Australia and England); risk-assessment questions/documents (England and Australia); and the information that was recorded on the custody record (in Australia and England and to a lesser extent in Ireland) (see Chapters 5 and 6 for further details). This is not to say that the police always operated within these rules, but the overall mentality with which they approached their role in police detention seemed to rest on an assumption that there were a set of rules, within which they should operate, as much as possible (see Chapter 5). These legal rules were largely inescapable because of how embedded they were in various communication tools that existed in police detention in the cities in these jurisdictions.

This embedding of legal rules in these forms of communication seemed less prevalent in the American city. These forms of communication did exist, including the police caution and the reading of rights, though this was only provided immediately prior to interrogation, as well as in custody records and medical checklists, though they were basic and poorly kept (see Chapter 5). However, staff did not seem to operate with the same level of regard for formal rules as they did in the other cities in the research (see Chapter 5). This was illustrated by practices, such as detaining but not arresting citizens, and by the uncertainties that existed about the length of police detention (see Chapters 5 and 6). As such, discretionary decisions about whether to formally arrest someone or how long they should be detained seemed to have a logic of their own, which existed beyond the formal legal rules. For example, as noted in Chapters 5 and 6, how long someone was detained or whether someone was detained but not arrested was often connected to the practicalities of the police investigation, rather than to any sense of importance attached to legal rules and the need for procedural correctness. At times then, formal legal rules seemed to be superfluous to police practices, existing only as part of the background to discretionary police decision-making. Hence, police officers in the American city can be characterised as largely operating with a set of values and beliefs that corresponded to the "beyond the rules" type.

American exceptionalism?

Thus far it has been suggested that relative to the other cities in the research, the US city was an outlier in terms of the scope of police officers' discretionary power, affecting decisions about *whether* they used their authority. This resulted in limited rights and entitlements, in practice, for those citizens who found themselves in police detention, which, as explored in Chapter 8, particularly affected vulnerable detainees. As noted in Chapters 5 and 7, the American city was also anomalous in terms of the relative coerciveness of its custody environment and with regard to the predominance of symbolic styles of authority. The findings presented in the book, therefore, raise the question of why the American city was so distinct from the other cities in the research. Based on the evidence presented in this book, these differences appear to be for two sets of interconnected reasons, relating, first, to traditions and beliefs about discretionary police decision-making, the police role and the rule of law. Second, they relate to the socio-cultural-political context of the police institution. Both of these are examined, in turn, next.

Traditions and beliefs about discretionary police decision-making, the police role and the rule of law

First, the outlier status of the US city can be explained by the historically discretionary nature of police work in the US. As noted in Chapter 4, localised and discretionary police work was part of the American response to living in a large and difficult-to-govern country, in which power became dispersed as part of the federal system. As such, unlike in England, discretion became the "hallmark" of American policing (Brodeur, 2010: 71; Scott, 2010; Walker, 2008; Haller, 1976). As Brodeur (2010: 70) notes, it depended on close connections between the police and citizens and on citizens' informal expectations of individual officers, rather than on formal or legal standards. There were certain factors that encouraged a similarly personalised and discretionary approach to police authority in England (e.g. localised policing structures) and in Ireland (e.g. Irish informalism). However, they were overridden by the desire for the police to be answerable to the law in England as part of the Peelian principles of policing, which continue to exert a significant influence on police work today, and also by the national, centralised structure of the police in Ireland. By contrast, in Australia, police reformers were quick to establish a centralised approach to police work controlled by government officials at the centre of each state, suggesting more of a top-down impersonal approach to police authority, than in the US.

Second, the more limited role of the law in police work in police detention in the American city might also be explained by the relative ineffectiveness of the law 'in the books' and the courts in safeguarding suspects' rights, compared to the more robust approach taken in Australia, England and Ireland (Dixon, 2019; Weisselberg, 2017). This is partly due to measures, such as the European Convention on Human Rights (ECHR) and European Union (EU) Directives on Procedural Rights of suspects in England and Ireland, which provide a broader array of rights to suspects, including, for example, that they be provided with legal counsel prior to police interrogation (Weisselberg, 2017). The ECHR also conveys the importance attached to human rights in Europe, a discourse which is absent from the US (Fineman, 2010).

However, the ineffectiveness of the law is also rooted in the greater emphasis in the US on ex post facto judicial interventions (by not admitting confessions or admissions), rather than on ex ante regulation of police detention practices through legislation (Dixon, 2019). As such, the rules of police detention in the US are part of an ever-changing legal terrain, which is never meaningfully consolidated into legislation, which could be used to prevent malpractice from happening in the first place. The American Constitution, its amendments and associated case law offer some clarification of the way that the police may use their powers in police detention. However, as discussed in Chapter 4, this is on a piecemeal basis, depending, for example, on which issues are considered by the courts and also on whether these court rulings are subsequently effectively communicated to police officers, such as through police training manuals and directives, and then put into practice. Simon (2011), moreover, describes the American Constitution as an "empty vessel" which has been filled by different interpretations, including by Republican-leaning judges in the Supreme Court. By contrast, legislation such as Police and Criminal

Evidence Act 1984 (PACE) in England, the Criminal Justice Act 1984 in Ireland and similar legislation in Australia, as well as updates to the associated Guidance and Codes of Practice ensure that changes to the law are communicated in a more systematic way to police officers, lawyers and detainees. As a result, relative to the other cities in the research, it may have been more difficult for police practices in the American city to keep pace with changes introduced via case law. This might explain why it was that the operational police officers in the American city in the research were unfamiliar with court rulings, for example, about the 48 hours of detention permitted before someone must be put before a judge.

As for the more coercive nature of the custody environment, in the city in the US, as well as the greater reliance on symbolic forms of authority, this can be explained with reference to the historical role of the police in American society. As noted in Chapter 4, the police in the US did not adopt the quiet kind of coercion (policing by consent) developed in England (Brodeur, 2010: 72). Hence, soon after the introduction of modern police organisations in the US, it became commonplace for them to be armed with a gun, albeit this also fitted with prevailing traditions of US settlers enforcing law and order for themselves and of the right to bear arms (Waddington, 1999a). As argued in Chapters 4 and 7, it is possible that such traditions, along with the historically racialised nature of policing in the US, continue to have relevance for contemporary police (detention) practices, setting the tone for a style of authority which rests on the symbolism of the might of the police. In contemporary times, custodial citizens – whose experiences *inside* police detention were illuminated in the present book – have also become socialised into this understanding of the police as an authoritarian, totalising institution, through multiple contacts with criminal justice institutions (Lerman and Weaver, 2014: 28). Together this seemed to result in detainees, in the city in the US, having an overriding sense that they had no other choice than to do what the police asked them to do

The socio-cultural-political climate

Since beliefs about discretionary police decision-making and the rule of law do not exist in a vacuum (see Chapter 2), it is vital to examine the ways in which the wider socio-cultural-political context might also explain the outlier status of the American city when it came to the use of discretion and the role of the law in police detention. First, perhaps the American city was culturally further apart from the other cities in the research. Ireland is geographically close to England, as well as being, in theory, forever joined to it geopolitically through Northern Ireland. As members of the EU, at least at the time of writing, Ireland and England are also linked together through a shared human rights framework, the ECHR. This has been central in clarifying the emphasis in England and Ireland (and across Europe) in relation to police custody (and other policing matters) on protecting not just due process rights, but human rights. Also important are the closer ties between Australia, England and Ireland, as a result of Australia's current and Ireland's past membership of the Commonwealth. Though to some extent the Commonwealth can be seen as a not necessarily welcome relic of the colonial past, through its networks, common laws, common values and common language of English, it continues to be a "radiating influence" (Letts, 2016). Taken together, it is no surprise to see that police custody policies and practices have been shared in the past and present across Australia, England and Ireland. For example, since the 1990s, changes to the right to silence in Ireland and in parts of Australia were in part a consequence of the precedent set by the introduction of a qualified right to silence in England, whilst in parts of Australia, the codification of police powers in police detention also drew directly on PACE 1984, including its terminology and principles, though there were also important points of variation, such as with regard to the length of detention provisions (Dixon, 1997: 225).

A second important explanation of the difference in police detention practices between the city in the US and the rest is its exceptionalism when it comes to neoliberalism. Drawing on a variety of indices, in Chapter 3, I argued that the US is exceptional in terms of its embracing of neoliberal policies, high levels of economic inequality and low levels of human development, according to the UN Human Development Index (UN, 2015), relative to the rest (see also Wilkinson and Pickett, 2010: 174). By contrast, the UK is less neoliberal, with Australia and Ireland being even less neoliberally orientated than the UK and fairly evenly matched with each other. A key question then is how does the neoliberal climate – encompassing values of personal responsibility, autonomy and the free market, as well as a declining welfare state and growing penal state – impact on police practices in police detention? That is, how do neoliberal values and practices become embedded in the day-to-day police detention practices of police officers, such as those in the American city in the research, which was also likely to be more neoliberal in its orientation than was the case in the other cities in the research?

It is possible to offer a few ideas, at this point, in answer to these questions. The wider discretionary power of the police in the city in the US, as already described in this chapter, potentially provided the vacuum into which neoliberal values absorbed from the wider sociocultural milieu were able to flourish and influence decision–making and behaviour. That is, these decisions and behaviour arose from an ideological position, which may have been tacit, rather than necessarily overt, yet still influential in terms of the social and political arrangements that were potentially advanced. One area in which this was apparent was with regard to the treatment of vulnerable detainees. As noted in Chapter 8, for these vulnerable detainees, there seemed to be a peculiarly high level of expectation in the American city that they would take personal responsibility for identifying themselves as vulnerable, rather than relying on staff to reach a judgement about this. If they did not, then detainees were seen as the ones to blame for anything untoward that subsequently happened to them in the criminal justice process, as a result of their vulnerability.[2] Hence, at the end of Chapter 8, I described these decisions about vulnerable detainees as more discretionary and individualised, than was the case for the rights and entitlements examined in Chapter 6, particularly in the American city.

This responsibilisation of vulnerable detainees and the tendency to blame them for their failings, in this case, to inform the police about their vulnerabilities, was also potentially enabled by a favourable police cultural climate – that is, neoliberal values chimed with the beliefs and values that staff in police detention had about the way things were done. For example, expectations about detainees taking personal responsibility for their actions seemed to affirm what the police already knew, namely, that part of their role was to police as well as socially discipline the disreputable and those lacking in self-reliance (Choongh, 1997: 100). This interaction between neoliberal values and police culture may also go some way towards explaining the more coercive conditions found in the American city, evident in the conditions, routines and rituals described in Chapter 5. To some extent, the police may have believed that such things were justified (or were at least not in need of challenge) because detainees 'deserved it.' Taken together, this suggests that the neoliberal climate has important consequences for the police; it empowers and legitimises their informal understandings of their job in police detention, whilst also symbolically and materially confirming detainees' low social positions, lack of credibility and spoiled identities.

The exceptional nature of the neoliberal climate in the US may also be a contributing factor to the wide discretionary power afforded to the police in the American city in the research, (along with some of the historical reasons described earlier in this chapter). In a neoliberal climate where there is an expectation that individuals should be autonomous and responsible for themselves, it logically follows that the police might see the decisions they take in the same vein, attaching greater importance to themselves, as the key decision-maker, rather than to the rules and structures that surround the decisions they take. That is, the exceptional neoliberal climate in the US may serve to accentuate the already greater discretionary power in the American city in the research, as part of a wider sociocultural context in which individuals feel that it is right and necessary that they are autonomous and responsible for their own decisions and behaviour. This suggests that neoliberal values may be being reproduced in police working cultures on the ground. As argued later in this chapter, this has implications for relationships between citizens and the state, with the staff in police detention thus playing a role in entrenching inequalities in neoliberal political economies. This was particularly potent in the American city in the research, given the wide discretionary powers of the police there.

State-citizen relations in neoliberal political climates

As noted above, the police have discretionary power in police detention, both in terms of *whether* but also *how* they use their authority. This was particularly evident in the American city in the research, as a consequence of the historical role ascribed to discretion in police work in the US, the complexities and ambiguities of the law and the neoliberal climate. The question explored here is what this means for citizens, in terms of their relationship with the state. One implication is that this discretionary authority places citizens in police detention in a disempowered position, relative to the police and, by implication, the state. For example, this discretionary authority, especially when combined with the symbolic and totalising aspects of police authority, meant that detainees were less likely to regard themselves as even having any rights and entitlements whilst detained by the police, let alone being able to assert them. Hence why the detainees mentioned at the start of Chapter 6 said "Rights? We ain't got no rights in here, you should know that by now" (AMEPO6). The largely coercive and unpleasant police custody environment, again, particularly in the American city, was a factor which further disempowered detainees relative to the police. This disempowered status of detainees has consequences for them as citizens. As argued later in this section, it has a cumulative effect on those multiply arrested, which may entrench existing inequalities, especially for those who were already vulnerable and especially in more neoliberal climates. As Lerman and Weaver (2014: 28) also note, these cumulative experiences also come to shape custodial citizens' notion of citizenship.

This greater degree of the police's discretionary decision-making in the American city cannot therefore be seen as indicative of less state involvement in the lives of citizens. Instead, it seemed that this discretionary power of the police, in fact, dispersed and thus enhanced the power of the state, as this power was simultaneously everywhere but nowhere. The higher degree of discretionary authority in the American city placed the police in a powerful position relative to (vulnerable) detainees, in the ways that I just described, particularly as this combined with poor physical conditions and the symbolic authority of the police to further undermine the role of detainees. In addition, the power of the police and, by implication, the state, was further enhanced by the rhetoric of Miranda rights. As shown in the present book, Miranda rights existed more in theory than in practice, thereby creating a mantle of fairness for the American Constitution, from which they derive. This prevents pertinent questions from being asked about this Constitution, which might expose its status as an "empty vessel," ripe for shaping by Supreme Court judges of different political persuasions (Simon, 2011) or by discretionary police practices at the local level. It is this shaping of police practices by different actors in different locations that enables state power to become dispersed rather than lessened, particularly for those regularly in contact with criminal justice institutions. In sum, in spite of the stated ideals of neoliberalism (including the need for less state interference in citizens' lives), these institutional practices and arrangements suggest the state to be all the more powerful in its influence. As shown by others in relation to prisons or welfare, for example (Wacquant, 2009b: xvi), this is particularly so for those on the margins, such as young, poor, black men or those who are vulnerable due to a learning disability or mental health condition. Over time, this may have a cumulative and disempowering effect.

The second main implication of the book for the state-citizen relationship is that police-citizen interactions in police detention may be a "teachable" moment – maybe even the "ultimate" teachable moment – in a neoliberal climate. In this context, detainees may be learning how to be a responsibilised and individualised subject rather than a citizen with a valued place in society (Skinns et al., 2017; Tyler et al., 2014). This may be particularly so in the more neoliberal climate of the US (see Chapter 3). As noted above and in Chapter 8, it was in the American city where police officers expressed the most reluctance to recognise their own responsibility towards identifying and responding to detainees' vulnerabilities, with their higher degree of discretionary power enabling them to impress upon vulnerable detainees the need to be responsible for themselves. This is one reason why police detention and police practices, more generally, cannot be seen as merely a "dragnet" which has contributed to the "hypertrophy of the penal state" (Wacquant, 2009a: 58). Rather, police-citizen interactions, including in police detention, can be seen as one of the mechanisms by which citizens learn about or have confirmed their place in the neoliberal world. In the case of detainees, particularly vulnerable detainees, this means that they may learn that they do not have access to the full complement of civil, political and social rights, which are the foundation of being a person of equal value (Faulkner, 2003; Marshall and Bottomore, 1992: 18). In this sense, then, police detention is one of the contexts in which neoliberal citizen-state relations are constituted and reproduced.

The third and final implication of the book is that whilst police detention may appear like a microcosm, which is, in some way, separate from its wider socio-cultural-political context, the present book suggests this to be a misunderstanding. The individuals who work in and are detained in police detention are intimately connected to wider societal institutions and the state. Just as the police institution is a litmus paper reflecting the unfolding dynamics of this wider context (Reiner, 1992), so too is police detention. As argued in the present book, historical precedents and traditions, such as the significance of discretion to police work in the US, as well as the climate of neoliberalism, become writ large on police detention practices. Therefore, since neoliberalism generates and entrenches inequalities, for example, through mass incarceration and the dissolution of the welfare state, so too can police detention. Alongside these neoliberal processes of governance, police detention serves to reproduce and entrench the inequalities of the wider neoliberal state. This is none more so than in relation to vulnerable citizens who, as shown in the present book, are more easily swept up in the police's "dragnet" with police detention, in particular, marking the entrance point to the rest of the criminal justice process. As such, echoing Kaplan-Lyman (2012), the police can be seen as a site of neoliberal governance, which is different from but also contributes to the neoliberal governance of the penal state.

Conceptualising the relationship between neoliberalism and police authority

The foregoing discussion about the outlier status of the American city in the research, both in terms of its police practices and its wider neoliberal climate, as well as about the implications of the present book for state-citizen relations, points to six hypotheses about how the relationship between neoliberalism and police authority might be conceptualised. As such, it provides some possible areas to explore in future research. These hypotheses are set out in brief next, though I also further unpack each of them in the discussion that follows. The more neoliberal the climate:

1   the greater the likelihood of the police operating with a strong sense of their discretionary power.
2   the greater the likelihood that the police engage in individualised, discretionary decisions about vulnerable citizens.
3   the greater the prevalence of police decision-making and behaviour that conforms to Ericson's (2007) "beyond the rules" type.
4   the more coercive the style of authority that the police employ, albeit this may vary, depending on the setting (e.g. deprived neighbourhoods vs. police detention).
5   the higher the likelihood that discretionary police decision-making becomes a vehicle for perpetuating neoliberal values of personal responsibility, autonomy and blame of (vulnerable) citizens.
6   the greater the likelihood that the outcomes of police actions will coalesce with other forms of exclusion, thereby entrenching existing inequalities and reconstituting notions of citizenship.

First, this discussion suggests that the more neoliberal the climate (based on the measures set out in Chapter 3), the more likely it is that the police operate with a higher degree of discretionary power. This is because, to some extent, this discretionary power becomes an outlet for the expression of neoliberal values about the importance of personal responsibility and autonomy, for example, which align with existing informal rules about the role of the police in socially disciplining the disreputable (Choongh, 1997: 100). That said, the expression of these neoliberal values may also be affected by other prevailing traditions and cultures, such as about the historical importance attached to the autonomy of the police.

Second, this greater discretionary power in more neoliberal climates is also likely to be especially abundant and evident in relation to vulnerable citizens for whom, as argued in Chapter 8, the law was seen as more fluid. Such decisions are also likely to be highly individualised, and citizens' vulnerability is also more likely to be seen in isolation, rather than as a whole, the more neoliberal the climate. As a result, vulnerable citizens, in more neoliberal climates, are also more likely to be blamed by the police and other criminal justice organisations for not identifying themselves as vulnerable or for not performing their vulnerability 'enough' so that it is recognised and attended to, at an appropriate point in the criminal justice process.

Third, of the different types of rule-following noted by Ericson (2007), the "beyond the rule" type is likely to be of the greatest relevance in more neoliberal climates, in terms of helping to explain the discretionary decisions of the police. In such contexts, the law is likely to be largely only a backdrop, rather than a guiding principle for those decisions. As noted in this chapter, this type seemed of particular relevance to explaining the discretionary nature of police practices in the American city in the research (which also existed in the most neoliberal climate).

Fourth, both the present research and existing research point to the likelihood of more coercive police practices in more neoliberal settings. Kaplan-Lyman (2012), for example, makes a strong case for social order maintenance practices in New York City (NYC) being more repressive in more deprived neighbourhoods, in part because of the wider context of neoliberal governance. The present research in some ways supports this conclusion, but also adds some nuance to it in relation to police detention. In the present research, aspects of police detention were more coercive in the American city in the research, though this was not necessarily through overt displays of coercive police authority of the kind that Kaplan-Lyman (2012) noted. Whilst the coercive authority of the police was greater in the American city in the research, it rested, to a much greater extent, on threats of coercive police practices and on the symbolism of this authority. This suggests that in neoliberal climates, police authority may be more coercive but will not necessarily be overt in its manifestation.

Finally, the more neoliberal the climate, the more likely it is that police discretionary decisions become a vehicle for the perpetuation of neoliberal values of personal responsibility, individualism, autonomy and the blame of those that cannot live up to such responsibilities. Not only is this likely to further entrench existing inequalities in society, but as examined above, the police are thus likely to play a role in constituting and reproducing neoliberal state-citizen relationships, thereby making them an important site of neoliberal governance in themselves, rather than just a "dragnet" for the penal state.

What is to be done?

It has been argued that the discretionary power of the police provides a mechanism through which neoliberal values, such as about the importance of personal responsibility, are imparted to citizens, especially vulnerable ones. The present book has shown that this seemed to be particularly the case in the American city in the research, which was also located in the most neoliberal climate according to the analysis provided in Chapter 3. This suggests that police-citizen interactions, including in police detention, have the potential to become a "teachable moment" in which those involved learn how to become responsibilised neoliberal citizens. As such, the police are more than just a "dragnet" for the penal state, they also play a role in constituting and reproducing neoliberal values in society, thereby also making them an important site of neoliberal governance. This final section of the book examines the question of what might be done to change this situation.

An obvious response might be to try to curtail the discretionary power of the police, especially in places where this discretion is wider than in others. This could be through additional layers of accountability, such as CCTV cameras, lay visitors and unannounced inspections by external bodies, which might render discretionary decision-making more visible inside police detention. Improvements could also be made to the regulatory process. This might entail, for example, the greater codification of police powers in single pieces of legislation, accompanied by clear guidelines, which are made available to the police, detainees and the wider citizenry, in order to make the formal rules clearer and less complex and thus more understandable. These improvements are of particular relevance to the American city in the research. Such changes might go some way towards closing the gap between the law in the books and the law in practice. However, as discussed in Chapter 2, the inevitability of discretion – for example, because any law or piece of guidance requires interpretation or because sometimes fairness requires bending rather than sticking to the rules – means that discretion will never be entirely eliminated and nor should it be. What is also required is greater reflexivity amongst police officers about the existence of discretion, the way they use their discretionary powers and its consequences, particularly for vulnerable citizens, in terms of the entrenching of existing inequalities. This would also require greater understanding, on the part of police officers, about the political aspects of police work, revolving around the exercise of power in an already unequal society. Furthermore, it might also involve the creation of "new stories," such as about the discretionary power of the police, by and for the police, which "create new and different sensibilities," with managers, for example, playing a role in challenging existing narratives and creating new ones (Shearing, 1995: 57).

One such narrative might emerge from a transformation in the way that vulnerability is conceptualised by the police. This is important given that decisions about vulnerable detainees were particularly prone to being made in an individualised and discretionary manner. Rather than expecting individual detainees or citizens to identify as vulnerable or to 'prove' their vulnerability, drawing on the work of Fineman (2008, 2010), the police could work from the assumption that to some extent, all citizens are vulnerable, meaning that only the least vulnerable are not provided with additional support or safeguarding. Such an approach would also enable better recognition of hidden forms of vulnerable (e.g. women and those with learning disabilities), as well as the overlapping nature of vulnerability for most policed populations in which substance misuse, mental health conditions, learning disabilities and language barriers overlap, to create deleterious consequences, if not properly recognised and attended to by the police. However, as noted in Chapter 8, in all of the cities in the research, vulnerability was not understood in this way. Changes of this kind would therefore require an almost total transformation of the law, policies, procedures, as well as the decision-making and behaviour of the police and other organisations that support vulnerable citizens.

To some extent, such changes to accountability frameworks to curtail discretion or to reorientate the way that the police see vulnerability are only likely to ever scratch the surface of the problems identified in the present book. At their root are existing inequalities which have grown more entrenched as a result of the ascendance of neoliberalism (see Chapter 3). These need to be tackled if the police are to become democratic and equal in their dealings with citizens, including in police detention, not least because equality is likely to have advantages for all of us. As Reiner says, "[s]ocial democracy is needed if we are to avert the barbarisms of excessive crime and repressive control that flow from the deeper evils of inequality and injustice produced by neoliberalism" (Reiner, 2012: 105).[3] Reiner (2012) also notes that, unlike in other fields, such as economics, or other parts of criminology, there has been a tendency in police studies to shy away from examining the role of political economy and the root causes of policing problems, opting instead for piecemeal reforms. Perhaps this was partly because tackling such root causes has seemed for a long time like an impossible dream. This was certainly the case when I began working on this book in 2010, shortly after the election of the Conservative-dominated coalition government in the UK. Since then, meaningful, but also increasingly viable, social democratic opposition has begun to emerge, with the ascendance of political figures, such as Bernie Sanders and Jeremy Corbyn, respectively in the US and the UK.[4] By expressing a commitment to the need to address the inequalities of neoliberalism, as they relate to police detention, it is hoped that this book will add to this growing social democratic momentum, which may make the possibility of tackling societal inequalities less of a dream and increasingly more of a reality.

Notes

1 See Gamble (2001) on why it is important not to reify neoliberalism and thus treat it as the only explanation for social actions and institutional practices.
2 To some extent, there was also an expectation that the courts would weed out any cases where evidence had been improperly obtained as a result of someone's vulnerability (see Chapter 8).
3 These advantages are likely to extend beyond the criminal justice sphere. This is because inequality has been shown to be linked to a range of health and social problems, such as less trust between members of the public, as well as worse mental and physical health and life expectancy (Wilkinson and Pickett, 2010: 52–53, 67, 81).
4 Corbyn's rise to prominence was partially aided by the boom of alternative forms of media (Twitter, YouTube, Facebook, etc.), which helped to more effectively deliver his message to a new and younger audience than might have been possible with conventional forms of media, which have traditionally been more hostile to politicians on the left (Chadwick and Stromer-Galley, 2016). Though potentially problematic, as highlighted by the Cambridge Analytica debacle (Greenfield, 2018), these alternative forms of media are something that left-leaning politicians need to continue to capitalise on in the future.

Methodology

This book draws on two different studies, the broad aims of which were to explore suspects' access to their due process rights whilst in police custody. The first was a mixed-methods study of two police custody areas in cities in the south of England, which explored the impact of inter-agency cooperation on suspects' access to their due process rights. Between February and July 2007, in each custody area, a week-long period of participant observation was followed by semi-structured hour-long interviews with police officers, other criminal justice practitioners and detainees. Some of these data were written up in Skinns (2011). In the second study, data were collected in August, October and November 2009 in cities in Ireland and in jurisdictions in Australia and the US.[1] This research was more exploratory in nature than the study in England. Limited research on police custody in these three jurisdictions meant that the aims of the research were to chart some of the similarities and differences between the jurisdictions in terms of how the police custody process operated, as well as exploring due process rights in practice. In a month spent in a large city in each of the jurisdictions,[2] as much data were collected as possible through observing in police custody areas in the day and at night, and by conducting semi-structured hour-long interviews with police officers. The data from both studies are summarised in Table A.1. These data were thematically coded and analysed using NVivo; primary coding was used to identify broad themes in the data, and this was followed by secondary coding, which attempted to identify sub-themes and the relationships between them.

As shown in Table A.1, more data of different kinds were collected in the first study in England. There were also other limitations to the comparative data collected in the second study. For example, in the comparative research, there were few opportunities to minimise the impact of observer effects on the data collected, simply because less time was spent in each police station. The layout of the detention facilities in the research, particularly in the American city, also enabled the observation of staff more than suspects. When combined with the fact that detainees were not formally interviewed in this second study, it meant that suspects had a limited voice. Furthermore, without the collection of data from relevant police data and documents such as custody records and police training manuals – which was largely due to a shortage of resources – it is impossible to quantify how many suspects accessed their rights and entitlements and the full extent to which police procedures and rules were being followed. Nevertheless, the data from the comparative study is sufficient to begin to document, assess and understand some of the similarities and differences between jurisdictions. These data paint a picture of staff and suspects' *perceptions* of the custody areas, whether the police abided by legal rules, how they used their authority and how they dealt with vulnerable detainees. That said, their exploratory nature, as well as their limited scope, means that they cannot be used to generalise much beyond the specific cities in which the data were collected.

Conducting research on police custody also presents many challenges and opportunities, some of which are accentuated and perhaps even worsened by conducting this kind of research in a comparative setting. Given the importance of these matters but the lack of space in the present book, they are explored in Skinns (forthcoming in 2019). Here, I provide critical reflections and an insider account of the messy and complicated nature of the research process, something which is particularly important given the additional demands of comparative research. In particular, I focus on the challenges of 'getting in' to conduct the research, 'getting on' with participants, 'getting your hands dirty' with regards participation and 'getting out' emotionally unscathed.

Table A.1 Data collected

Jurisdiction	No. of police custody areas	Date of data collection	Hours spent observing	Semi-structured qualitative interviews with police officers (as well as detainees and other practitioners in England)
2 cities in 2 police force areas in England	2	Feb–Sep 2007	336 (42 shifts)	51
1 city in 1 Australian state	3	Aug 2009	44 (4 shifts)	6
1 city in the Republic of Ireland	6	Oct 2009	41 (6 shifts)	8
1 city in 1 American state	7	Nov 2009	59 (7 shifts)	6
Total	18		480 (59 shifts)	71

Notes

1 Like the first, the second study was located in common-law jurisdictions to min-imise differences in the findings attributable to differences in the legal systems. English-speaking jurisdictions were also selected to eliminate language barriers.
2 For reasons of confidentiality, the individual jurisdictions and sites of the re-search are not named.

References

Aas, K. (2013) *Globalization and crime*. London: Sage.

Adebowale, V. (2013) *Independent Commission on Mental Health and Policing Report*. Published online at: http://news.bbc.co.uk/1/shared/bsp/hi/pdfs/10_05_13_report.pdf [last accessed 19 July 2017].

Allen, K. (2012) The model pupil who faked the test: social policy in the Irish crisis, *Critical Social Policy*, 32(3), 422–439.

Amnesty International (2016) *Deadly force: police use of lethal force in the US*, executive summary. New York City, NY: Amnesty International US.

Andreas, P. and Nadelman, E. (2006) *Policing the globe: criminalization and crime control in international relations*. Oxford: Clarendon.

Angiolini, E. (2017) *Report of the Independent Review of Deaths and Serious Incidents in Police Custody*. Published online at: https://www.gov.uk/government/publications/deaths-and-serious-incidents-in-police-custody [last accessed 21 July 2018].

Archer, M. (2010 [1982]) Morphogenesis versus structuration: on combining structure and action, *The British Journal of Sociology – The BJS: Shaping Sociology over 60 Years*, 61(1), 225–252. [Originally published in 1982 *British Journal of Sociology*, 33(4), 455–483].

Ashworth, A. and Redmayne, M. (2014) *The criminal process*. Oxford: Oxford University Press.

Asquith, N. and Bartkowiak-Théron I. (2012) Vulnerability and diversity in policing. In I. Bartkowiak-Théron and N. Asquith (eds.) *Policing vulnerability*. Annandale, NSW: Federation Press, 3–19.

Australian Bureau of Statistics (2016a) Regional population growth, 2010–11. Available at: www.abs.gov.au/ausstats/abs@.nsf/Previousproducts/3218.0Main%20Features12010-11?opendocument&tabname=Summary&prodno=3218.0&issue=2010-11&num=&view= [last accessed 16 August, 2016].

Australian Bureau of Statistics (2016b) *Cultural diversity in Australia*. Available online at: www.abs.gov.au/ausstats/abs@.nsf/lookup/2071.0main+features902012-2013 [last accessed 16 August 2016].

Australian Bureau of Statistics (2017) *Recorded crime – Offenders 2015–2016 – Indigenous Status*. Online at: www.abs.gov.au/ausstats/abs@.nsf/Lookup/by%20Subject/4519.0~2015-16~Main%20Features~Indigenous%20status,%20selected%20states%20and%20territories~5 [last accessed 19 January 2018].

Australian Human Rights' Commission (2016) How are human rights protected in Australian law? Available online at: www.humanrights.gov.au/how-are-human-rights-protected-australian-law [last accessed 12 August 2016].

Ayling, J., Grabosky, P. and Shearing, C. (2009) *Lengthening the arm of the law: enhancing police resources in the twenty-first century*. Cambridge: Cambridge University Press.

Bartels, L. (2012) Twenty years on: indigenous deaths in police custody and lessons from the frontline. In I. Bartkowiak-Théron and N.L. Asquith (eds.) *Policing vulnerability*. Annandale, NSW: Federation Press, 181–197.

Bartkowiak-Théron, I. and Asquith, N.L. (2012) The extraordinary intricacies of policing vulnerability, *Australasian Policing: A Journal of Professional Practice and Research*, 4(2), 43–49.

Bartkowiak-Théron, I. and Crehan, A.C. (2012) "For when equality is given to unequals, the result is inequality": the socio-legal ethics of vulnerable people. In I. Bartkowiak-Théron and N.L. Asquith (eds.) *Policing vulnerability*. Annandale, NSW: Federation Press, 33–46.

Bass, S. (2001) Policing space, policing race: social control imperatives and police discretionary decisions, *Social Justice*, 28(1), 156–176.

Bayley, D.H. (1996) What do the police do? In W. Saulsbury, J. Mott and T. Newburn (eds.) *Themes in contemporary policing*. London: Policy Studies Institute, 29–41.

BBC (2012) Votes for prisoners: Cameron says he will fight the European court, *BBC News Online*. Available online at: www.bbc.co.uk/news/uk-politics-18177776 [Last accessed 4 June 2015].

Beck, U. (1981) *The risk society: towards a new modernity*. London: Sage.

Beck, U. (2000) *What is globalization?* Cambridge: Polity Press.

Beetham, D. (1991) *The legitimation of power*. London: Macmillan Press.

Bellamy, R. (2008) *Citizenship: a very short introduction*. Oxford: Oxford University Press.

Best, D. (2004) *Analysis of ethnic minority deaths in police custody*. Home Office Report. London: HMSO.

Bibby, P. (2015) Overflowing prisons see people locked for days in harsh, threatening temporary cells. *The Sydney Morning Herald*. Available online at: www.smh.com.au/nsw/overflowing-prisons-see-people-locked-for-days-in-harsh-threatening-temporary-cells-20150522-gh7ocl.html [last accessed 22 December 2017].

Birmingham, G. (2006) *Report of the Commission of Investigation (Dean Lyons Case)*. Set up Pursuant to the Commissions of Investigation Act 2004. Available online from the Department of Justice and Equality at: www.justice.ie/en/JELR/Pages/dean_lyons_commission_of_investigation [last accessed 10 July 2017].

Bittner, E. (1970) *The functions of the police in modern society*. Rockville, MD: National Institute of Mental Health.

Bittner, E. (1990) *Aspects of police work*. Boston, MA: Northeastern University Press.

Black, D. (1976 [2010]) *Behavior of law*. Bingley: Emerald Publishing Group Ltd.

Blackstock, J., Cape, E., Hodgson, J., Ogorodova, A. and Spronken, A. (2014) *Inside police custody: an empirical account of suspects' rights in four jurisdictions*. Cambridge: Intersentia Ltd.

Blagg, H., Morgan, N., Cunneen, C. and Ferrante, A. (2005) *Systemic Racism as a Factor in the Overrepresentation of Aboriginal People in the Victorian Criminal Justice System*. Victorian Equality and Human Rights Commission. Available online at: www.humanrightscommission.vic.gov.au/our-resources-and-publications/reports/item/1391-systemic-racism-as-a-factor-in-the-over-representation-of-aboriginal-people-in-the-victorian-criminal-justice-system-sep-2005 [last accessed 30 May 2017].

Body-Gendrot, S. and de Wenden, C. (2014) *Policing the inner city in France, Britain and the US*. Basingstoke, Hampshire: Palgrave Macmillan.

Bosworth, M. (2018) "Working in this place turns your racist": staff, race and power in detention. In M. Bosworth, A. Parmar and Y. Vasquez (eds.) *Race, criminal justice and migration control: enforcing the boundaries of belonging*. Oxford: Oxford University Press.

Bottomley, K. (1991) The detention of suspects in police custody: the impact of the Police and Criminal Evidence Act 1984, *British Journal of Criminology*, 31(4), 347–364.

Bottoms, A.E.B. and Tankebe, J. (2012) Beyond procedural justice: a dialogic approach to police legitimacy in criminal justice, *Journal of Criminal Law and Criminology*, 102(1), 119–170.

Bourdieu, P. and Wacquant, L. (2001) NeoLiberalSpeak: notes on the new planetary vulgate, *Radical Philosophy*, 105 (Jan/February), 2–5.

Bowling, B. (2010) *Policing the Caribbean: transnational security cooperation in practice*. Oxford: Clarendon.

Bowling, B. and Sheptycki, J. (2012) *Global policing*. London: Sage.

Bowling, B. and Weber, L. (2011) Stop and search in global context: an overview, *Policing and Society*, 21(4): 480–488.

Bowling, B., Parmar, A. and Phillips, C. (2008) Policing minority ethnic communities. In T. Newburn (ed.) *Handbook of policing*. Cullompton: Willan, 611–641.

Bradford, B., Jackson, J. and Hough, M. (2014) Police futures and legitimacy: redefining 'good policing'. In J. Fleming (ed.) *The future of policing*. London: Routledge, 29–100.

Bradford, B., Jackson, J., Hough, M. and Farrall, S. (2009) Trust and confidence in criminal justice: a review of the British research literature. In A. Jokinen, E. Ruuskanen, M. Yordanova, D. Markov and M. Ilcheva (eds.) *JUSTIS project working papers review of need: indicators of public confidence in criminal justice for policy assessment*. Helsinki: HEUNI, 141–190.

Bradley, K. (2009) *The Bradley report: Lord Bradley's review of people with mental health problems or learning disabilities in the criminal justice system*. London: The Department of Health, 214–228.

Bridges, L. and Cape, E. (2008) *CDS direct: flying in the face of the evidence*. Other. Centre for Crime and Justice Studies. London: Centre for Crime and Justice Studies. Available online at: http://eprints.uwe.ac.uk/10488 [last accessed 11 January 2018].

Brodeur, J.-P (2010) *The policing web*. Oxford: Oxford University Press.

Bronitt, S. and Finnane, M. (2012) Comparative perspectives on Australia-American policing, *Journal of California Law Enforcement*, 46(3), 18–22.

Bronitt, S. and Stenning, P. (2011) Understanding discretion in modern policing, *Criminal Law Journal*, 35, 319–332.

Brookman, F. and Pierpoint, H. (2003) Access to legal advice for young suspects and remand prisoners, *Howard Journal of Criminal Justice*, 42(5), 452–470.

Brown, D. (1989) *Detention at the police station under the Police and Criminal Evidence Act 1984*. London: Home Office.

Brown, D. (1994) The incidence of right of silence in police interviews: The research evidence reviewed. *Research bulletin* 35: 57. London: Home Office.

Brown, D. (2011) Neoliberalism as a criminological subject, *Australian and New Zealand Journal of Criminology*, 44(1), 129–142.

Brown, G.R. (2016) The blue line on thin ice: police use of force modifications in the era of camera phones and YouTube, *British Journal of Criminology*, 56(2), 293–312.

Brunson, R.K. and Miller, J. (2006) Young black men and urban policing in the United States, *British Journal of Criminology*, 46(4), 613–640.

Bucci, N. and Willingham, R. (2013) 200 people held in police cells, *The Age, Victoria*. Available online at: www.theage.com.au/victoria/200-people-held-in-police-cells-20130704-2pel5.html [last accessed 22 December 2017].

Bucke, T. and Brown, D. (1997) *In police custody: police powers and suspects' rights under the revised PACE Codes of Practice*. London: Home Office.

Bucke, T., Brown, D. and Britain, G. (1997) *In police custody: police powers and suspects' rights under the revised PACE Codes of Practice*. London: Home Office.

Buvik, K. (2016) The hole in the doughnut: a study of police discretion in a nightlife setting, *Policing and Society*, 26(7), 771–788.

Campbell, E. (1999) Towards a sociological theory of discretion, *International Journal of the Sociology of Law*, 27(1), 79–101.

Campbell, J. L. (2010) Neoliberalism's penal and debtor states, *Theoretical Criminology*, 14(1), 59–73.

Cape, E. (2006) *Defending suspects at police stations: the practitioner's guide to advice and representation*. London: Legal Action Group.

Cassell, P. G. and Hayman, B. S. (1996) Police interrogation in the 1990s: an empirical study of the effects of Miranda, *UCLA law Review*, 43, 839–931.

Cassell, P.G. and Fowles, R. (2017) Opening address: still handcuffing the cops? A review of fifty years of empirical evidence of Miranda's harmful effects on law enforcement, *Boston University Law Review*, 97(3), 685–849.

Cassell, P.G. and Hayman, B.S. (1996) Police interrogation in the 1990s: an empirical study of the effects of Miranda, *UCLA Law Review*, 43, 839–931.

Cavadino, M. and Dignan, J. (2006a) Penal policy and political economy, *Criminology and Criminal Justice*, 64(4), 435–456.

Cavadino, M. and Dignan, J. (2006b) *Penal Systems: A comparative approach*. London: Sage.

Cedrone, M.A. (2016) Technology's effect on the forty-eight-hour rule and the administrative steps incident to arrest, *Rutgers University Law Review*, 69, 289–324.

Central Statistics Office (2012) *This is Ireland: highlights from the 2011 census, part 1*. Dublin: Stationery Office.

Chadwick, A. and Stromer-Galley, J. (2016) Digital media, power, and democracy in parties and election campaigns: party decline or party renewal? *The International Journal of Press/Politics*, 21(3), 283–293.

Chan, J. (1996) Changing police culture, *British Journal of Criminology*, 36(1), 109–134.

Chan, J. (1997) *Changing police culture: policing in a multicultural society*. Cambridge: Cambridge University Press.

Chan, J. (1999) Governing police practice: limits of the new accountability, *British Journal of Sociology*, 50(2), 251–270.

Charman, S. and Corcoran, D. (2015) Adjusting the police occupational cultural landscape: the case of An Garda Síochána, *Policing and Society*, 25(5), 484–503.

Chavey, V.W. (1992) The forty-eight hour rule and County of Riverside v. McLaughlin, *Boston University Law Review*, 72, 403–416.

Choongh, S. (1997) *Policing as social discipline*. Oxford: Clarendon.

City Mayors Statistics (2016) The largest US Cities: ranked 1 to 100. Available online at: www.citymayors.com/gratis/uscities_100.html [Last accessed 16 August, 2016].

Clare, I.C.H., Gudjonsson, G.H. and Harari, P.M. (1998) Understanding of the current police caution (England and Wales), *Journal of Community and Applied Social Psychology*, 8(5), 323.

Clark, D. (2014) Filling in the doughnut? Police operational discretion and the law in Australia, *Oxford University Commonwealth Law Journal*, 14(2), 195–224.

Conservative Party (2014) Protecting human rights in the UK: the conservatives' proposals for changing Britain's human rights laws. Available online at: https://fullfact.org/law/conservative-partys-bill-rights/ [last accessed 15 August 2016].

Conway, V. (2010) *The blue wall of silence: the Morris Tribunal and police accountability in Ireland*. Dublin: Irish Academic Press.

Conway, V. (2014) *Policing twentieth century Ireland: a history of An Garda Síochána*. London: Routledge.

Conway, V. (2017a) *Personal communication*, Discussion over the telephone and email, 17 July 2017.

Conway, V. (2017b) 'The right to legal advice in the Garda Station: DPP v Doyle', Blog post on Human Rights in Ireland. Available online at: http://humanrights.ie/constitution-of-ireland/the-right-to-legal-advice-in-the-garda-station-dpp-v-doyle/ [Last accessed 17 July 2017].

Corston, J. (2007) *The Corston Report: a report by Baroness Jean Corston of a review of women with particular vulnerabilities in the criminal justice system*. London: Home Office.

Crewe, B. (2009) *The prisoner society: power, adaptation and social life in an English prison*. Oxford: Clarendon Studies in Criminology, Oxford University Press.

Cribb, J., Disney, R. and Sibieta, L. (2014) The public sector workforce: past, present and future, IFS Briefing Note BN145. Published by the Institute for Fiscal Studies online at: www.ifs.org.uk/publications/7113 [last accessed 18 July 2017].

Cummins, I. (2008) A place of safety? Self-harming behaviour in police custody, *The Journal of Adult Protection*, 10(1), 36–47.

Cummins, I. (2012) Mental health and custody: a follow on study, *The Journal of Adult Protection*, 14(2), 73–81.

Cummins, I. and Edmondson, D. (2016) Policing and street triage, *The Journal of Adult Protection*, 18(1), 40–52.

Cunneen, C. (2001) *Conflict, politics and crime: aboriginal communities and the police*. Crows Nest, NSW: Allen and Unwin.

Cunneen, C., Baldry, E., Brown, D., Brown, M. Steel, A. and Schwartz, M. (2013) *Penal culture and hyperincarceration: the revival of the prison*. London: Ashgate.

Dalton, V. (1999) *Aboriginal Deaths in Prison 1980 to 1998: National Overview*. Canberra: Australian Institute of Criminology. Online at: www.aic.gov.au/publications/tandi/tandi131 [Last accessed 19 January 2018].

Daly, Y. (2014) The right to silence: inferences and interference, *Australian and New Zealand Journal of Criminology*, 47(1), 59–80.

Davis, K.C. (1969) *Discretionary justice: a preliminary inquiry*. Baton Rouge: Louisiana State University Press.

Davis, K.C. (1975) *Police discretion*. St. Paul, MN: West Publishing Co.

de Maillard, J. and Roché, S. (2016) Studying policing comparatively: obstacles, preliminary results and promises, *Policing and Society*, 28(4), 385–397.

de Maillard, J., Hunold, D., Roché, S. and Oberwittler, D. (2016) Different styles of policing: discretionary power in street controls by the public police in France and Germany, *Policing and Society*, 28(2), 175–188.

Dehaghani, R. (2016) He's just not that vulnerable: exploring the implementation of the appropriate adult safeguard in police custody, *Howard Journal of Criminal Justice*, 55(4), 396–413.

Dehaghani, R. (forthcoming) *Vulnerability in police custody: definition, identification and implementation in the context of the appropriate adult safeguard.* Abingdon: Routledge.

Dickinson, D. (2006) Descriptive legal theory, *IVR Encyclopedia of Jurisprudence, Legal Theory and Philosophy of Law.* Available online at: www.academia.edu/9746248/J_Dickson_Descriptive_Legal_Theory_2006_IVR_Encyclopaedia_of_Jurisprudence_Legal_Theory_and_Philosophy_of_Law_..._ [last accessed 8 December 2017].

Dixon, D. (1997) *Law in policing: legal regulations and police practices.* Oxford: Clarendon, Oxford University Press.

Dixon, D. (2008) Authorise and regulate: a comparative perspective on the rise and fall of a regulatory strategy. In E. Cape and R. Young (eds.) *Regulating policing.* Oxford: Hart, 21–44.

Dixon, D. (2019) Interrogation law and practice in common law jurisdictions. In D. Brown, J.I. Turner and B. Weißer (eds.) *The Oxford handbook of criminal process.* Oxford: Oxford University Press.

Dixon, D. and Cowdery, N. (2013) Silence rights, *Australian Indigenous Law Review*, 17(1), 23–37.

Dixon, D. and Travis, G. (2007) *Interrogating images: audio-visually recorded police questioning of suspects.* Sydney: University of Sydney.

Dixon, D., Bottomley, K., Coleman, C., Gill, M. and Wall, D. (1990) Safeguarding the rights of suspects in police custody, *Policing and Society*, 1(2), 115–140.

Dixon, D. with Travis, G. (2007) *Interrogating images: audio-visually recorded police questioning of suspects.* Sydney, NSW: University of Sydney.

Donner, C., Maskaly, J., Fridell, L. and Jennings, W.G. (2015) Policing and procedural justice: a state-of-the-art review, *Policing: An International Journal of Police Strategies and Management*, 38 (1), 153–172.

Durkheim, E. (1973 [1899–1900]) Two laws of penal evolution, *Economy and Society*, 2(3), 285–308.

Dworkin, R. (1977) *Taking rights seriously.* Cambridge, MA: Harvard University Press.

Elks, L. (2008) *Righting miscarriages of justice? Ten years of the criminal cases review commission.* London: Justice.

Elmsley (1996) *The English police.* Hemel Hempstead: Harvester Wheatsheaf.

Engel, R.S. and Cohen, D.M. (2014) Racial profiling. In M.J. Reisig and M.J. Kane (eds.) *The Oxford handbook of police and policing.* New York City, NY: Oxford University Press, 383–408.

Ericson, R.V. (1982) *Reproducing order: a study of police patrol work.* Toronto, ON: University of Toronto Press.

Ericson, R.V. (2007) Rules in policing: five perspectives, *Theoretical Criminology*, 11(3), 367–401.

Ericson, R.V. and Haggerty, K.D. (1997) *Policing the risk society.* Oxford: Clarendon, Oxford University Press.

Eterno, J.A. and Barrow, C.S. (2018) Contemporary police and minorities in the United States: causes, theories and solutions. In J.D. Ward (ed.) *Policing race in America: economic, political and social dynamics.* Lanham, MD: Lexington Books, 31–54.

Eterno, J.A. and Silverman, E.B. (2006) The New York City police department's compstat: dream or nightmare? *International Journal of Police Science and Management*, 8(3), 218–231.

European Committee on the Prevention of Torture (1995) *Report to the Irish Government on the visit to Ireland carried out by the European Committee for the Prevention of Torture and Inhuman or Degrading Treatment or Punishment (CPT) from 26 to 5 October 1993*. Dublin/Strasbourg: Council of Europe.

European Committee on the Prevention of Torture (1999) *Report to the Irish Government on the visit to Ireland carried out by the European Committee for the Prevention of Torture and Inhuman or Degrading Treatment or Punishment (CPT) from 31 August to 9 September 1998*. Dublin/Strasbourg: Council of Europe.

European Committee on the Prevention of Torture (2003) *Report to the Irish Government on the visit to Ireland carried out by the European Committee for the Prevention of Torture and Inhuman or Degrading Treatment or Punishment (CPT) from 20 to 28 May 2002*. Dublin/Strasbourg: Council of Europe.

European Committee on the Prevention of Torture (2007) *Report to the Irish Government on the visit to Ireland carried out by the European Committee for the Prevention of Torture and Inhuman or Degrading Treatment or Punishment (CPT) from 2 to 3 October 2006*. Dublin and Strasbourg: Council of Europe.

Evers, A. and Guillemard, A.-M. (2012) Introduction: Marshall's concept of citizenship and contemporary welfare reconfiguration. In A. Evers and A.-M Guillemard (eds.) *Social policy and citizenship: the changing landscape*. Oxford: Oxford University Press, 3–34.

Fagan, J. (2016) Terry's original sin, *University of Chicago Legal Forum*, 2016, Article 3, 43–97. Available online at: http://chicagounbound.uchicago.edu/uclf/vol2016/iss1/3 [last accessed 14 December 2017].

Fagan, J. and Geller, A.B (2015) Following the script: narratives of suspicion in Terry stops in street policing, *University of Chicago Law Review*, 82(1), 51–88.

Fassin, D. (2013) *Enforcing order: an ethnography of urban policing*. Cambridge: Polity Press.

Faulkner, D. (2003) Taking citizenship seriously: social capital and criminal justice in a changing world, *Criminal Justice*, 3(3), 287–315.

Fineman, M. (2008) The vulnerable subject: anchoring equality in the human condition, *Yale Journal of Law and Feminism*, 20(1), 1–23.

Fineman, M. (2010) The vulnerable subject and the responsive state, *Emory Law Journal*, 60, 251–275.

Fineman, M. and Grears, A. (2014) *Vulnerability: reflections on a new ethical foundation for law and politics*. London: Routledge.

Fineman, M., Andersson, U. and Mattsson, T. (2016) *Privatization, vulnerability, and social responsibility: a comparative perspective*. London: Routledge.

Finnane, M. (1990) Police and politics in Australia – the case for historical revisions, *Australian and New Zealand Journal of Criminology*, 23(4), 218–228.

Finnane, M. (1994) *Police and government: histories of policing in Australia*. Melbourne, VIC: Oxford University Press.

Forst, B. and Manning, P.K. (1999) *The privatization of policing: two views*. Washington, DC: Georgetown University Press.

Foster, J. (2003) Cop cultures. In T. Newburn (ed.) *Handbook of policing*. Cullompton: Willan, 196–227.

Foucault, M. (1991 [1977]) *Discipline and punish*. London: Penguin.

Frampton, T.W. (2012) The uneven bulwark: how (and why) criminal jury trial rates vary by state, *California Law Review*, 100, 183–222.

Gamble, A. (2001) Neoliberalism, *Capital and Class*, 25(3), 127–134.

Garda Inspectorate (2014) *Crime Investigation*. Available online at: www.gsinsp.ie/en/GSINSP/Pages/published_reports [last accessed 17 July 2017].

Garland, D. (1990) *Punishment and modern society*. Oxford: Oxford University Press.

Garland, D. (2001) *The culture of control*. Oxford: Oxford University Press.

Gearty, C. (2007) *Civil liberties*. Oxford: Oxford University Press.

Giddens, A. (1984) *The constitution of society*. Cambridge: Polity Press.

Giddens, A. (1991) *Modernity and self-identity*. Cambridge: Polity Press.

Goldsmith, A.T. (2010) Policing's new visibility, *The British Journal of Criminology*, 5(5), 914–934.

Goldstein, J. (1960) Police discretion not to invoke the criminal process: low-visibility decision in the administration of justice, *The Yale Law Journal*, 69(4), 542–594.

Goodman-Delahunty, J. and Martschuk, N. (2016) Risks and benefits of interpreter-mediated police interviews, *Varstvoslovje*, 18(4), 451–471.

Grabosky, P. (2012) Foreword. In I. Bartkowiak-Théron and N. Asquith (eds.) *Policing vulnerability*. Annandale, NSW: Federation Press, v–viii.

Green, D.A. (2009) Feeding wolves: punitiveness and culture, *European Journal of Criminology*, 6(6): 517–536.

Greenfield, P. (2018) The Cambridge Analytica files: the story so far, *The Guardian Online*. Available online at: www.theguardian.com/news/2018/mar/26/the-cambridge-analytica-files-the-story-so-far [last accessed 25 July 2018].

Gudjonsson, G., Clare, I.C.H., Rutter, S. and Pearse, J. (1993) *Persons at risk during interviews in police custody: the identification of vulnerabilities*. Royal Commission on Criminal Justice Report. London: HMSO.

Guthrie Ferguson, A. and Leo, R.A. (2017) The Miranda app: metaphor and machine, *Boston University Law Review*, 97(3), 935–993.

Hall, S., Critcher, C., Jefferson, T., Clarke, J. and Roberts, B. (1978) *Policing the crisis: mugging, the state and law and order*. London: Macmillan.

Haller, M.H. (1976) Historical roots of police behavior: Chicago, 1890–1925, *Law & Society Review*, 10(2), 303–323.

Hallsworth, S. and Lea, J. (2011) Reconstructing Leviathan: emerging contours of the security state, *Theoretical Criminology*, 15(2), 141–157.

Hamilton, C. (2013) Punitiveness and political culture: notes from some small countries, *European Journal of Criminology*, 10(2), 154–167.

Hancock, P. and Jewkes, Y. (2011) Architectures of incarceration: the spatial pains of imprisonment, *Punishment and Society*, 13(5), 611–629.

Hannan, M., Hearnden, I., Grace, K. and Bucke, T. (2010) *Deaths in or following police custody*. IPCC Research Series, Paper 17. London: IPCC.

Harcourt, B.E. (2010) Neoliberal penality: a brief genealogy, *Theoretical Criminology*, 14(1), 74–89.

Hart, H.L.A. (1994 [1961]) *The concept of law*. Oxford: Oxford University Press.

Harvey, D. (2005) *A brief history of neoliberalism*. Oxford: Oxford University Press.

Healy, D., Hamilton, C., Daly, Y. and Butler, M. (2016) *The Routledge Irish handbook of criminology*. London: Routledge.

Hennessey, M. (2014) 'What do our 5,500 peace commissioners actually do?', *thejournal.ie*. Available online at: www.thejournal.ie/peace-commissioners-1265204-Jan2014/ [last accessed 30 May 2017].

Herbert, S. (2006a) *Citizens, cops and power: recognizing the limits of community.* Chicago, IL and London: University of Chicago Press.

Herbert, S. (2006b) Tangled up in blue, *Theoretical Criminology,* 10(4), 481–504.

HMIC (2011) *Who's looking out for the children? A joint inspection of appropriate adult provision and children in detention after charge.* Available online at: www.justiceinspectorates. gov.uk/hmiprobation/inspections/who-s-looking-out-for-the-children-a-joint-inspection-of-appropriate-adult-provision-and-children-in-detention-after-charge/ [last accessed 19 July 2017].

HMIC (2015) *The welfare of vulnerable people in police custody.* Available online at: www.justiceinspectorates.gov.uk/hmic/publications/the-welfare-of-vulnerable-people-in-police-custody/ [last accessed 19 July 2017].

Hodgson, J. (1992) Tipping the scales of justice: the suspects' right to legal advice, *Criminal Law Review,* December, 854–862.

Hodgson, J. (1994) Adding injury to injustice: the suspect at the police station, *Journal of Law and Society,* 21(1), 85–101.

Hodgson, J. (2013) Making custodial legal advice more effective in France, *Criminal Justice Matters,* 92(1), 14–15.

Holdaway, S. (1980) The police station, *Urban Life,* 9(1), 79–100.

Holdaway, S. (1983) *Inside the British police.* Oxford: Blackwell.

Home Office (2017) *PACE Codes of Practice: Code C.* London: TSO.

Horspool, K., Drabble, S.J. and O'Cathain, A. (2016) Implementing street triage: a qualitative study of collaboration between police and mental health services, *BMC Psychiatry,* 16(1), 313–323.

Huff, C. and Naughton, M. (2017) Wrongful conviction reforms in the U.S. and UK: Taking Stock. In E. Plywaczewski (ed.) *Current problems of the penal law and criminology.* 7th Edition. Poland: Wolters Kluwer, 482–504.

Humpage, L. (2015) *Policy change, public attitudes and social citizenship.* Bristol: Policy Press.

Irving, B.L. and McKenzie, I. (1989) *Police interrogation: the effects of the Police and Criminal Evidence Act 1984.* London: Police Foundation.

Jackson, J. (2009) Re-conceptualizing the right to silence as an effective fair trial standard, *International and Comparative Law Quarterly,* 58(4), 835–861.

Jackson, J., Bradford, B., MacQueen, S. and Hough, M. (2015) Truly free consent? On the nature of duty to obey, *Social Science Research Network,* 18 June 2015. Available online at SSRN: http://ssrn.com/abstract=2620274 or doi: 10.2139/ssrn.2620274 [last accessed 20 May 2016].

Jackson, J., Bradford, B., Stanko, B. and Hohl, K. (2013) *Just authority? Trust in the police in England and Wales.* London: Routledge.

Jacobson, J. (2008) *Police responses to suspects with learning disabilities and learning difficulties: a review of policy and practice.* London: Prison Reform Trust.

Johnston, L. and Shearing, C. (2003) *Governing security.* London: Routledge.

Jones, T. and Newburn, T. (2002) The transformation of policing: understanding current trends in policing systems, *British Journal of Criminology,* 42(1), 129–146.

Kaplan-Lyman, J. (2012) A punitive bind: policing, poverty and neoliberalism in New York City, *Yale Human Rights and Development Journal,* 15(1), 177–221.

Kassin, S. M., Drizin, S.A., Grisso, T., Gudjonsson, G.H., Leo, R. and Redlich, A. (2010) Police-induced confessions: Risk factors and recommendations, *Law and Human Behavior,* 34(3), 3–38.

Kemp, V. and Balmer, N. (2009). *Legal Advice and representation in the CJS.* London: Legal Services Research Centre.

Kemp, V. and Hodgson, J. (2016) England and Wales: empirical findings. In M. Vanderhallen et al. (eds.) *Interrogating young suspects: procedural safeguards from an empirical perspective*. Cambridge: Intersentia. Available online at: http://young suspects.eu/project-publications/ [last accessed 18 October 2017].

Kemp, V., Balmer, N.J. and Pleasence, P. (2012) Whose time is it anyway? Factors associated with duration in police custody, *Criminal Law Review*, 10, 736–752.

King, A. (2010) The odd couple: Margaret Archer, Anthony Giddens and British social theory, *British Journal of Sociology*, 61(1), 253–260.

Kleinig, J. (1996) Introduction. In J. Kleinig (ed.) *Handled with discretion: ethical issues in police decision making*. New York: Rowman and Littlefield, 1–12.

Lankevich, G.J (1998) *American metropolis: a history of New York City*. New York City, NY: New York University Press.

Lea, J. and Hallsworth, S. (2013) Bringing the state back in: understanding neoliberal security. In P. Squires and J. Lea (eds.) *Criminalisation and advanced marginality: critically exploring the work of Loic Wacquant*. London: Routledge, 19–40.

Legal Services Commission (2007) *Duty solicitor call centre and CDS direct expansion march 2007*. London: Legal Services Commission.

Leo, R. (1996a) Inside the interrogation room, *Journal of Criminal Law and Criminology*, 86(2), 266–303.

Leo, R. (1996b) Miranda's revenge: Police interrogation as a confidence game, *Law and Society Review*, 30(2), 259–288.

Leo, R. (2008) *Police interrogation and American Justice*. Cambridge, MA: Harvard University Press.

Lerman, A.E. and Weaver, V.M. (2014) *Arresting citizenship: the democratic consequences of American crime control*. Chicago, IL: University of Chicago Press.

Letts, Q. (2016) What's the point of the Commonwealth, Radio 4 programme broadcast on 17 August 2016. Available online at: www.bbc.co.uk/programmes/b07nrlql [last accessed 18 August 2016].

Levin, R.M. (2005) The administrative law legacy of Kenneth Culp Davis, *San Diego Law Review*, 42, 315–347.

Lipsky, M. (2010 [1980]) *Street-level bureaucracy: dilemmas of the individual in public services*. New York, NY: Russell Sage Foundation.

Lister, R. (2012) Social citizenship in new labour's new 'active' welfare state: the case of the UK. In A. Evers and A.-M. Guillemard (eds.) *Social policy and citizenship: the changing landscape*. Oxford: Oxford University Press, 121–149.

Loader, I. (2016) In search of civic policing: recasting the 'Peelian' principles, *Criminal Law and Philosophy*, 10(7), 427–440.

Loader, I. and Mulcahy, A. (2006) *Policing and the condition of England: memory, politics and culture*. Oxford: Oxford University Press.

Loader, I. and Sparks, R. (2016) Ideologies and crime: political ideas and the dynamics of crime control, *Global Crime*, 17(3–4), 314–330.

Loftus, B. (2009). *Police culture in a changing world*. Oxford, Oxford University Press.

Loftus, B. (2010) Police occupational culture: classic themes altered times, *Policing and Society*, 20(1), 1–20.

Loftus, B., Skinns, L., Munck, T. and Rice, L. (2014) *Policing partnerships: evidence review*. Leeds: University of Leeds, N8 Policing Research Partnership. Available online at: https://n8prp.org.uk/about_us/evidence-reviews/ [last accessed 19 December 2018]

Lustgarten, L. (1986) *The governance of the police*. London: Sweet and Maxwell.

MacCoun, R.J. (2005) Voice, control and belonging: the double-edged sword of procedural fairness, *Annual Review of Law and Social Science*, 1, 171–201.

Macdonald, S. (2008) Constructing a framework for criminal justice research: learning from Packer's mistakes, *New Criminal Law Review: An International and Interdisciplinary Journal*, 11(2), 257–311.

Maclin, T. (2017) The prophylactic fifth amendment, *Boston University Law Review*, 97(3), 1047–1085.

Maguire, M. (1988) Effects of the PACE provisions on detention and questioning: some preliminary findings, *British Journal of Criminology*, 28(1), 19–43.

Manning, P.K. (2010) *Democratic policing in a changing world*. Boulder, CO: Paradigm Publishers.

Manning, P.K. (2011) *The technology of policing: crime mapping, information technology and the rationality of crime control*. New York City, NY: New York University Press.

Manning, P. (2012) Trust and accountability in Ireland: the case of An Garda Síochána, *Policing and Society*, 22(3), 346–361.

Marshall, G. (1978) 'Police Accountability Revisited' In D. Butler and A.H. Halsey (eds.) *Policy and Politics*. London:Macmillan, 51–65.

Marshall, T.H. and Bottomore, T. (1992) *Citizenship and social class*. Chicago, IL: Pluto Press.

Mawby, R.I. (1990) *Comparative policing issues: the British and American experience in international perspective*. London: Unwin Hyman Ltd.

Mazerolle, L., Bennett, S., Davis, J., Sargeant, E. and Manning, M. (2013) *Legitimacy in Policing: A Systematic Review*, The Campbell Collaboration research study no. 141. Available online at: www.campbellcollaboration.org/lib/project/141/ [last accessed 22 August 2016].

McBarnet, D. (1981) *Conviction*. London: Macmillan.

McCausland, R. and Baldry, E. (2017) 'I feel like I failed him by ringing the police': criminalising disability in Australia, *Punishment and Society*, 19(3), 290–309.

McConville, M., Sanders, A. and Leng, R. (1991) *The case for the prosecution*. London: Routledge.

McKinnon, I.G. and Grubin, D. (2012) Health screening of people in police custody: evaluation of current police screening procedures in London, UK, *European Journal of Public Health*, 23(3), 399–405.

Meares, T.L. and Neyroud, P. (2015) *Rightful policing*, Executive Session on Policing and Public Safety, February 2015. Cambridge, MA: Harvard Kennedy School.

Meares, T.L., Tyler, T.R. and Gardener, J. (2016) Lawful or unfair? How cops and laypeople perceive good policing, *The Journal of Criminal Law and Criminology*, 105(2), 297–344.

Messner, S.F. (2012) Morality, markets and the ASC: 2011 presidential address to the American society of criminology, *Criminology*, 50(1), 5–25.

Millie, A. (2013) The policing task and the expansion (and contraction) of British policing, *Criminology and Criminal Justice*, 13(2), 143–160.

Moskos, P. (2008) *Cop in the hood*. Princeton, NJ: Princeton University Press.

Moston, S. (2009) Investigative interviewing of suspects in Australia. In T. Williamson, B. Milne and S.P. Savage (eds.) *International developments in investigative interviewing*. Cullompton: Willan, 3–23.

Muhammad, K. G. (2010). *The condemnation of blackness: race, crime and the making of modern urban America.* Cambridge, MA: Harvard University Press.

Mulcahy, A. (2007) Crime, policing and social control in Ireland. In S. O'Sullivan (ed.) *Contemporary Ireland: a sociological map.* Dublin: University College Dublin Press, 120–135.

Mulcahy, A. (2013) *Policing Northern Ireland: conflict legitimacy and reform.* Oxon: Routledge.

Mulroy, S.J. (2013) "Hold" on: the remarkably resilient, constitutionally dubious 48-hour hold, *Case Western Reserve Law Review*, 63(3), 815–867.

National Appropriate Adult Network (NAAN) (2015) *There to help.* Available online at: www.appropriateadult.org.uk/index.php/news/9-public-articles/154-theretohelp.

Nelken, D. (2010) *Comparative criminal justice.* London: Sage.

Nettelbeck, A. and Ryan, L. (2018) Salutary lessons: native police and the 'civilising' role of legalised violence in colonial Australia, *The Journal of Imperial and Commonwealth History*, 46(1), 47–68.

Newburn, T. (2010) Diffusion, differentiation and resistance in comparative penality, *Criminology and Criminal Justice*, 10(4), 341–352.

Newburn, T. and Hayman, S. (2002) *Policing, surveillance and social control: CCTV and police monitoring of suspects.* Cullompton: Willan.

Nickels, E.L. (2007) A note on the status of discretion in police research, *Journal of Criminal Justice*, 35(5), 570–578.

Noone, G. (2015) An Garda Síochána model of investigative interviewing of witnesses and suspects. In J. Pearse (ed.) *Investigating terrorism: current political, legal and psychological issues.* Chichester: Wiley-Blackwell, 100–122.

O'Malley, P. (2014) A review essay: prisons, neoliberalism, neoliberal states: reading Loic Wacquant and prisons of poverty, *Thesis Eleven*, 122(1), 89–96.

O'Neill, M. and Loftus, B. (2013) Policing and the surveillance of the marginal: everyday contexts of social control, *Theoretical Criminology*, 17(4), 437–454.

Office for National Statistics (2015) People identifying as 'other white' has increased by over a million since 2001. Available online at: www.ons.gov.uk/people populationandcommunity/culturalidentity/ethnicity/articles/peopleidentifying asotherwhitehasincreasedbyoveramillionsince2001/2015-06-26 [last accessed 24 July 2018].

Office for National Statistics (2016a) London data store. Available online at: http://data.london.gov.uk/dataset/office-national-statistics-ons-population-estimates-borough [last accessed 16 August 2016].

Office for National Statistics (2016b) Ethnicity and national identity in England and Wales: 2011. Available online at: www.ons.gov.uk/peoplepopulationand community/culturalidentity/ethnicity/articles/ethnicityandnationalidentityin englandandwales/2012-12-11 [last accessed 16 August 2016].

Olano, A.B. (1992) Determination of probable cause of a warrantless arrest: a case-note on County of Riverside v. Mclaughlin, *Louisiana Law Review*, 52, 1311–1319.

Packer, H. (1968) *The limits of the criminal sanction.* Oxford: Oxford University Press.

Panzavolta, M., de Vocht, D., Van Oosterhout, M. and Vanderhallan, M. (eds.) (2015) *Interrogating young suspects: procedural safeguards from a legal perspective.* Cambridge: Intersentia. Available online at: http://youngsuspects.eu/project-publications/ [last accessed 7 July 2017].

Parmar, A. (2018) Policing belonging: race and nation in the UK. In M. Bosworth, A. Parmar and Y. Vasquez (ed.) *Race, criminal justice and migration control: enforcing the boundaries of belonging.* Oxford: Oxford University Press, 108–124.

Pattenden, R. and Skinns, L. (2010) Choice, privacy and publicly funded legal advice at the police station, *Modern Law Review*, 73(3), 349–370.

Payne-James, J.J., Green, P.G., Green, N., McLachlan, G.M.C. and Moore, T.C.B. (2010) Healthcare issues of detainees in police custody in London, UK, *Journal of Forensic and Legal Medicine*, 17(1), 11–17.

Peak, K.J. (2009) *Policing America: challenges and best practice.* Sixth edition. Upper Saddle River, NJ: Pearson.

Peck, J. and Tickell, A. (2002) Neoliberalizing space, *Antipodes*, 38(3), 380–404.

Phelan, S. (2007) The discourses of neoliberal hegemony: the case of the Irish Republic, *Critical Discourse Studies*, 4(1), 29–48.

Phillips, C. and Bowling, B. (2017) Ethnicities, racism, crime and criminal justice. In S. Maruna, L. McAra and A. Liebling (eds.) *Oxford handbook of criminology.* Oxford: Oxford University Press, 190–212.

Phillips, C. and Brown, D. (1998) *Entry into the criminal justice system: a survey of police arrests and their outcomes.* London: HMSO.

Picketty, T. (2014) *Capital in the twenty-first century.* Cambridge, MA: Harvard University Press.

Pierpoint, H. (2006) Reconstructing the role of the appropriate adult in England and Wales, *Criminology and Criminal Justice*, 6(2), 219–237.

Pleasence, P., Kemp, V. and Balmer, N.J. (2011) The justice lottery? Police station advice 25 years on from PACE, *Criminal Law Review*, 1, 3–18.

Primus, E.B. (2017) Disentangling Miranda and Massiah: how to revive the sixth amendment right to counsel as a tool for regulating confession law, *Boston University Law Review*, 97(3), 1085–1129.

Punch, M. (1979) The secret social service. In S. Holdaway (ed.) *The British police.* London: Edward Arnold, 102–117.

Quinn, K. and Jackson, J. (2003) *The detention and questioning of young persons by the police in Northern Ireland.* Belfast: Northern Ireland Statistics and Research Agency.

Quinn, K. and Jackson, J. (2007) Of rights and roles: police interviews with young suspects in Northern Ireland, *British Journal of Criminology*, 47(2), 234–255.

Quirk, H. (2017) *The rise and fall of the right to silence.* London: Routledge.

Rawlings, P. (2002) *Policing: a short history.* Cullompton: Willan.

Reiner, R. (1992) Policing a postmodern society, *Modern Law Review*, 55(6), 761–781.

Reiner, R. (1995) From sacred to profane: the thirty years' war of the British police, *Policing and Society: An International Journal*, 5(2), 121–128.

Reiner, R. (2010) *The politics of the police.* Oxford: Oxford University Press.

Reiner, R. (2012) Policing and social democracy: resuscitating a lost perspective, *Journal of Police Studies*, 25(4), 97–114.

Reiner, R. (2015) Do the powerful still need the police? *Criminal Justice Matters*, 100(1), 33.

Reiner, R. (2017) Political economy, crime and criminal justice. In S. Maruna, L. McAra and A. Liebling (eds.) *The Oxford handbook of criminology.* Oxford: Oxford University Press, 116–137.

Rigakos, G.S. (2002) *The new parapolice: risk markets and commodified social control.* Toronto: University of Toronto Press.

Roberts, K. and Herrington, V. (2012) Detention and investigation of vulnerable suspects. In I. Bartkowiak-Théron and N. Asquith (eds.) *Policing vulnerability*. Annandale, NSW: Federation Press, 198–213.

Ross, J. (2007) The place of covert surveillance in democratic societies: a comparative study of the United States and Germany, *The American Journal of Comparative Law*, 55(3), Summer, 493–579.

Rossman, D. (2017) Resurrecting Miranda's right to counsel, *Boston University Law Review*, 97(3), 1129–1157.

Royal Commission on Criminal Procedure (1981) *The investigation and prosecution of criminal offences in England and Wales: The law and procedure*. London: HMSO.

Royal Commission into Aboriginal Deaths in Custody (1991) *National Report: Volume 1*. Available online at: www.austlii.edu.au/au/other/IndigLRes/rciadic/ [last accessed 19 July 2017].

Royal Commission on Criminal Justice (1993) *Royal Commission on Criminal Justice Report*, chaired by Viscount Runciman of Doxford. London: HMSO.

Sanders, A. and Young, R. (2007) *Criminal justice*. Third edition. Oxford: Oxford University Press.

Sanders, A. and Young, R. (2008). Police powers. In T. Newburn (ed.) *Handbook of Policing*. Cullompton, Willan, 281–312.

Sanders, A., Young, R. and Burton, M. (2010) *Criminal justice*. Fourth edition. Oxford: Oxford University Press.

Saunders, C. (2011) *The constitution of Australia: a contextual analysis*. Oxford: Hart.

Scarman, L.G. (1981) *The Scarman report: the Brixton disorders 10–12 April 1981*. London: Home Office.

Scott, J.E. (2010) Evolving strategies: a historical examination of changes in principle, authority and function to inform policing in the twenty-first century, *The Police Journal*, 83(2), 126–163.

Shearing, C. (1995) Transforming the culture of policing: thoughts from South Africa, *The Australian and New Zealand Journal of Criminology*, 28(1), 54–61.

Simon, J. (2007) *Governing through crime: how the war on crime transformed American democracy and created a culture of fear*. New York City, NY: Oxford University Press.

Simon, J. (2011) *Mass Incarceration and the US Constitution: Can Courts Lead the US out of Its Culture of Control (and can the European Court of Human Rights keep your version in check)*, Public Seminar Series, Centre for Criminological Research, University of Sheffield, 3 March 2011.

Skinns, L. (2009a) "I'm a detainee get me out of here": predictors of access to custodial legal advice in public and privatized police custody areas, *British Journal of Criminology*, 49(2), 399–417.

Skinns, L. (2009b) "Lets' get it over with": early findings on the factors affecting detainees' access to custodial legal advice, *Policing and Society*, 19(1), 58–78.

Skinns, L. (2010) Stop the clock? Predictors of detention without charge in police custody areas, *Criminology and Criminal Justice*, 10(3), 303–320.

Skinns, L. (2011a) *Police custody: governance, legitimacy and reform in the criminal justice process*. Cullompton: Willan.

Skinns, L. (2011b) *The overnight detention of children in police cells: Full Report*, London: Howard League.

Skinns, L. (2012) The role of the law in policing, *Journal of Police Studies: Tides and Currents in Police Studies*, 2012/4, no. 25, 225–247.

Skinns, L. (forthcoming in 2019) Researching inside police custody detention in a comparative setting: "getting in", "getting on", "getting your hands dirty" and "getting out", *International Journal of Social Research Methodology*.

Skinns, L. and Rice, L. (2016) *Power, policing agents and police custody: findings from phase 2 of the 'Good' police custody study*, paper presented at the American Society of Criminology Conference, New Orleans, LA, 16–19 November 2016.

Skinns, L., Rice, L. and Sprawson, A. (2016) 'Power and suspect compliance', in *Key dimensions of police custody: an unpublished report from Phase 2 of the 'good' police custody study*.

Skinns, L., Rice, L., Sprawson, A. and Wooff, A. (2017a) Police legitimacy in context: an exploration of 'soft power' in police custody in England, *Policing: An International Journal of Police Strategies and Management*, 40(3), 601–613.

Skinns, L., Sprawson, A., Sorsby, A., Smith, R. and Wooff, A. (2017b) Police custody delivery in the twenty-first century in England and Wales: current arrangements and their implications for patterns of policing, *European Journal of Policing Studies*, 4(3), 325–349.

Skinns, L. and Sorsby, A. (2017) *Making a difference to detainees: preliminary findings on the use of authority in police custody suites in England and Wales*, Conference paper at the Stockholm Criminology Symposium, June 2017.

Skinns, L. and Wooff, A. (2017) *Policing risk inside police detention in England and Wales*, Paper presented at the American Society of Criminology Conference, Philadelphia, 15–18 November 2017.

Skinns, L. and Wooff, A. (forthcoming in 2019) 'The pains of police detention': towards an understanding of the pains of confinement, submitted to *Policing and Society*.

Skogan, W.G. (2006) Asymmetry in the impact of encounters with police, *Policing and Society*, 16(2), 99–126.

Skogan, W.G. and Frydl, K. (2004) Explaining police behavior: people and situations. In W. Skogan and K. Frydl (eds.) *Fairness and effectiveness in policing: the evidence*. Washington, DC: National Academies Press, 109–154.

Skolnick, J. (2005) A sketch of the policeman's "working personality". In T. Newburn (ed.) *Policing: key readings*. Cullompton: Willan, 264–279.

Slobogin, C. (2017) Manipulation of suspects and unrecorded questioning: after fifty years of Miranda jurisprudence, still two (or maybe three) burning issues, *Boston University Law Review*, 97(3), 1157–1197.

Softley, P., Brown, D., Forde, B., Mair, G. and Moxon, D. (1980) *Police interrogation: an observational study in four police stations*. London: HMSO.

Sommerlad, H. (2004) Some reflections on the relationship between citizenship, access to justice, and the reform of legal aid, *Journal of Law and Society*, 31(3), 345–368.

Squires, P. and Lea, J. (2013) Introduction: reading Loic Wacquant – opening questions and overview. In P. Squires and J. Lea (eds.) *Criminalisation and advanced marginality: critically exploring the work of Loic Wacquant*. Bristol: Policy Press, 1–18.

Stanford, S. (2012) Critically reflecting on being 'at risk' and 'a risk' in vulnerable people policing. In I. Bartkowiak-Théron and N. Asquith (eds.) *Policing vulnerability*. Annandale, NSW: Federation Press, 20–32.

Stedman Jones, D. (2012) *Masters of the Universe: Hayek, Friedman, and the birth of neoliberal politics*. Princeton, NJ: Princeton University Press.

Storch, R.D. (1975) The plague of the blue locusts: police reform and popular resistance in Northern England, 1840–57, *International Review of Social History*, 20(1), 61–90.

Sunshine, J. and Tyler, T. (2003) The role of procedural justice theory and legitimacy in shaping public support for policing, *Law and Society Review*, 37(3), 513–548.

Swaine, J. (2016) Police officers will be required to provide officer-involved deaths under the new US system. Available online at: www.theguardian.com/us-news/2016/aug/08/police-officer-related-deaths-department-of-justice [last accessed 19 August 2016].

Sykes, G.M. (2007 [1958]) *The society of captives: a study of a maximum security prison*. Princeton, NJ: Princeton University Press.

Talbot, J. (2008) *No one knows: report and final recommendations*. London: Prison Reform Trust.

Tankebe, J., Reisig, M.D. and Wang, X. (2016) A multi-dimensional model of police legitimacy: a cross-cultural assessment, *Law and Human Behavior*, 40(1), 11–22.

Taylor, N. and Bareja, M. (2005) *The 2002 National police custody survey*, Technical and Background Paper No. 13. Canberra: Australian Institute of Criminology.

The Guardian (2016) The counted: people killed by the police in the US. Available online at: www.theguardian.com/us-news/ng-interactive/2015/jun/01/the-counted-police-killings-us-database# [last accessed 19 August 2016].

Thomas, G.C. and Leo, R.A. (2002) The effects of Miranda v. Arizona: "embedded" in our national culture? *Crime and Justice: A Review of Research*, 29, 203–271.

Tong, C.R. (2018) 'Personal communication', discussion over email with a public defender in New York State, 1 August 2018.

Tonry, M. (1999) Why are U.S. incarceration rates so high? *Crime and Delinquency*, 44(4), 419–437.

Turnbull, P. and Skinns, L. (2010) Drug intervention programme, In A. Hucklesby and E. Wincup (eds.) *Drug interventions in criminal justice*, Milton Keynes: Open University Press, 64–83.

Turner, B.S. (1990) Outline of a theory of citizenship, *Sociology*, 24(2), 189–217.

Tushnet, M. (2009) *The constitution of the United States of America: a contextual analysis*. Portland, OR: Hart.

Tyler, T. (2004) Enhancing police legitimacy, *The Annals of the American Academy of Political and Social Science*, 593, 84–99.

Tyler, T. (2011) Trust and legitimacy: policing in the USA and Europe, *European Journal of Criminology*, 8(4), 254–266.

Tyler, T.R., Fagan, J. and Geller, A. (2014) Street stops and police legitimacy: teachable moments in young Urban men's legal socialization, *Journal of Empirical Legal Studies*, 11(4), 751–785.

Tyler, T.R., Goff, P.A. and MacCoun, R.J. (2015) The impact of psychological science on policing in the United States: procedural justice, legitimacy and effective law enforcement, *Psychological Science in the Public Interest*, 16(3), 75–109.

United Nations (2015) *Human development report 2015: work for human development*. New York City, NY: United Nations.

United Nations (2015) *Human development report 2015: work for human development*. New York City, NY: United Nations Publications.

United States Census Bureau (2016) Quick facts. Available at: https://www.census.gov/quickfacts/table/PST045215/00 [last accessed 16 August 2016].

United States Department of Justice (2016) *The presidential task force on 21st century policing*, May 2015. Available online at: http://cops.usdoj.gov/policingtaskforce [last accessed 19 August 2016].

UNODC (2016) UNODC statistics online. Available online at: www.unodc.org/unodc/en/data-and-analysis/statistics/crime.html [last accessed 4 May 2016].

van Dijk, J., van Kesteren, J. and Smit, P. (2007) *Criminal victimisation in international perspective key findings from the 2004–2005 ICVS and EU ICS*. Available online at: http://wp.unil.ch/icvs/key-publications/key-publications/ [last accessed 17 July 2017].

Vanderhallan, M., Van Oosterhout, M., Panzavolta, M. and de Vocht, D. (eds.) (2016) *Interrogating young suspects: procedural safeguards from an empirical perspective*. Cambridge: Intersentia. Available online at: http://youngsuspects.eu/project-publications/ [last accessed 7 July 2017].

Wacquant, L. (2009a) *Prisons of poverty*. Minneapolis, MN: University of Minnesota Press.

Wacquant, L. (2009b) *Punishing the poor*. Durham, NC, and London: Duke University Press.

Waddington, P.A.J. (1999a) Armed and unarmed policing. In R.I. Mawby (ed.) *Policing across the world: issues for the twenty-first century*. London: UCL Press limited, 151–166.

Waddington, P.A.J. (1999b) *Policing citizens*. London: Routledge.

Wahlquist, C. (2016) 'Aboriginal deaths in custody: 25 years on, the vicious cycle remains', *Guardian Online*. Available online at: www.theguardian.com/australia-news/2016/apr/15/aboriginal-deaths-in-custody-25-years-on-the-vicious-cycle-remains [last accessed 19 January 2018].

Walby, S. (1994) Is citizenship gendered? *Sociology*, 28(2), 379–395.

Walker, A. (2008) Democracy's double-edge: police and procedure in the United States. In M. R. Haberfeld and I. Cerrah (eds.) *Comparative policing: the struggle for democratization*. London: Sage, 325–340.

Walker, S. (1993) *Taming the system: the control of discretion in criminal justice, 1950–1990*. New York City, NY: Oxford University Press.

Walker, S., Spohn, C. and DeLone, M. (2012) *The color of justice: race, ethnicity and crime in America*. Fifth Edition. Belmont, CA: Cengage.

Walsh, D. (1998) *The Irish police: a legal and constitutional perspective*. London: Sweet and Maxwell.

Walsh, D. (2009) *Human rights and policing in Ireland: law, policy and practice*. Dublin: Clarus Press.

Weisselberg, C. (2008) Mourning Miranda, *California Law Review*, 96, 1519–1601.

Weisselberg, C. (2017) Exporting and importing Miranda, *Boston University Law Review*, 97(3), 1235–1293.

Weitzer, R. (2017) Theorizing racial discord over policing, before and after Ferguson, *Justice Quarterly*, 34(7), 1129–1153.

Weitzer, R. and Tuch, S.A. (2006) *Race and policing in America*. Cambridge: Cambridge University Press.

Western, M., Baxter, J., Pakulski, J., Tranter, B., Western, J., van Egmond, M., Chester, J., Hoskins, A., O'Flaherty and van Gellicum, Y. (2007) Neoliberalism, inequality and politics: the changing face of Australia, *Australian Journal of Social Issues*, 42(3), 401–418.

Westmarland, W. (2008) Cop cultures. In T. Newburn (ed.) *Handbook of policing*. Cullompton: Willan, 253–280.

White, R. (2009) Ethnic diversity and differential policing in Australia: the good, the bad and the ugly, *Journal of International Migration and Integration*, 10(4), 359–375.

Whitfield, J. (2007) The historical context: policing and black people in post-war Britain. In M. Rowe (ed.) *Policing beyond Macpherson.* Cullompton: Willan, 1–17.

Wikström, P.-O (2010) Explaining crime as moral action. In S. Hitlin and S. Vaisey (eds.) *Handbook of the sociology of morality.* New York: Springer, 211–240.

Wilkinson, R. and Pickett, L. (2010) *The spirit level. Why more equal societies almost always do better.* London: Allen Lane.

Wilson, D. (2009) Histories of policing. In R. Broadhurst and S.E. Davies (eds.) *Policing in context: an introduction to police work in Australia.* Melbourne, VIC: Oxford University Press, 18–31.

Wooff, A. and Skinns, L. (2017) The role of emotion, space and place in police custody in England: towards a geography of police custody, *Punishment and Society.* doi: 10.1177/1462474517722176

World Justice Project (2016) *World justice project: rule of law index 2016.* Available online at: https://worldjusticeproject.org/our-work/wjp-rule-law-index/wjp-rule-law-index-2016 [last accessed 18 December 2017].

Wyld, G., Lomax, P., and Collinge, T. (2018) *Understanding women's pathways through the criminal justice system.* NPC: Available online at: www.thinknpc.org/publications/ [last accessed 17 July 2018].

Young, J. (1999) *The exclusive society.* London: Sage.

Young, S., Goodwin, E.J., Sedgwick, O. and Gudjonsson, G.H. (2013) The effectiveness of police custody assessments in identifying suspects with intellectual disabilities and attention deficit hyperactivity disorder, *BMC Medicine,* 11, 248–259.

Zedner, L. (1995) Comparative research in criminal justice. In M. Maguire and M. Levi (eds.) *Contemporary issues in criminology.* Cardiff: Cardiff University Press, 8–25.

Cases

California v. Beheler 463 US 1121 (1983)

County of Riverside, California. v. McLaughlin, 59 LW 4413 (May 13, 1991)

Dietrich v. The Queen [1992] HCA 57, 177 CLR 292.

Director of Public Prosecutions v. Doyle [2017] IESC 1

Escobedo v. Illinois, 378 U.S. 478 (1964).

Fed. R. Crim. P. 5(a)

Frazier v. Cupp, 394 U.S. 731 (1969)

Gerstein v. Pugh 420 U.S. 103 (1975) 1

Massiah v. United States, 377 U.S. 201 (1964)

Miranda v. Arizona (1966) 384 US 436 12, 57, 164.

Murray (John) v. UK (1996) 22 EHRR 29, 10, 16, 86, 118, 127, 132, 155.

S and Marper v. United Kingdom [2008] ECHR 1581.

Salduz v. Turkey (2008) 49 EHRR 19 86

Stansbury v. California 511 US 318 (1994)

Index

Note: Boldface page numbers refer to tables and page numbers followed by "n" denote endnotes.